"I drowned. I could feel the water closing over my face....Yes, I remember being dead."

Ruth MacGuire, a Connecticut housewife, was recalling a former life as a British officer's wife in nineteenth-century India. Hypnotized under the most stringent scientific conditions, she told in exhaustive detail how she lived in Calcutta, was raped in a bloody Hindu uprising, and finally died in a fall overboard from her England-bound ship. Hers is only one of the many *verified* instances of reincarnation described in this book by one of America's leading parapsychologists.

"Bizarre dreams and ghostly experiences...a loaded portfolio of eyebrow-lifting case histories." —*Publishers Weekly*

D1008032

BORN AGAIN:
The Truth About Reincarnation
was originally published by Doubleday & Company, Inc.

Books by Hans Holzer

*Born Again: The Truth About Reincarnation
ESP and You
Ghost Hunter
Ghosts I've Met
Ghosts of the Golden West
*Gothic Ghosts
Life After Death: The Challenge and the Evidence
The Lively Ghosts of Ireland
Predictions—Fact or Fallacy?
Psychic Investigator
Psychic Photography—Threshold of a New Science?
Star in the East
*The Truth About Witchcraft
*Window to the Past
Yankee Ghosts

*Published by POCKET BOOKS

 *Are there paperbound books you want
but cannot find in your retail stores?*

You can get any title in print in **POCKET BOOK** editions. Simply send retail price, local sales tax, if any, plus 25¢ to cover mailing and handling costs to:

MAIL SERVICE DEPARTMENT
POCKET BOOKS ● A Division of Simon & Schuster, Inc.
1 West 39th Street ● New York, New York 10018

Please send check or money order. We cannot be responsible for cash. *Catalogue sent free on request.*

Titles in this series are also available at discounts in quantity lots for industrial or sales-promotional use. For details write our Special Projects Agency: The Benjamin Company, Inc., 485 Madison Avenue, New York, N.Y. 10022.

Hans Holzer

BORN
AGAIN

The Truth About Reincarnation

PUBLISHED BY POCKET BOOKS NEW YORK

BORN AGAIN:
The Truth About Reincarnation

Doubleday edition published 1970
POCKET BOOK edition published July, 1973
4th printing.......................January, 1974

This POCKET BOOK edition includes every word contained
in the original, higher-priced edition. It is printed from
brand-new plates made from completely reset, clear, easy-to-
read type. POCKET BOOK editions are published by POCKET
BOOKS, a division of Simon & Schuster, Inc., 630 Fifth
Avenue, New York, N.Y. 10020. Trademarks registered
in the United States and other countries.

L

Standard Book Number: 671-77461-1.
Library of Congress Catalog Card Number: 71-119920.
Cover photograph by Kenn Mori; montage by Elias Eliopulos.
Printed in the U.S.A.

Contents

Introduction

"Reincarnation?" said the secretary I had just fired. "You mean, I could come back as a pig?"

I shook my head. She didn't have to come back, but misconceptions such as this one are the reasons why it is so difficult to explain reincarnation on a scientific, factual basis.

Some people, just as this little girl, think reincarnation is the same as transmigration. People have read about the Indian philosophy of reincarnation and karma, and think that any form of scientific inquiry into the subject of re-birth must, of necessity, be based on Eastern philosophy.

In reality, it is exactly the opposite. Eastern philosophy is based on certain facts that the people of those countries have learned concerning reincarnation. It is not the tail wagging the dog, but the dog wagging the tail and know-ingly winking an eye, for the East is centuries ahead of the West when it comes to an understanding of human personality, the soul as we know it, and that which makes us tick. To the Easterner, it seems perfectly natural that man lives more than one life, whereas the Westerner finds the entire idea preposterous, if not completely out of context with what he has been brought up to believe. Some Westerners think that the idea of reincarnation is contrary to their religious faith. This is not so. Many Western religions also hold that reincarnation is a fact.

As far back as the Stone Age, the ancient Celtic religion of witchcraft, or Wicca, held that man's ultimate goal is to return again and again in reincarnation cycles to fulfill that which he was unable to fulfill in an earlier lifetime.

Even Christianity, at least in its early forms, has over-tones of rebirth, but we must speak of this at the proper time.

Reincarnation, then, as a subject at least in the Western world, somehow has always been linked with the East, and to this very day there are serious scientists who think that all examples of reincarnation, that is to say, all those cases that seem to have the ring of truth about them, must of necessity come from India or, at the very least, the East.

It will therefore come as a shock to those who think this way that not a single case in this book occurred in the Eastern part of the world, but, to the contrary, every single one is of Western origin, mainly American, recent, and, of course, factual as far as I am able to determine.

Religious philosophy has played absolutely no part in my work. The purpose of this book is not to reaffirm any religious concept, but to determine by analysis whether reincarnation is a fact or a fallacy; to establish whether there are sufficient grounds, sufficient material and evi-dence, to support a conviction that people are reborn into other bodies, that life does not end at death's door, but that all of us do return to continue the cycle of life and rebirth.

True, there are many books dealing with the subject, some of them in a philosophical manner, others quite fac-tually; some of them are of quite recent origin. The prob-lem, then, is not so much to write a book that will present facts never discussed before, but to present them in such a manner that an open-minded person can accept them as true. By open-minded, I mean neither committed to reincarnation nor dead set against it. An open-minded per-son is one who has not yet made up his mind and who is willing to examine the evidence at face value.

I am such a person. Even though I had strong feelings that the facts would bear out reincarnation, I had not come to any final conclusion as I was writing this book. It was only toward the end of the book that I became fully and wholly convinced that there is indeed no other explanation than reincarnation—no other explanation for the many facts reported herein. Still, I am not a mission-ary in the cause of reincarnation. I have set down the facts as I found them, and I have done so in the hope that others will do likewise in other books. The difficulty is not only of defining what is reincarnation, but also what constitutes *proof* of reincarnation. First of all, as we have just seen, reincarnation is not the return in an animal's body, but in human form. This may occur at various times in one's life cycle, and it does not follow that everyone reincarnates in exactly the same manner. Far from it! The variety of reincarnation material suggests that each case is different and must, therefore, be examined on its own merits.

To define my quest, then, scientifically, I would say first that reincarnation is the return of a human being in another life. Proof must be of a kind that cannot be explained away by ordinary means. It cannot be vague or subject to another explanation, such as having read books dealing with a particular period, or knowledge of the person one feels one has come back as because of some family connection. All these things have to be taken into account when one weighs the evidence, of course; for proof must be absolute, or reasonably absolute. Man is fallible, and nothing is one hundred per cent correct in our lives, but one must strive to attain at least a reasonable amount of evidence before one accepts reincarnation as a fact.

The purpose of this work is to show that reincarnation occurs frequently, if not for everyone; and that it is by no means a freak situation or something that can happen only once in millions of cases. True, only a small number of cases come to the attention of someone properly trained to evaluate the material; and of that number of cases, only a small part is worthy of consideration; an even smaller portion is capable of evidential proof. Nevertheless, reincarnation memories and other indications of previous lifetimes do exist by the thousands, if not, indeed, by the hundreds of thousands. It is only a question of collecting this material properly and evaluating it at some future date.

There seems to be no geographical or ethnic distinction when it comes to cases of reincarnation. East and West, as I have already pointed out, are equally involved; young and old, rich and poor, people of every kind, may at one time or other have reincarnation experiences. Later on, I will examine the nature of this material in detail and also explain how one can evaluate it—how one can encourage the coming to the surface of suppressed material dealing with reincarnation.

In this introduction, however, I feel it important to point out what it would mean to mankind in general if reincarnation were accepted broadly, universally, and without questioning. It is clear that those who reject scientific evidence for survival of human personality will find it even harder to accept the possibility of more than one survival; that is to say, a number of lives of a soul in a number of bodies at various times. Thus, the evidence must speak for itself if it is to convince large segments of our population. By population I don't necessarily mean just the average person, but also the scientific establishment, or at least that part of the establishment capable of accepting new theories and not yet committed to a defense of what has already been attained.

There are always some scientists who are ahead of their times, who are willing, open-mindedly, to discuss possibilities that seem to be contrary to the accepted theories of the orthodox establishment. I am one of those, and I will admit that the struggle for recognition has never been an easy one and isn't bound to be much easier in the future, but we must present the evidence and hope that, as time goes on, man will indeed recognize these universal truths that alone make life livable.

It is clear that reincarnation answers many questions religion has left unanswered; for example, why people suffer terribly in their lifetimes when they are patently innocent of any wrongdoing, or when they are trying very hard to accomplish things and yet fail. To an average person, this seems unjust, unfair; and only reincarnation and the religions based upon it have an answer: what one has done in one lifetime may very well reflect upon the results one obtains in another lifetime. That is the law of just retribution, which extends over one's entire life cycle: the soul may reap in one lifetime what it has sown in another, and vice versa.

Now, this is a very comfortable theory, and it does indeed take care of all the injustices a man might suffer.

Orthodox religions do not offer such a practical solution to man's problems. Most religions refer to the inscrutable wisdom of the deity as the answer to what seems to be rather unfair. Only reincarnation and the religions accepting it as fact come up with a solution involving man's own failures, man's own deeds, as being responsible for success or failure in his lifetime. Whereas in orthodox religions the deity has decided to punish or to elevate a person, in reincarnation and the Eastern religions based upon it, it is man himself who makes his later life. In a way, then, reincarnation gives man the power of free will and of decision making, which orthodox religions have deprived him of.

Those who believe in reincarnation may invoke the law of karma in order to blame even the slightest discomfort upon something they might have done in a previous existence. One has to use common sense as well as scientific appraisal to evaluate the truth of such relationships. But it is conceivable that there exists a law, a natural law, governing all our actions, thoughts, and reactions, and that such a law might very well set up a system of retribution, of compensation, extending even to minor and seemingly unimportant details of our life. Again, the purpose of this book is to examine the evidence that such a law is in operation. Those who laugh at the concept of rebirth sometimes shrug off the evidence of reincarnation as wishful thinking or as a "cop out" for the man who does not wish to face his future on rational grounds. But logic works with the mind, not the emotional part of self— the soul. On the inner, mystical level, man does know, even if at times dimly, that there is another part of him responding not to logical thinking, but to something beyond that state. There seems to be a link beyond personality, beyond one lifetime. To determine whether this link is individual or part of a universal mind, a world mind, a pool of information, whence comes some of the material regarded as evidence for reincarnation, is one of the reasons why I have examined the cases in this book very carefully. I wanted to be sure that no alternate explanation will fit.

Reincarnation, if generally accepted as factual, would,

of course, greatly influence our personal conduct. I am referring especially to the conduct in times of war, under conditions of violence, or whenever there is a possibility of taking another person's life. Whenever a man or a woman is faced with the commission of a crime or of an evil deed (I mean evil in terms of contemporary morality), there is the possibility of "accumulating karma," that is to say, of mortgaging one's future lifetime in a negative sense. Now, if reincarnation is subject to a universal law of retribution and justice, then an evil deed committed in one lifetime may very well have dire consequences in the next one. The knowledge of this might influence people toward a better life, toward a more moral existence. It may prevent crimes of violence, perhaps even war. This may only be wishful thinking on my part, but it stands to reason that a universal and scientifically accepted conviction that reincarnation is factual would have deep and long-lasting consequences in our entire way of life. The common attitude toward death, for instance, would undergo rapid and profound changes, for if there is more than one lifetime to live, surely one could not fear death as the inevitable end. Surely one might even welcome it at times if the existence one suffers could be exchanged for a better one within a short time. The hopelessly ill might very well welcome the continuing life cycle.

Musical comedy writer Alan Jay Lerner wrote of a man who, convinced of the reality of reincarnation, wanted to leave his money to himself in another body in the next life. This, of course, was in jest. But it is not entirely outside the law of probability that, at some future date, people may plan their lives and consider the multiple existence of the soul in a number of bodies as the basis for monetary considerations.

All this is for the future. My job in this book is merely to pinpoint the evidence *for* reincarnation and to present it as best I can. I hope that my reading public will look back into their own lives and report to me some of their own reincarnation experiences, if they so desire, so that we may have an even greater number of evidential cases on file. Let there be no mistake about this: Reincarnation is a very important subject today. It may very well be the most important subject tomorrow.

I
"Come Back to Scotland!"

One day in October of 1967, I was going through my fan mail, which had been piling up rather dangerously for a few weeks. I get about three hundred to four hundred letters a week from readers all over the country and even from abroad, and I cannot devote as much time to these letters as I wish I could, but on this brisk October morning I felt compelled to go over the mail and try to pick out the most urgent letters for an immediate reply. Somehow my hands picked up a letter from Harvey, Illinois. It looked just like any other letter that I might get from a reader, but I proceeded to open it and read it. I read it three times, and then I wondered what had made me open this particular letter of all the hundreds that lay on my desk that morning.

Dear Mr. Holzer,

I am writing to you about an experience I had, which may not really mean anything. I have seen what looks like a Scottish girl, standing at the foot of my bed, three times. I don't know if she actually talked to me, but after I'd seen her, these words keep coming back to me: "castle," "perch" or "purth,"

"Ruthvin," "Cowrye," "sixteen," and "towers." Also, something which sounds like "burn night." I've never mentioned this to anyone, because they probably would not believe me.

If you can make anything out of this, I would appreciate it if you would let me know.

Sincerely, Pamela Wollenberg.

What puzzled me about this short letter was the fact that the words mentioned by Miss Wollenberg had no immediate meaning for me either. It didn't sound like the usual ghost story, or the usual psychic experience relating simply to something left behind in the atmosphere of a particular room or house. It didn't sound like an ordinary dream either, since Miss Wollenberg was so precise in mentioning what appeared to be place names.

I was intrigued by her letter, and I wrote back requesting additional information, asking her whether she could remember any more details about this girl, or any further communications from her.

I must confess that anything having to do with Scotland has always interested me. I am a Scotophile. For no reason whatever, I am emotionally involved whenever I hear Scottish music, especially bagpipes, and in 1953 I felt myself compelled to write a series of what appeared to be Scottish folk songs. These songs were totally alien to my ordinary background, which happens to be Austrian, and the songs themselves have the earmarks of authentic seventeenth-century ballads. Some of them have been performed on television and radio, and one or two have been published. I consider them my most original compositions, even though I have a strong feeling that they were "dictated" to me by some unknown entity outside my own personality. I cannot prove any of this, or at any rate, I couldn't at the time when Miss Wollenberg wrote to me, but strange as it seemed at the time, the girl she described as having come to her in a dream also rang a bell with me.

One of the ballads I wrote in 1953 was called "The Maid of the Meadow," and it told of a lovely young lady who is not of this world and who appears to a weary

traveler in a meadow in Scotland. I have always seen
this girl, with my inner eye, and can describe her as a
tall, white-skinned, redheaded girl, of impish and irre-
sponsible character, who somehow had something to do
with me in an earlier lifetime. I have never taken this
idea very seriously, but, intrigued by the possibility of
reincarnation, I have often wondered whether some day I
might not find a Scottish grave with some meaning for me
personally. I have always had a dim feeling of homecom-
ing to Scotland some day, and have taken an unusual
interest in the story of Bonnie Prince Charlie and other
Scottish heroes. Was I perhaps a reincarnated Scotsman
who lived several centuries before the present? Curiously
enough, there were several instances at sittings with mediums and psychics who knew nothing about me, when
reference was made to my having lived in Scotland at an
earlier time. One might put this down to mind reading, if
indeed there is such a thing, but the impression of a Scottish incarnation at an earlier date has always been very
strong within me.

I remember the time I went to see the Broadway musical *Brigadoon.* I was so overcome with emotion afterward
that I made arrangements to go to Scotland immediately.
I arrived in Edinburgh a short time later and demanded
to be shown "Brigadoon," only to discover that there was
no such thing, at least not in the sense in which the musical had presented it. There was indeed a "Brigadoon,"
but the term signified Bridge of Doon, the Doon being a
small river in western Scotland. Eventually I got to see
this river and I found that it was enchanting, but hardly
enchanted.

As time went on, I relegated the idea of finding my
"Maid in the Meadow" to some future date, hoping instead that the ballad I had written would some day
achieve fame. But my interest in matters Scottish has
never waned, and Miss Wollenberg's letter revived it.

The lady from Harvey, Illinois, answered my letter
immediately. I had asked her whether there were any witnesses to the experience she had reported in her first letter,
but apparently there weren't any, since she was asleep at
the time.

I have no witnesses to the Scottish girl I see, because no one else has seen her. The girl I see seems to have red hair and seems to be very elegantly dressed, with long white gown and gold braid. I saw her the other night. It seems she said to me the word "handsel." It seems as though she's lost. She keeps saying "ruthven," "gowrie," "sixteen hundred," "two towers." She also said, "glamis—angus." She also said, "I leaped." I don't believe I have any Scottish background, but it's possible, because on my mother's side they are all English. On my father's side they are all German. I do not know if I have ESP, but I seem to see some things before they happen.

I hope this will help you.

Sincerely, Pamela Wollenberg.

The matter rested there for a while, but I was determined to go to Scotland in the future and investigate this material. It meant nothing to me at the time, but I knew some research historians in Scotland, and thought that perhaps they might be able to shed some light on the mysterious words of Miss Wollenberg's letters.

We had no further correspondence until I was able to go to Scotland in the summer of 1969. I took the two letters with me, although I really didn't know where to begin the search. One of my dearest friends is a writer named Elizabeth Byrd, author of *Immortal Queen* (a history of Mary, Queen of Scots), who now resides in the Scottish Highlands. I thought that perhaps Elizabeth could shed some light on the material I was bringing along with me. She read the two letters, but could not offer anything concrete except the promise to look into it further.

We were luncheon guests of Mr. and Mrs. Maurice Simpson at their castle in northeastern Scotland called Muchalls. The occasion was a casual invitation of the Simpsons to visit their castle because of a possible haunted room. It turned out that there was no such room, but the Simpsons were amiable people, whose hospitality we enjoyed.

For no reason in particular, I mentioned my letters from the lady in Harvey, Illinois, wondering whether, perhaps, Mr. Simpson had some idea as to the meaning of those letters. To my amazement, Mr. Simpson caught on immediately and seemed to remember a legend or story involving "a maiden's leap" in one of the castles in Scotland.

"You mean, there is something to this?" I said, getting more and more interested. Evidently, fate had destined us to come to Muchalls, not because of a haunted room, but because of a link supplied by the owner, leading me to an understanding of what Miss Wollenberg's letter was all about.

"I think I have a guidebook here, a book dealing with Scottish castles," he said. "Let me look for it."

A few minutes later he returned, holding triumphantly what seemed to be a slender booklet. The booklet was called *Huntingtower Castle* and was the work of J. S. Richardson, formerly Inspector of Ancient Monuments for Scotland. Huntingtower Castle is now under the supervision of the Ministry of Public Buildings and Works. As I leafed through this little booklet I realized that we had discovered the key to Pamela Wollenberg's strange dream/vision.

What is now called Huntingtower Castle was originally known as Ruthven Castle. The name goes back to the first half of the thirteenth century. The third and fourth Lords Ruthven apparently had some part in the murder of Rizzio, Queen Mary's favorite, and the father subsequently died while the son eventually returned from England, whither he had fled, and received a full royal pardon. This fourth Lord Ruthven, whose first name was William, was created the first Earl of Gowrie by King James in 1581. The King was then still legally an infant, and his regents actually created the title.

The following year the newly created Earl repaid the favor in a rather peculiar fashion. He and some associates captured the young King and held him a prisoner for almost a year at Ruthven Castle. The reasons were political. Gowrie and his associates disapproved of the government of the Earl of Arran and the Duke of Lennox, who were then running Scotland. They took power away from those two nobles and into their own hands, with the young King, of course, unable to do much about it. They forced the King to listen to their complaints and to sign a declaration denouncing the former government. When the young man remonstrated against this enforced order, the Master of Glamis, who was among those detaining the young King, is reported to have said, "Better bairns greet than bearded men," meaning, Young man, you had better talk to children than to grown-ups. Allegedly, King James never forgot these words.

This "Raid of Ruthven" was an important event in Scottish history, that is, important to those who specialize in sixteenth-century Scottish history and do research into this turbulent era.

Eventually, it appears, when King James found his freedom, he returned under the sway of the Earl of Arran, so the detention at Ruthven really didn't change anything, except, perhaps, the King's feelings toward the man he had just created the first Earl of Gowrie.

At first he showed a forgiving spirit to those who had been connected with the raid, for he issued a proclamation offering them all a full pardon. But two years later the Earl of Gowrie was ordered to leave the country. Having retired only to Dundee, he was arrested by one William Stewart, taken by ship to Leith, and thence to the royal palace of Holyrood. There he stood trial on the accusation of being implicated in a plot to seize Stirling Castle, was found guilty, and was beheaded at Stirling on May 4, 1585, his property being forfeited to the Crown.

A year later, the estates and honors of the first Earl were restored to his son James, who died, however, shortly after. He was succeeded in 1588 by his brother John, the third and last Earl of Gowrie. All the Gowries, incidentally, had the reputation in their time of being adepts of necromancy and witchcraft.

Evidently, King James's revenge did not stop there. The last Earl of Gowrie and his brother, Alexander Ruthven, were killed upon his orders in their Perth town house in August of 1600. The reason given at the time was "an alleged attempt on the life of the King," which was apparently without foundation. No details are known of this so-called "Gowrie conspiracy," but contemporary reports speak of some papers taken from the belt of the dead Earl that contained magic spells no one but an adept in the black arts could properly read. The dead bodies of the two brothers were then carried to Edinburgh, where indictments for high treason were read publicly.

Not satisfied with having executed the two Ruthven brothers, the King ordered their bodies to be publicly hanged, drawn, and quartered, and the remnants to be distributed to various parts of Scotland, thus insuring, according to the belief of the times, that their souls could not rest in peace.

The early seventeenth century was a hard and rough period in history. People were not gentle to each other, and political tempers rose high at times. Religious differences had not been settled, and Scotland was torn by the Protestant and Catholic factions. The King's continuing vengefulness must be understood against this violent background. The Parliament of 1600 abolished the name of Ruthven, ordering that the castle change its name to Huntingtower and remain a property of the Crown of Scotland. Finally, in 1643, the castle passed into the hands of William Murray, and was generally known from that time onward only as Huntingtower Castle.

It required the knowledge and skill of a Scottish historical specialist to recall the earlier designation as Ruthven Castle and the connection between the names Ruthven and Gowrie, and yet a young lady who had never left her native Illinois was able to speak of Ruthven and Gowrie and the year 1600 and the two towers, all in one and the same breath. She was even able to speak of Glamis and Angus, not realizing the connection between the Master of Glamis, which is in Angus County, and the Gowrie family. How could she know that Perth, which was mentioned in her very first letter to me, was the place where the Earl of Gowrie was slain?

But Pamela Wollenberg had also written, "I leaped." Again, the official Huntingtower Castle booklet was able to give me some clues as to the meaning of this cryptic remark:

A daughter of the first Earl of Gowrie was courted by a young gentleman of inferior rank, whose intentions were not countenanced by the family. When a visitor at the castle, he was always lodged in a separate tower from the young lady. One night, however, before the doors were shut, she conveyed

herself into her lover's apartment, but some prying duenna
acquainted the Countess with it, who, cutting off, as she
thought, all possibility of retreat, hastened to surprise them.
The young lady's ears were quick. She heard the footsteps of
the old Countess, ran to the top of the leads, and took the
desperate leap of nine feet four inches, over a chasm of sixty
feet, and luckily landing on the battlements of the other
tower, crept into her own bed, where her astonished mother
found her, and, of course, apologized for her unjust suspicion.
The fair daughter did not choose to repeat the leap, but the
next night eloped and was married. This extraordinary exploit
has given the name of "the maiden's leap" to the space between the two towers, which were originally separate.

After I had read the contents of the official booklet,
there was a moment of silence when we all realized the
importance of the information contained therein.

What remained to be found was further corroboration
of the material—perhaps some knowledge concerning the
further events of the Gowrie conspiracy itself, and the
girl's name. All this had to be investigated further, but at
least I knew then that Pamela Wollenberg either had authentic experiences reaching out into an earlier time or
there had to be a logical explanation for her knowledge. I
decided not to tell Miss Wollenberg anything whatsoever
about my research, and to arrange for an early meeting
with her so that we could begin hypnotic regression. At
this point I knew nothing whatsoever about Miss Wollenberg, not even her age or status, and I could only hope
that there would be no reason why she could not submit
to the experiment I intended to undertake.

Also present at the delightful dinner at Muchalls were
Mr. and Mrs. Alastair Knight. Mrs. Knight, whose first
name is Alanna, is highly psychic. She is a writer of historical novels, and offered to help me with the research
this unusual case would require. In addition, Elizabeth
Byrd enlisted the voluntary aid of historian Carson
Ritchie, but Mr. Ritchie made it plain to her that finding
girls' names is a difficult matter. In those days, girls'
birth were not registered unless they were royal.

Fortified by such a formidable team of helpers, I was
confident I could crack the mystery of Pamela Wollen-

berg's strange visions. The Knights decided to go to Gowrie Castle at the first opportunity. Alastair Knight bought a map of the area and looked at it to familiarize himself with the roads he was to take. His eyes fell upon a strip of land marked Ruthven Field Meadow. When he mentioned this casually to Elizabeth Byrd, she became very excited. "Why, Hans' song is about a maid in the meadow," she explained. Mr. Knight, a practical man and a scientist, smiled.

Two phrases in Pamela's original vision had not yet been fully explained or placed. There was, first of all, the expression "burn night." Elizabeth Byrd thought that it might refer to Robert Burns, for there is indeed a Burns Night celebration in Scotland. I was also tempted by an explanation of this kind, for in 1790 a certain Captain Francis Grose, a friend of Robert Burns, visited Gowrie Castle and recorded in a drawing a portion of the building that no longer exists. But the date seemed completely out of place to me. I suspect that what Pamela Wollenberg tried to convey was not Burn Night, but Bairns Night, the night when the young King James was told to address his remarks to children of his own age—the night he formulated his long-range plans for revenge on the Ruthven family. But this is merely an assumption on my part.

Far more interesting is the word "Handsel." The term seemed completely unfamiliar to me. Where was I to find an explanation for this strange word? At first I thought Pamela tried to say "Hansel," which is a child's nickname for my first name, Hans, but even my considerable ego rejected this solution although I still had a vague feeling that "The Maid of the Meadow" had something personal to do with me as well.

Through Elizabeth Byrd, I had met authoress Margaret Widdemer some years before. Elizabeth asked for permission to consult Miss Widdemer, who is widely read and who has a fine research library. "From my Chambers' Scottish Dictionary," Miss Widdemer wrote, "I can give you an explanation for 'Handsel': an inaugural gift, a present, on Handsel Monday, a coin put in the pocket of a new coat or the like. Handsel means to inaugurate, to make a beginning, a gift." I was, of course, elated at this news that there was such a word as handsel. Miss Widdemer had an opinion of her own. "My first reaction to the word was earnest money, or something given as a sealing of a bargain, money or not. Possibly the red-haired girl you speak of was Handselled to the man she leaped to." So there was such a word after all.

More and more pieces of the jigsaw puzzle began to fall into place now, even though I had not yet met Miss Pamela Wollenberg in person. While my wife and I were still traveling through the Austrian Alps, Mr. and Mrs. Knight prepared for a visit to Gowrie Castle on my behalf. This came about in a most unusual way. On August 6, they found themselves on a routine trip connected with Mr. Knight's work as a geologist. They were looking for Scone Palace, and having a hard time finding it, so they decided to go instead to visit a relative in Dundee. They decided to take a short cut but suddenly found themselves completely lost, and after a bewildering number of side roads, halted at a signpost reading HUNTINGTOWER CASTLE—TWO MILES. It was only much later that they realized that they had arrived at what had once been Gowrie Castle, on the anniversary of the execution of the last two Gowrie Lords.

Now, Alanna Knight does not take her psychic abilities too seriously, although I have seen her at work using her sixth sense to good advantage. She is apparently able to pierce the veil of time and to relive events in the distant past. As soon as they arrived at the castle, she experienced a strange sense of familiarity. The moment she set foot into Huntingtower Castle she was sure she had been in it before, except that she knew it furnished. Her husband assured her that they had never been there. Suddenly Mrs. Knight knew her way inside.

"This was a bedroom. The bed was over there," she said, and pointed. As she went from room to room she found herself singing under her breath. Her son, Christopher, asked, "What is it that you are singing?" She couldn't tell him, but it was the same tune that had been running through her mind ever since I had mentioned I had written a song entitled "The Maid in the Meadow." Mrs. Knight has never heard my song nor has she seen any sheet music of it. All she knew was that I had written such a song and that there was some connection with Scotland, but when they came across the custodian of the castle, she immediately asked her about Ruthven Field Meadow, as it is marked on the map. Following the custodian's directions, they meandered along some pretty lanes, which again seemed rather too familiar to her. Her feelings of déjà vu were rather vague, and yet, at the same time, they were definite.

When they started to leave the area and her husband wondered how they would get out of there, having been lost once that afternoon, she immediately replied, "About twenty yards further on there is an old stone bridge on the right, which leads to the main road eventually," and there was. As they drove away, she could not help but go over the events of the last hour in her mind.

Once inside the castle she had immediately gone up to the battlements, practically on hands and knees, as the steps were very steep. There she had perched on the edge of the battlements, about sixty feet above the ground. Today the two original towers, which were separate at one time, are connected by a somewhat lower central portion. In the early seventeenth century, however, there was a chasm between the two portions of the castle measuring over nine feet. Anyone wishing to leap from the right-hand tower onto the lower, left-hand tower would still have to cover a distance of nine feet, but since the left-hand portion was one story below the right-hand portion, the leap would have been downward. Also, there is a ledge along both battlements, and as the buttresses protrude and overlap, it reduces the distance by a couple of feet. Thus it is not entirely impossible to make such a leap safely and without falling off the roof, but it is somewhat of a feat, just the same. Eventually, Alanna Knight had left the battlement and returned to the inside of the castle.

In what she considers a bedroom, she had had a very strong impression of a girl with reddish-gold hair, pale rather than dark, with freckles. She was what, in modern parlance, would be called a tomboy, Alanna reports—mischievous rather than passionately amorous. "The sort of girl who would do anything for a dare," Alanna felt, "and who would enjoy leading a man on, feeling rather superior to the poor creature. I think she was merry, laughed a lot, was strongly disapproved of by her family. I feel that the sixteenth century wasn't her time; she was a misplacement, and would have been happier living now, who even then yearned for some equality with men, and watched them go out to fight with envy in her soul. I think also that her name is Margaret or Isabelle or both, but these names are particularly Scottish, so there is really nothing exciting about this feeling. I only hope that one day you'll know the answer."

I asked Alanna Knight about the song that kept going through her mind and that she felt had something to do with my ballad "The Maid of the Meadow." Since she is not a musician, she asked a friend, Ann Brand, to transcribe it for her. I looked at the musical composition with interest. There are four bars, and they resemble greatly four bars from my ballad, written in 1953, and certainly unknown to Alanna Knight or her friends. To be sure, it wasn't the entire song; it was merely a portion of it, but the similarity was striking.

Alanna had one other bit of news to add: Dr. Ritchie had found some reference to one of the Ruthven girls. In Robertson's *History of Scotland,* published in 1759, he had found a reference to the sister of the Earl of Gowrie by the name of "Mistress Beatrix." Of course, there might have been more than one sister, but the name is on record. In the meantime, Elizabeth Byrd had promised further inquiries in Edinburgh.

While all this feverish activity on my behalf was going on across the ocean I went to Chicago to finally meet Pamela Wollenberg in person. She had agreed to come to the Knickerbocker Hotel, where I was then staying, and to submit to hypnotic regression. I had told her that I had found some interesting evidence relating to her dream vision, but declined to say any more.

On October 17, 1969, Pamela Wollenberg came to my suite at the Knickerbocker Hotel. When she entered, I was somewhat surprised, for she didn't look at all like the person I had somehow imagined her to be. Instead of a fey, somewhat romantic individual of indeterminate age, I found her to be a young girl of twenty or twenty-one, lively and practical, and not at all interested in the occult. I explained that I would interview her first and then attempt to put her into hypnotic regression. Since she was agreeable, we proceeded immediately.

In the following pages I am presenting the exact transcript of our interview and of what happened when Pamela Wollenberg became another person.

"Pamela," I began the conversation, "where were you born?"

"Chicago Heights."

"What does your father do?"

"My father is deceased. He worked in a factory which built locomotives, and my mother works in a hospital as a dietary worker."

"What is your background?"

"My father's family are from Germany, the Black Forest, and my mother's side of the family are English."

"Was she born here?"

"Yes."

"Is there anybody of Scottish ancestry among your family?"

"Not that I know of."

"Do you have any brothers and sisters?"

"I have half sisters and a half brother."

"What is your family's religion?"

"Well, my father's side of the family is Lutheran, and my mother's family is Baptist."

"And you, yourself?"

"I consider myself a Mormon."

"You're twenty-one. Do you work?"

"I was doing work in a hospital. I was going to nursing school, and now I'm just taking care of a woman part time. She's ill, and once I get the money I want to go back into nursing."

"What is your schooling like? What did you do? You went to public school?"

"I went to school in Glenwood, right outside of Chicago Heights, and the rest of my schooling was all in Harvey, where I live now."

"Did you ever have any flashes, or visions, or feelings of having been in places that you hadn't really visited?"

"I've seen people that I'd swear that I'd seen somewhere before, and no possibility of it."

"Have you ever been to Europe?"

"No."

"Have you ever had any desire to go to Europe?"

"Oh yes, I'd love to go to Europe. I want to see castles."

"When did you first notice this desire?"

"Oh, I'd say maybe three years ago, when I was eighteen."

"Do you know the first time you had this sudden desire to see castles?"

"I had a castle, all in my mind, a big, white castle with towers."

"How many towers?"

"Two or three, I think, and it was like up on a stone, a mountain or something."

"What kind of books do you read?"

"Well, I read a lot of mysteries."

"Do you read any history?"

"No, history doesn't really interest me too much. I read about Waterloo one time, but that's about the first one I read."

"What kind of music do you like?"

"Classical music and folk songs. I don't mean folk songs like you hear now. I mean of the European countries, the British Isles."

"Do you ever have a particular song running through your mind?"

"I hear bagpipes sometimes."

"When do you hear these bagpipes?"

"Usually at night, when I'm getting ready to go to sleep."

"How long has that been going on?"

"I would say off and on now for maybe a year and a half, two years."

"Have you ever had a feeling of strangeness in your present surroundings?"

"Yes, I'd say so. I don't think I've ever belonged *around here.*"

"Can you be more specific as to when this feeling started?"

"I would say I've noticed it for the last couple of years, two or three years, possibly, but I don't really feel like I know anybody *here*. It seems I know people that are in other places of the world, and I *don't*."

"What places would you say they are at?"

"Well, I think I'm really drawn more to the British Isles than I am to Europe. There's just something about the British Isles that fascinates me."

"Have you ever had a feeling, perhaps when you were very tired, of looking in the mirror or walking, seeing yourself *different* from what you look like now, see any change in yourself, personality, character, or in face?"

"Yes, I know one time I can remember very, very clearly, because it startled me. The girl that I talked about in the dream I had, with the red hair—I looked in the mirror one day—I don't know if I pictured myself *as her,* or if I saw her there, but it set me back."

"How long ago was that?"

"Oh, I'd say maybe nine months ago."

"Is that the only time you had this feeling?"

"I have had the feeling that I'm somebody besides who I am."

"How long have you had this feeling?"

"I'd have to go back two or three years."

"Anything, do you think, that started it off?"

"No, not that I can think of."

"Now, let us talk about the dreams."

"The dream happened the first time about two years ago. I've had it quite a few times since then. I've seen a girl with red hair. She has a long, white gown on, and it has gold braiding on it, and she's kind of walking like she's dazed. When I have this dream I also see two towers there, and I hear her say, 'Handsel to me,' and then I hear her mention 'Glamis, Angus,' and she'll say, 'Ruthven, Gowrie,' and one time she said, 'I leaped.' Sometimes she seems very peaceful and sometimes she seems very angry."

"How old a girl would you say?"

"I'd say somewhere around twenty."

"Is she short or tall?"

"I would say short, somewhat petite."

"Pretty, ugly, anything special about her?"

"No, nothing really. She has beautiful red hair. That's the thing."

"Short or long?"

"Long hair, very thick."

"Does the dream vary at all, or is it exactly the same each time?"

"I will say it is basically exactly the same every time, except there's times when she'll seem angry."

"How many times have you had the dream altogether?"

"I'd say five or six times."

"When was the last time?"

"The last time, let's see, July I think."

"Of this year?"

"Yes."

"Was she angry then?"

"Very angry."

"Do these dreams last all night, or are they short dreams?"

"Very short. I mean, I'll just see her and she'll say what she has to say, and then she's gone."

"How is it that you remember this particular dream so vividly? Do you remember all your dreams as well?"

"Her I do, because I'm not really sure if you can classify it as a dream. I don't really think I'm asleep."

"Does it happen early in the night, middle of the night, or late at night?"

"I would say after eleven-thirty and before two to two-thirty."

"Outside of those dreams, did you have any feeling of a presence around you in any way? While awake, I mean?"

"I don't know if I can say specifically *her* or not, but I have had the feeling at times that *someone's* around me. I mean, when I'm home by myself."

"When you contacted me, do you think that someone made you do it?"

"I felt I just *had* to write you, for no reason."

"Did it make any sense to you, personally?"

"The only thing I ever really thought about was the 'Handsel to me.' I thought the 'to me' must mean something. Maybe 'Handsel' means come to me, but I wouldn't know why she'd want me coming to her."

"Have you any particular tastes in clothes, accessories,

music, habits, phrases, anything you find is alien to your own personality, especially since you were eighteen, let us say?"

"I love to cook anything which is from the English Isles. I have three English cookbooks. As for clothes, the old-style dress really appeals to me."

"Do you have any boy friends who are of English or Scottish background? I don't mean American English, but I mean true native."

"No, none whatsoever."

"Have you ever done any reading about Britain to any extent—history, background, geography?"

"I read one time about the Tower of London, and I've read about the royal family, but really nothing else."

"What is your own view of the meaning of these phenomena that have occurred in your life? What do you suppose it means?"

"I don't really know, unless someone's trying to tell me something. I feel that I know her. I don't know *how* I know her, or *why* I know her, but feel *I know her.*"

"When the first dream occurred, the very first time, was it out of the blue? There was nothing that would indicate any reason for it?"

"The first time, I really didn't pay much attention to it. I noticed it, and I knew it was there, but I thought, 'Well, one of these wild things,' but then it kept coming back, and every time it would come back I'd feel closer to her."

"Are you ready to be hypnotically regressed now?"

"Yes, I am."

A few moments later, Pamela was in deep hypnosis, fully relaxed and obeying my commands. "You are going to go back a hundred years, two hundred years, three hundred years. Go back until you see the redheaded girl."

After a moment, she spoke. "Ruthven . . . ," she said quietly.

"Do you live there?" I began questioning.

"I live there."

"Who is your father?"

"He's not there."

"Is there anyone else there?"

"My mother."

"What is her name? What is your mother's name?"

"I don't know. We can't talk about it."

"Why not?"

"Because they're conspiring against us and we're not supposed to talk about them."

"What year are we in?"

"Sixteen hundred."

"Sixteen hundred what?"

"Just sixteen hundred."

"What country do you live in?"

"In Scotland."

"Why are you worried?"

"We're going to have to leave."

"Why do you have to leave?"

"They'll kill us if we don't leave."

"Who will kill you?"

"I don't know. Father just said, 'the men.' "

"What are you going to do?"

"I don't know. Mother's packing."

"Where are you going to go?"

"To Glamis."

"Why there?"

"The royal family is there."

"Will they help you?"

"I don't know."

"Describe your home."

"Stones."

"What is it called?"

"Breasten."

"What does the building look like?"

"Two towers, garden."

"Have you been up in the towers?"

"I used to play up there."

"How did you play?"

"I had little china cups."

"How old were you then?"

"Four, five."

"How old are you now?"

"Twenty-two."

"Are you single or married?"

"Single."

"Do you know any man you would like to marry?"

"Yes."

"What is his name?"

"I can't tell his name."

"Why not?"

"I'm not supposed to see him."

"Why not?"

"The family says no."

"What is his first name?"

"Mother said I'll be punished if I tell."

"And what will you do? Have you seen him lately?"

"Yes."

"Where?"

"By Loch Catherine."

"Is that far away?"

"Not too far."

"Has he ever been in the castle?"

"Yes."

"Where? In what part of it?"

"In the main hallway."

"Never upstairs?"

"Only once, but he's not allowed in the castle."

"Was he upstairs in the tower at any time?"

"Only once, when Mother wasn't supposed to know he was there."

"What did you do?"

"We talked."

"And will you marry him?"

"I can't."

"Why not?"

"The family won't allow it. They want me to marry someone else."

"Who?"

"I don't know him."

"Why do they want you to marry this other person?"

"The family is very wealthy."

"And your friend isn't?"

"Yes, but not to their wealth."

"Why is it that you have come to speak through this instrument? What is your connection with her? Are you her, or are you speaking *through* her?"

"I am *her*."

"Where have you been in between? Have you been anyone else?"

"No, I was caught in the wind."

"How did you die?"

"I jumped from the tower."

"Did you die in jumping?"

"Yes, I died after."

"Where did you jump to?"

"I was trying to jump to the other one."

"Didn't you make it?"

"No."

"Where did you fall?"

"In front of the door."

"Was that the first time that you ever jumped from one tower to the other?"

"No."

"You've done it before?"

"Yes."

"And it worked?"

"Yes."

"And this time it didn't, and you died? How old were you then?"

"Twenty-two."

"Was it an accident, or did you want to jump?"

"I wanted to jump."

"Were you unhappy?"

"Yes."

"When you were down there dead, what happened to you next? What did you see next?"

"Nothing."

"What was your next memory after you had fallen? What is the next thing that you remember?"

"I was in wind."

"Did you see yourself as you were?"

"Yes."

"Where did you go?"

"Nowhere."

"Did you see anyone?"

"No."

"Did you stay outside, or did you return to the castle?"

"I went to the castle once."

"Did anyone see you?"

"No."

"And what happened after that? Where did you live?"

"I was caught in the wind again."

"And what was the next thing you remember after that?"

"I saw people."

"What sort of people?"

"Funny people, walking around."

"Were they also dead?"

"No."

"Where were you?"

"I was in a city."

"Were you in another body?"

"No."

"You were still as you were?"

"Yes."

"What was the city?"

"I don't know."

"Were the people dressed in the same way as the people you knew in your time?"

"No."

"Were you the same way as you were in your time?"

"Yes, I could see my gown."

"These funny people, did they notice you?"

"No, they walked by me."

"What was the next thing you remember after that?"

"I wanted someone to take me back."

"Back where?"

"To Ruthven."

"Did you find anyone?"

"Yes—Pamela."

"How did she take you back?"

"She'll take me back."

"How did you get *into* Pamela? Did you select her yourself?"

"Yes, she looked like she'd go back."

"Who told you about Pamela? How did you find her?"

"I found her when I went into the building."

"Which building?"

"In her building."

"But, what makes you so sure that she can?"

"She'll feel sorry and take me back."

"Are you within her? Are you in her body?"

"Yes, I've got to go back with her."

"Who sent you to her?"

"No one."

"Then how did you know where to find her?"

"I don't know."

"Did you talk to anyone and ask for help?"

"No one could hear me. They walked right by."

"There was no one, no person who said, 'You must go back to earth,' or anything like that?"

"No."

"Do you remember being reborn as a baby?"

"No."

"What was the thing you remember after you saw Pamela?"

"She looks like someone."

"Like who? Does she look like you?"

"No."

"Then, what does she look like to you?"

"She looks like the clan McGibbon."

"Which one of the clan McGibbon?"

"She looks like Catherine."

"Catherine of the clan McGibbon? What was Catherine to you?"

"I didn't know her too well. I met her only in Angus."

"Why did you go to Angus?"

"We had to go to Glamis."

"And did you pass through Angus?"

"No, Glamis is in Augus."

"What was she doing in Glamis?"

"She lives there."

"What does she do there?"

"A maid."

"Whose maid was she?"

"At the castle of the royal family."

"And Pamela reminds you of her?"

"Yes."

"But, what is it that binds you to Pamela? Is it your own destiny?"

"Yes, I must go back."

"And do what?"

"I've got to look for something."

"What do you have to look for?"

"My ring."

"Who gave you the ring?"

"I can't talk about it."

"What does it look like?"

"It's round, an opal."

"Is there anything inscribed in it?"

"No."

"Why is it so important to get this ring?"

"*He* gave it to me."

"Who did?"

"I'd be punished if I tell."

"You will not be punished . . . on my honor. Give me his name so I can help you."

"I can't find him again. I only want my ring."

"Call out for him and he will come to you."

"I'll be punished if I tell."

"And when you find the ring, what will you do then?"

"I'll go away."

"Where will you go to?"

"Loch Catherine. I was happy there."

"With whom?"

"*He* would take me there. We would talk about going away."

"Where would you go to, if you could?"

"Away from Perth."

"And where to?"

"He'd like to go to London."

"What sort of work does he do?"

"He wants to be an architect."

"Has he studied?"

"Only a little, but without permission."

"He's not a nobleman?"

"He's a nobleman, but his father does not want him to do that."

"Why is it that you came to Pamela when she was about eighteen, and not before?"

"She's old enough to go away now."

"Will you help her go there? Why did you seek *me* out?"

"Maybe you would make her go."

"Is that what you want me to do?"

"I want to go back."

"Suppose I promise to help you, will you then tell me who the young man was?"

"Can I go back?"

"I will try to find a way for her to back, yes. I have already made contact over there and I know you are telling the truth."

"Will she take me back?"

"I will do my best for her to take you back within a year's time."

"I've waited too long."

"How long have you waited?"

"For hundreds of years."

"Then you can wait another year. But a lot of time has gone on. Perhaps the ring isn't there any more. Then what?"

"I'll look till I find it."

"Are you happy being in Pamela's person now? Are you reconciled to being her? Do you like being her?"

"Only to go back."

"I am still curious why it is, and how it is, that you found her over here. Do you know in what country you are? Do you?"

"No."

"Where do you think you are? Do you know the name of the country in which you are? It is not Scotland."

"I'm not in the Isles?"

"No. Do you know how much time has gone on since you lived? Do you know how much?"

"Hundreds of years."

"Do you want to tell me the name of the young man?"

"I can't have him again. You won't bring him back."

"Tell me more about this conspiracy that frightened you so. Who was involved?"

"Father just said they were against him."

"Who?"

"I only know him as Gowrie."

"What rank did he have?"

"I don't know. When they came, I had to go to the tower."

"And when they called for you, what name did they use?"

"I want him back!"

"I will help you. You can tell me your name now, your true name."

"I have to look in the Bible."

"Go and look at the Bible and tell me what is written in it."

"No, I have to go see him."

"You will see him, if he *wants* you to see him."

"No, I want Peter."

"Peter shall be yours. I have promised it. Now, your name."

"I want Peter."

"Peter, come to her. If you have been reborn, let her know where you are, so that she may come to you again. You have to say, 'I,' and say your name, 'want you.' Then he will come to you."

"We can't tell any people."

"You and I are the only ones to know."

"No; when we left the castle, Mother said, 'No.'"

"Speak your name."

"No, I'll be hit."

"What did the servants call you?"

"They always called me by my proper name of Ruthven."

"But what did they say when they meant you were there?"

"They called me 'Lady.'"

"Lady what? What is your Christian name?"

"I can't."

"You know it?"

"Yes."

"What is the initial? The first letter of your name?"

"I'll be punished."

"You will not be punished to speak your own name."

"I can't tell you."

"You would like to find the ring. Is there anything else you want?"

"No."

"Then will you be at peace? If you find the ring, or when you find there is no more ring, will you be at peace then?"

"Yes, if I may go to the Loch."

"Alone?"

"Yes."

"Be patient, and I will see whether it can be done. Have you any other requests?"

"No."

"If I ask you a question, will you answer it truthfully? Do you promise to answer it truthfully?"

"Yes."

"Are you *Beatrix?*"

"I can't tell you."

"You must say yes or no."

"But I'll be punished."

"You will not be punished, because you are not *telling* me. You are simply saying yes or no. If you say yes, and it is the truth, you will not have said it, and if you say no, and it is the truth, you will have perjured yourself, and lied, and invited damnation, so you had better tell the truth. For the third and last time, I ask you, *are you Lady Beatrix?*"

"Yes."

"I will now release you, and I will see to it that as soon as it is possible, you shall see your favorite place again."

"Yes."

"Then go in peace with my blessing."

After Pamela woke up, remembering absolutely nothing of her hypnotic regression, I asked her how she happened to get the name Pamela in the first place.

"My mother couldn't decide on a name, and she wanted a name no one in the family had, and she read a society page, and there was a girl by the name of Pamela being married."

"I'm going to name a few women's names. Tell me if any of them rings a bell in some way, or means anything special, all right? Dorothy or Dorothea."

"My grandmother is named Dorothy."

"You like that name?"

"It's all right."

"How about Barbara?"

"No."

"How about Beatrix?"

"That's pretty. *I like that.*"

"You like that better than the others?"

"Yes, as long as people didn't call me Bea. I don't care for that."

The material obtained from Pamela while in hypnotic regression was very interesting indeed. Now I knew what the handsel was, the ring that meant so much to her because of the one who had given it to her. When I realized that she wasn't going to give me her name, it was best to try to see what reaction I might get from her by mentioning several names. Although I do not consider the evidence thus obtained in the same light as spontaneous admission of facts or names, it is nevertheless of interest in the context of this entire investigation that she did react to the name Beatrix significantly differently from the reaction to other names mentioned by me in the same tone of voice.

After a while, Pamela sat up and joined me for a cup of coffee. Only then did I open the latest letter from Elizabeth Byrd, which had reached me the day before in New York. In it was enclosed a communication from the Lord Lyon of Scotland, that is to say, the nobleman in charge of registering claims and the coats of arms of noble families.

"The daughter after which the maiden's leap at Huntingtower was named was Dorothea, who married before June 8, 1609, John Wemyss, of Pittencrieff. Dorothea, however, though the thirteenth child, was not apparently the youngest daughter, and information on Barbara, the fourteenth child, and youngest of that family, can be found on pages 266 and 267 of Volume Four of the Scots Peerage, referred to above."

Thus read the report from the Lord Lyon of Scotland. Of course, the list of Gowrie daughters is by no means complete. A further thought entered my mind. True, Pamela, in her other identity as Lady Gowrie, had spoken of leaping, but was she the one for whom the Maiden's Leap was famous? Could she not have been another person, leaping and falling, where another had leaped and landed safely? On re-examining the testimony, it appears to me that the Lady Gowrie who spoke to me in Chicago, and who fell to her death from the battlements of Gowrie Castle, was not in the habit of practicing the leap to reach her love, but then again, the true evidence may be confused. Nigel Tranter, in his book *The Fortified House in Scotland,* speaks only of the battlements and the buildings themselves, so the legend of the Maiden's Leap was not as far-spread as we might think.

Before I parted company with Pamela Wollenberg, I asked that she observe anything that might happen to her after our hypnosis session. In particular, I asked that she record any dream/visions that she might have in the future, for it is possible that a memory can be stirred up as a consequence of hypnotic regression.

Four days after our meeting, I received a letter from Pamela. Now, I had briefly told her that her Scottish memories had been confirmed by experts, and that she apparently had lived once before as one of the ladies Gowrie. Thus, anything duplicating that which she already knew would be of no evidential value, of course.

I don't know if this will mean anything or not, but I felt compelled to write you. It's almost 2:30 a.m., but I have just awoken from a dream which seems very real to me. In my dream I found myself on a horse in a place I don't know, but still I feel I know it. I started riding, and after about forty miles or so I stopped and tied my horse to a tree. I started walking in what seemed to be a valley, and it was very wooded. I also saw mountains around me. As I was walking, there were thorns, or something sharp scratching my leg. I started to approach a river, and then I began running. After that I found myself in bed again, and the thing that startled me most is that I felt the most terrible burning sensation on my legs. Then I was taken back by the most awful crying and moaning sounds, which I thought would awaken the entire neighborhood.

Two words have impressed themselves strongly onto my mind. One is either "dab" or "daba." I don't know where it came from, but it's been bothering me. The other word is "Beitris," which I saw clearly on the ceiling of my room last night, with the lights turned off. I don't know if all this will mean anything or not, but I had to write you.

Since the words did not have any meaning for me either, I asked Elizabeth Byrd to check them out in Jamison's English-Scottish Dictionary. "Daddown" means to fall forcibly and with noise. Did the term have reference to her fatal fall from the battlements of Gowrie Castle? But there is also "dablet," which means an imp, a little devil. Didn't Alanna Knight describe the girl she saw in her visions as something of that sort?

In early November Pamela had another dream/vision. The same image impressed itself upon her mind twice in a row, and she was a little worried about the message it contained.

"You will die by *Newa Vleen,*" the girl said in the dreams. Pamela wondered *who* was to die, the redhead or herself, and what, if anything, did Newa Vleen signify?

I immediately contacted Elizabeth Byrd in Scotland and asked her to check it out. Realizing that Pamela was reproducing phonetically what she had heard, I asked her to disregard the spelling.

There is a village of New Alyth situated six miles from the village of Ruthven, which in turn is twenty-five miles distant from Huntingtower Castle. Where Americans might say "at" in referring to a place, Scotsmen would prefer "by" for the same meaning. Thus, someone was to die at that place. But who?

Perhaps there is also a New Avleen or something sounding like that, but so far I have not been able to locate it. There is, however, a Loch Catherine not far from Huntingtower, and it is not a very well-known place, adding still more authenticity to the material obtained from Pamela.

I am satisfied that Pamela Wollenberg had no access to the information she gave me when she first wrote to me. I am also satisfied that she had no ulterior motive in contacting me. No money has changed hands between us; no fame or publicity is likely to come to her. She cannot be reached, and her telephone is unlisted, so the only explanation remaining to any fair-minded individual is that Pamela Wollenberg did indeed remember a previous lifetime.

What is to be done about getting her to Scotland to carry out that which this inner self, representing Lady Gowrie, demands? It is difficult to foretell how soon

Pamela will be able to go to Scotland in her present incarnation, but if Lady Gowrie continues in her forthright
manner to get attention for that which she considers important, no doubt she will also find a way of getting her
present incarnation, Pamela, to go and do her bidding
over there. I can only hope that one way or another both
ladies will live in peace ever after in their present abode.

II
How People Feel About Reincarnation

First we must consider the cultural attitudes of people of all ages, of all cultures, from the beginning of time to the present day, because reincarnation and all the consequences of accepting this theory inevitably involve cultural considerations. One fashions one's outlook after one's beliefs.

It is not particularly surprising to find that reincarnation is among the oldest beliefs held by mankind. As a matter of fact, Stone Age practitioners of "the old religion," better known as witchcraft, already believed in reincarnation. It is such a basic part of their religion that witchcraft is unthinkable without the firm conviction that man does return time and again, and that the life cycle continues forever or at least until such time as an individual has fully discharged his obligations toward self, or perhaps toward the deity.

Speaking of the Western world, that is to say Europe and that part of the world that today is considered an offshoot of European cultures, the ancient beliefs in reincarnation gradually diminished, as Christianity and modernization of thought took roots. Only in the so-called

31

underground religions, that is to say, the folk religions
that persisted through the centuries side by side and sometimes in opposition to the official creed, did the conviction
that reincarnation was part and parcel of one's life continue. Because so much of early cultural life is inter-
woven with religious belief, it seems natural that the cultural attitudes of primitive people were colored by what
had been taught by their respective priests. I am speaking
of people who lived perhaps a hundred thousand to fifty
thousand years before our time, who lived a compara-
tively primitive life and yet had philosophical concepts
far beyond their time and development. Whence this
knowledge comes can only be guessed at. But one need
only look at the magnificent Stone Age creations in the
caves of southern France and elsewhere in order to realize
that these artists were indeed motivated by high concepts
of life and afterlife.

The culture of Stone Age man involved a conviction
that whatever he did in the physical world in which he
lived had some bearing both on his progress into the next
world and on his return to earth after he had completed
a certain waiting period and been told by the deity, or
some force representing the deity, that it was his time to
return to earth again. Consequently, the killing of enemies
was a matter of necessity rather than wanton aggression,
because one never knew whom one might meet in the next
stage of life. Everything had to be motivated properly in
terms of what, to these people, seemed to be justified
and proper.

Some primitive civilizations included human sacrifice
among their rituals. This did not deter them from a belief
in return of the spirit in another body, since it was ob-
vious to them that they were sacrificing only the physical
shell and not the soul of their victim. To the contrary,
some cultures even believed that they were doing the victim a favor by allowing him to sacrifice his physical self
to the deity and thus earn extra credits for his return trip
to earth. This was particularly prevalent among North
American and Central American Indian cultures. In Western Europe the people practicing witchcraft were eventually replaced by the Druidic cultures of Britain, western

France, and Scandinavia, who also accepted reincarnation as part of their religion.

You may, perhaps, have wondered why I have started this account only with the Stone Age people, that is to say, the people of whom we do have records, even though they are not written records, and whom we generally refer to as people living in the prehistoric period of our earth. There may very well have been prior people, prior cultures, perhaps cultures that have been totally destroyed. More and more indications point toward the existence of a highly civilized world far beyond the generally accepted dates, far beyond the world of the Stone Age man. For the present, however, let us consider only those cultures of which we have certain records.

While the Greeks readily accepted a world populated by numerous gods and demigods, there is no central motive in the Greek religion emphasizing the need to return to earth. Only in some of their myths, in some of their exceptional stories, do the Greeks refer to someone coming back or someone appearing in the body of an animal, but these accounts were to be taken symbolically rather than literally, and in no way compare to the universal and firm belief in reincarnation encountered among the practitioners of "the old religion." It was, therefore, fashionable in the Greek world to live for today and for the one incarnation one happened to be in at the time. Thus we have, among Greeks, a strong reliance upon the physical, upon the here-and-now world, in which one is to enjoy the pleasures and blessings of civilization and culture, and not to concern oneself with *what lies beyond*. This was not a materialistic culture in the sense in which we understand the word today, but it was a practical culture, in which man's salvation lay in his accomplishments in this world, far more than in any hope for an improvement of his position in a return engagement at some later date.

What to the Greek world was a matter of general civilization and pleasure, and enjoyment of the fruits of a good life, became a matter of political necessity when the Roman state religion became paramount throughout the civilized world, as it was then known, principally around the Mediterranean. A religion advocating the return through a cycle of reincarnation would not serve at all from the point of view of the state religion. To the Roman Empire it was important that every man do his best to help build a greater empire, and to serve loyally the Emperor and his representatives. Thus, individual responsibility and a restriction to one life were political necessities, and any form of mystical belief in reincarnation was frowned upon by those who upheld the Roman state religion. The luxury of belief in reincarnation was left to poets and occasionally philosophers, so long as they did not divulge their views too publicly.

When Christianity became a power both religiously and culturally, certain things began to change in the attitude toward such beliefs as reincarnation. Christianity, of course, was based upon the Jewish faith. The Jewish faith itself did not particularly emphasize reincarnation, but certain passages in both the Old and the New Testaments do seem to indicate that the return of a particularly great soul in another body was a belief held by the faithful. In general, however, the Jewish faith and the early Christian faith did not preach reincarnation. They preached, instead, a belief in a supreme deity and a deity that was not necessarily in accord with the interests of the Roman state.

In the Jewish faith, rewards and punishments are meted out according to one's doings on earth, and the place to which one proceeds is never fully explained, although something more than physical life is promised. This is even more emphasized in the Christian religion, where this place is very clearly defined as an "upstairs" and a "downstairs," so to speak, depending upon one's life on earth, and there is no doubt left in anyone's mind as to why Christians must live a moral life: they make their own heavens and their own hells, depending upon their deeds. But with Judaeo-Christian monotheism, the life cycle ends right then and there. You go to heaven or you go to hell, and that's where you stay. True, there is resurrection, but resurrection comes at one particular time for everyone in exactly the same way. Quite clearly, then, one's chances at this faraway resurrection will depend on one's position toward the church, and if church and state are one, one's position in relation to the state.

This, indeed, must have been one of the motivating factors that turned Constantine to the Christian religion and caused him, in a genial stroke of political matchmaking, to establish Christianity as the state religion. Until that very moment in the middle fourth century, Christianity was the underdog, the persecuted, minority religion that had been considered a menace to the very existence of the Roman state. Now with one stroke Constantine had made it his own; if you can't beat them, join them. Constantine not only joined the Christians, but he used the concept of Christian rewards for his own ends without ever turning Christian himself until the very moment of his own death. Constantine, nevertheless, practiced Christianity in his affairs of state. Those who did not conform to the established doctrines of the early church were also in contempt of his state, and very few people were brave enough to fight both church and state.

When it was the thing to be a Christian, therefore, it was no longer the thing to accept reincarnation, and the early Christian culture of the late Roman and Byzantine periods neglected that very ancient idea of rebirth and multiple life cycles, while they devoted themselves almost exclusively to the doctrinal and fanatical interpretations of Christian teachings, the teachings of the early saints, and the pronouncements of Christian theoreticians. This took up their time. This was the food for their intellect, and only the very brave or the very advanced souls would dare dabble in mystery religions or in any form of cult advocating belief in reincarnation.

To be sure, there were always individuals who continued the old pagan traditions derived from witchcraft—both the Western European kind, and the Greek kind better known as the cult of Dionysus. But on the surface at least, the world had become Christian, and Christianity said, You die and you will then go to heaven or hell and your body lies in your grave until the bugle blows and you are resurrected to join other souls out there somewhere, up there somewhere, perhaps it wasn't a healthful thing to question such a doctrine.

As the Middle Ages replaced the classic period in Europe, Christianity became more and more deeply involved with doctrines, and the early teachings of Jesus were supplemented and often replaced by medieval concepts in which the form was more important than the philosophy underlying it. In a period when all intellectual life was restricted to religious interpretation within the framework of the existing church, there was certainly no room for any delving into the deeper layers of human consciousness or in the exploration of man's purpose.

What was merely a frowned-upon subject in the late Roman period became a forbidden subject in the Middle Ages, when the church enforced her views in the most fanatical and cruel manner. Anyone advocating reincarnation during the centuries of medieval oppression was a heretic and had to be destroyed, and indeed many were destroyed as heretics in a period when anyone differing ever so slightly with the official line was automatically suspect. Centuries of persecution for any aberration, be it ever so slight, from the official religious line made people cautious. The majority no longer had any knowledge of the traditions concerning reincarnation, and those who did hid their convictions well indeed. No one was particularly eager to speed up the process of reincarnation, even if he believed in it. Millions were sacrificed by the church to her fanatical need to stamp out any form of opposition.

While Europe lay in spiritual chains, matters stood somewhat differently in the East. A continuing tradition of belief in an afterlife followed by other lives and afterlives had been established at an early date in India and the Far East. Chinese traditions, going back at least ten thousand years, have always held that man goes through many cycles and that, therefore, one must continue close relationships with one's ancestors and worship and honor them, for they do continue to exist in another world.

To the Easterner, life has always been a dual affair, the physical and the spiritual intermingling at various levels in one's lifetime and continuing to have influence upon one's further development after death and beyond. In India, belief in reincarnation was so universal that people kept looking for signs to recognize those whom they thought they had known in a previous incarnation. Great leaders were always thought to be the reincarnated leader of a previous period, and it was accepted as perfectly natural that great minds should again be present as great minds in some later period in history.

This concept rose to even greater heights in Tibet, where the Dalai Lama was, and still is, the reincarnated person of a predecessor, and where years are spent in search to locate the proper child into whose body the spirit of the departed Dalai Lama has entered. An elaborate ritual has been devised to make sure that the right child is found, and the system has worked so well that Tibet has been ruled by a number of Dalai Lamas for several centuries without the slightest challenge to their authority. In fact, one of the great difficulties the Red Chinese conquerors of Tibet have encountered is the attitude toward life among Tibetans, which is so far removed from Communist doctrine and, therefore, in some ways superior when it comes to resisting the aggressor. The Tibetan knows that, no matter what happens to him in this life, if he does right, he will return in another life to be rewarded for his sufferings. Marx does not promise any such thing.

Certainly the signs by which the people of India would recognize a reincarnated person were in no way comparable to modern scientific tests, but for them it seemed to work. Hindu culture was, and is, built around the concept of reincarnation, and even the system of separate classes (castes) is based upon the firm conviction that one may jump over the barrier separating the classes in a different life even if one is barred from doing so in this lifetime. Thus, it makes acceptance of one's fate or one's restrictions much easier to bear.

The Egyptian cultural-religious establishment was, in a way, a thing unto itself, totally different from its surrounding cultures. A very complicated system of multiple personalities took care of one's progress after physical death. To the Egyptian, dying was a very important part of life. *The Art of Proper Dying* could have been written for the Egyptians. To them, proper funeral arrangements insured a happy afterlife. The thought of reincarnation was not so strong, for the average Egyptian preferred a continuing afterlife, with all the amenities, to a return engagement and all the toil and sweat that accompanies a return to earth.

Nevertheless, Egyptians accepted the theory of transmigration of the soul. That is to say, the person had to come back, as it were, in animal form, for three thousand years, until, through periods of purification, he or she could again return to human form. There are varying theories as to the meaning of the elaborate embalming and funeral arrangements, but the Egyptian did not accept reincarnation in the same way as did the Celtic people of the Stone Age period. In a similar way, the Zoroastrians, the people of ancient Persia, also believed in a form of limited reincarnation, more than one existence of the human soul; and even among the Greeks there were those who had learned Eastern philosophy, or who, like Plato, had been East and absorbed some of the reincarnationist teachings. Thus there was, even in Greece, an element that believed in reincarnation as it was practiced in Asia and Africa.

In America, a highly civilized race of Indians arrived at an early date, perhaps over the land bridge from Asia, or perhaps it developed by itself in some as yet mysterious manner in Asia. These Indians were quite different from what the Wild West Indians were like. There were common bonds between the Indians of North and South America. There seemed to have been a similarity of religion and culture between Aztec, Toltec, and Inca empires, and a level comparing favorably to that of ancient Egypt. These were not primitive people living in the jungles, unable to do anything beyond hunting and fishing, the mere sustenance of life.

To the contrary, these Indians built entire cities, buildings of several stories, temples, pyramids. They had roads similar to the Roman roads, and their communities were complex and highly sophisticated, but, unfortunately, though they did have a form of ideographs, we do not have any writings or books telling us their more intimate thoughts on religion and philosophy. We cannot be sure of their attitude toward reincarnation as I have defined the term. But, as in all other cultures, there was a belief among these Indians that the gods could sometimes manifest themselves through human bodies; that the gods could descend into human form and thus live on earth for a period before returning to their lofty abode. This is a universal concept, of course. It can be found among the Greeks and Romans. It can even be found among Christians. A particularly inspired preacher or minister may indeed be "possessed of the Lord" and speak for him. Among Hebrew prophets were those who were spokesmen for the Lord for a limited time and clearly stated that they were indeed not acting on their own volition, but as messengers of a higher authority.

Cultural and religious attitudes are intermingled at all times, but religious attitudes, in addition, depend upon the official attitude of one's church toward the subject of reincarnation. In many cases, these are identical with the attitudes displayed by the society or state in which one lives. Occasionally they are different.

In the Stone Age societies practicing witchcraft, or "the old religion," there was unity both on the cultural and on the religious level. Reincarnation was a part of daily life. But if an individual member of the group decided not to accept such a concept, he or she would not be prosecuted for this, for witchcraft was a democratic religion that did not believe in having missionaries or in forcing anyone to accept it. Not so with the later religions of the Greeks and Romans; one could worship additional gods only so long as one also worshiped the official ones. During the period of the Roman Republic, it was still possible to have a religious affiliation different from that of the majority. But with the arrival of the Roman Empire, this was no longer prudent, and thus religious dogma and state concept became one and the same.

In Christianity, holding any belief other than the official line laid down by the church was, of course, grounds for expulsion from the religious community. While the state would destroy any individual expelled by the church as being equally dangerous to the state, it relied on the church to pronounce judgment. Thus, the religious position during the Middle Ages was one of condemnation for any thought that reincarnation might, indeed, be factual. Only with the advent of the Renaissance and the Protestant movement was it possible even to discuss such concepts. For six or seven hundred years, the curtain of silence covered the subject, and covered it so thoroughly that we have almost no written record of its ever having been discussed during that time. What we do have are obscure and well-camouflaged allusions in some of the esoteric writings, especially of the alchemists. But books of this sort were, by themselves, considered not suitable for general reading, and the church cast a wary eye on those who wrote them.

Today Christianity, of course, no longer dictates what one is to believe, but there are many clergymen who will insist that the Bible does not make reference to reincarnation. Yet Solomon believed that he had lived before on earth, and said so in Proverbs. Jeremiah reported that God had told him he had been on earth before in another body. John the Baptist was believed to have been a reincarnation of the prophet Elijah, and Jesus said to Nicodemus, "No man has ascended up to heaven but he that came down from heaven."

Both Eastern and Western believers in reincarnation hold that, at a certain stage in a soul's development, that soul may remain in the world of spirit and need no longer return in the form of reincarnation. In the Apocalypse, we find: "Him that overcometh will I make a pillar in the temple of my God, and he shall go no more out," again referring to the possibility of remaining in the world of spirit without the need for further earthly incarnations.

All of early Christianity accepted the possibility of both reincarnation and transmigration to some degree, and it was only later, when the church strengthened dogma, that these references were no longer alluded to. Today there are very few religions built upon the acceptance of reincarnation as part of one's faith, but the Vedic religion, practiced by most Hindus, does hold that karma and reincarnation are fact, and that, in accepting them, one practices one's religion properly.

In more recent times, the religious cult known as theosophy is built upon the concept of reincarnation, very much as ancient witchcraft was. Theosophy holds that only through reincarnation can we redeem ourselves, and that only in accepting a cycle of lives on earth can we properly understand the meaning of our individual existences. Theosophy is a gentle and purposeful cult. It is a philosophy that has done much good and that today maintains lodges throughout the world. The nineteenth-century Russian writer Madame Blavatsky was among its founders, and her books form the major base for the philosophy promulgated by this cult.

Finally, we must concern ourselves with the *scientific attitudes* toward the reality of reincarnation. In past centuries, science was not sufficiently free to inquire into the factuality of this concept. Only during the nineteenth century did any kind of serious scientific inquiry begin, and even then, only sporadically. Today the subject comes properly within the areas investigated by psychic research societies and is part of parapsychology. As such, it must be subject to the same stringent tests of validity as any other form of extrasensory perception or extraphysical activity. By the same token, the scientific inquirer must be free of prejudice and be willing to accept evidence, provided it is presented tangibly and free from alternate explanations.

A number of good books have been written on the subject during the past two decades, but it was the work of Edgar Cayce that drew public interest to the subject in recent times. Edgar Cayce was instrumental in riveting attention on the subject because of his incredible accuracy in diagnosing medical problems in people whom he had never met in the flesh. Since Cayce's readings dealing with disease were proven to be true on medical authority, one was led to accept his reincarnation findings as well. Certainly they represent the most complete body of detailed information yet on this very difficult subject. The Association for Research and Enlightenment, in Virginia Beach, Virginia, has carefully and painstakingly edited this material, and it is available to anyone seeking information on Cayce's views and readings dealing with reincarnation. But these were readings given specifically for individuals, and do not necessarily apply in the same manner to other individuals.

The second most important work in this field is a book called *Twenty Cases Suggestive of Reincarnation,* by Dr. Ian Stevenson, a professor of parapsychology and head of the department at the University of Virginia, at Charlottesville. Professor Stevenson's conclusions, while couched in careful language, nevertheless indicate that, in his opinion, there is sufficient evidence to say that reincarnation does indeed occur. The majority of parapsychologists are not fully convinced of its reality, but there is a growing segment of investigators who have delved into the subject.

World interest in the subject has never been greater. Whether this is a consequence of the insecure times we live in and the wars and destruction around us, which make people focus their attention on the spirit within them, or whether this is merely a normal cycle of returning interest in the occult, the fact remains that more people than ever ask questions about reincarnation. The orthodox scientific establishment is not about to answer them. To the contrary, it even ignores their questions. What makes the entire subject more difficult is the undeniable fact that there are also quacks and dreamers among those who speak of reincarnation, and sometimes material is offered that is clearly fraudulent, or, at the very best, fantasy.

The path, then, is a difficult one. But if one remains scientifically minded and a cautious and keen observer free from prejudice either against or for reincarnation, one is bound to discover that even so difficult a subject as rebirth can be proven by the same rules that orthodox science has always accepted as its guideline. There is no need to deviate from the norm in scientific inquiry, even when discussing reincarnation, for there are, in my view, sufficient cases on hand offering proof and evidence of the kind that makes for a positive statement concerning the reality of reincarnation.

III
Reincarnation vs.
Déjà Vu and ESP

One of the most difficult problems confronting me when I started to assemble material for this book was to eliminate that which was unsuitable for verification because it presented either no case at all, or, at the very best, only a weak case.

From the beginning we must eliminate fraud, either conscious or unconscious. Conscious fraud I have really never encountered in this investigation. Perhaps people know me too well and respect me as an investigator, but the fact is, no one has tried to tell me a manufactured story about reincarnation memories. Unconscious fraud is another matter; that is to say, where people, either consciously or under hypnosis, will manufacture likely stories in order to come up with what is expected of them and thus please the investigator. This excuse, or rather this explanation, has been used many times by investigators and parapsychologists hostile to the theory of life after death. But it does not hold water, at least not in the cases that I am personally familiar with.

As soon as a subject develops unmistakable signs of

embellishing or furnishing material without also giving me the kind of data that I can check out, I drop the case.

I should, perhaps, explain how material dealing with reincarnation comes to me. I do not advertise for it. I do not encourage it. People come to me, usually unsought, usually by writing to tell me of experiences that they have had in their lives that seem to hint at some former existence. I investigate them as thoroughly as I can. That is to say, I make sure I'm dealing with level-headed people, regardless of their social or economic status. Whenever the handwriting or the general tone of communication hints at emotional or mental disturbances, I will respectfully and tactfully drop the case. There is a great deal of such material in my files; only a small part of it has been used here.

Some of the people who contact me of their own volition do so because they are disturbed by what has happened to them and want an explanation that they can accept. Because the prevailing climate is hostile to reincarnation, doctors and ministers, by and large, will discourage any thought that what has happened to these people may be explained by reincarnation. Instead, they suggest anything from momentary disorientation to mental disease, from wishful thinking and dreaming to consciously manufacturing stories.

I take into account all kinds of psychological reasons that might prompt someone to write to me of reincarnation experiences. For one thing, it interrupts the humdrum existence of someone who has very little excitement to look forward to. It is an attention getter. It creates a feeling of importance in the person, and it is a mysterious last frontier of the mind that promises adventure and excitement. Only if I am satisfied that these are not the reasons for a person's contacting me, I proceed with the investigation of the case.

Those who come to me are, in a way, better off than those who have gone to one of the many purveyors of fantastic reincarnation records that prey on the gullible in this country and abroad. These latter are, perhaps, people who need the crutch of a glamorous and illustrious previous lifetime and are willing to pay the price in self-delusion and money. I am less charitable toward those who sell such information, because they nourish a negative and destructive force within those they sell to instead of explaining reality, even the reality of reincarnation, to their clients. Some of the people who have bought manufactured case histories of earlier lives without the slightest proof or evidence that it really happened, have come to me afterward and asked me what I think of a certain "reader." Perhaps if the manufacturers of false information would simply furnish an average life before the present one, without recourse to such glamorous companions as Queen Cleopatra, Julius Caesar, and other luminaries of earlier ages, the damage would not be so great, but then, of course, the customer would not be satisfied. Many of the people who buy such false reincarnation material need the assurance that they were very important in earlier lifetimes, even though it cannot be proven to them or to anyone else. Then, too, there are those who did not quite make it as Cleopatra or Julius Caesar, but nevertheless were present at their courts and took part in the goings on from a less lofty perch, but still in person.

As if manufacturing reincarnation records involving well-known personages in history were not enough, the fraudulent readers have also gone into copying the apparently genuine Edgar Cayce material pertaining to Atlantis and other forgotten cultures, and I see increasing evidence of manufactured reincarnation lives having been spent in Atlantis, Lemuria, and other hard-to-check areas. Now, I am not saying that reincarnation may not be possible in these places, that someone may not have lived in Atlantis, or in Lemuria, but I am insisting on adequate scientific evidence and the kind of information that a professional investigator can put before the world without fear of being ridiculed. This involves names, dates, conditions, places, linguistic material, anything that can be checked out by a professional, the kind of material that a person should have in his unconscious mind if, indeed, we are dealing with reincarnation memories. But all the material of this kind that I have examined is vague and general, and never comes to grips with a level of reality that alone permits an investigator to proceed in the hope of obtaining positive results.

Apart from fraud of this kind, the genuine material can also be subject to perfectly normal explanations that would do away with any paranormal basis for it. For example, if a person, in reporting a previous lifetime, has actually absorbed similar situations in his early life and has forgotten them, such a person would be unconsciously perpetrating a fraud upon himself. A well-known case in point was the much-publicized Bridey Murphy case of some years ago. After Morey Bernstein had published the book *The Search for Bridey Murphy, Life* magazine proceeded to debunk it, or attempt to destroy it, by sending a team of investigators to the Middle West. True to their mission, these dedicated investigators came up with information according to which the subject of Mr. Bernstein's book had actually absorbed much about life in Ireland in the nineteenth century from Irish neighbors in her home town in the Middle West. But, before the public could absorb this negative report, the Denver *Post* assigned one of their reporters to an investigation of *Life*'s investigation. The reporter went to Ireland and was able to verify much of Mr. Bernstein's material and, in fact, add to it. In the end, *The Search for Bridey Murphy* was not only confirmed, but enlarged, and has recently been republished with the appended material. However, people do unconsciously pick up bits of information, characters, names, materials about people and places during their years of adolescence and childhood, and sometimes this material rests untapped in the subconscious until at some later date it is brought to the surface for one reason or another. In all cases that I have investigated, I disposed of this explanation very carefully, so that I was able to proceed under the assumption that the material was indeed paranormal in nature.

Some orthodox doctors and psychiatrists still feel that reincarnation memories are aberrations of the mind and should be treated as hallucinations and other forms of delusion. Those who follow the Freudian school will insist that these "illusions" represent suppressed sexual desires, while the Jungian analyst would interpret them as dream material come to the surface in the waking state and representing suppressed desires and other material of importance to the individual's personality development.

Only a handful of medical doctors and psychiatrists today accept the theory of reincarnation, but their number is increasing daily. Dr. Ian Stevenson is probably among the most prominent of those who accept the validity of such investigations. His books, unfortunately, are not popularly written and, therefore, reach only his own colleagues. If they were done in a way that would appeal to a broader segment of the population, I have no doubt that, in time, popular interest in the subject would, in turn, force larger segments of the medical establishment to look into the subject seriously and without prejudice.

Having eliminated fraud, self-delusion, wishful thinking, accidental picking up of material during childhood or adolescence, there remains a sufficiently large backlog of material to which these criteria do not apply, but all this material is still not necessarily reincarnation material. We have to deal with another phenomenon, bordering on reincarnation but not part of it. This is called the *déjà vu* (already seen) phenomenon. It is the feeling that one has seen a certain situation before but cannot remember where or when, or having heard certain words spoken before in exactly the same manner as one now hears, or having been to a place before, where consciously and logically one knows one has never been. The feeling of déjà vu is so universal and so common that almost everyone will come up with an example when asked.

Orthodox psychiatrists, of course, explain this simply as a matter of "opening a false memory door," but they never explain how one accomplishes this neat feat. True, in *some* cases one might explain the experience as one involving a pseudo memory, or a false memory, in that someone feeling that he has seen a face before, or said something before, or met someone before and in fact has not, is actually having a false impression of the event. Fortunately, there are thousands of cases where witnesses bear out the fact that a false memory is entirely out of the question. An excellent case in point, and perhaps a typical déjà vu experience, involves a young man from upstate New York by the name of Del Cook, who is a senior in high school at the present time, going on to college. Here, then, is Mr. Cook's report:

In the spring of 1965 several friends of mine, Joseph D., Christy D., Peter P., Margaret P., Joanne B., and myself, Del Cook, were on our way to a Christian camp at Beaver Falls, New York, accompanied by Father George K., our group supervisor. We were going to visit this camp to inquire about spending two weeks there. Upon arriving, it occurred to me that the main building, which was four stories high, was familiar to me, but at that time we went to see the director of the camp so I ignored the impression. After meeting the director, we went to look around the area. Then the feeling that I had been there before began to increase, but I didn't tell the others. We went to the side of the large building. There was a pool there, but it was relatively new, and I didn't recognize it.

As time went on I felt more and more that I had been there before, even though I had never been in the area. I told the others to follow me around to the back of the house. Just before going into the door I realized it was the door to the kitchen. We went through the kitchen, but it was not very familiar. At this time I didn't think much about it being unusual that I recognized the area. Then we went through the dining room to the stairs, and I told the others that I had seen the place before, even though I had never been there. I told them that I would show them around, so they agreed, but were a bit hesitant. Next I showed them the second and third floors, recognizing the rooms as we went. While on the third floor I told them that I would then show them the next floor. They asked where it was, as no stairs were apparent. I told them that the door to one side was the one that led up to the attic. They asked how I knew, and I told them that I remembered it from somewhere. We opened the door and there were the stairs. We went halfway up and I told them that as they went through the door at the top of the stairs they would see some old pictures, and to the left there would be two trunks placed end to end. The first one had china, and the second had clothes in it. Then we went up the rest of the way, and the room was just as I described. The trunks were there containing the china and the clothes. All of this was out of the line of sight of where we were on the stairs when

I told them there was a door at the top of the stairs as well. Then we went through a bit more of the house and went out. Outside I saw a dog, a Russian wolfhound, and I remembered its name. I can't remember the name now, though. It began barking, and a lady came out of the house and called it by the name, to stop barking. At this time I was fourteen years old.

It is true that many cases here classified as déjà vu experiences may in fact be also reincarnation memories, but I have chosen to label as reincarnation memory only those cases in which alternate explanations will *not* work. Sometimes the line between prevision or clairvoyance, and later verification in objective reality, is very thin, and the memory of the earlier impression is not entirely erased or suppressed. There is, then, a vague or uncertain feeling of having heard someone say something or having seen something or someone before, and when the event actually takes place, one realizes that this has not really happened until this very moment. A good case of this kind occurred to a colleague and friend of the previous communicator. John Leadley is also a senior in an upstate New York high school, and will attend the University of Notre Dame. Here is his report:

Del Cook and I were in English workshop on May 15, 1969. For several days previous to this particular afternoon, I had been thinking that something Del had said to me was very unusual. This thing that he had said was, "Did you know that gluttony was a moral affection?" I didn't give this too much thought during these days, except that it was such an unusual thing for him to say. Also, I had a mental picture of him turning to a certain page in the book and then saying that. Then on the fifteenth I was sitting at a desk in the English room, when it seemed as though I had seen the whole scene, with the people in exactly those positions, before. Then Del said, "Did you know that gluttony was a moral affection?"

Now, a phrase of such unusual connotation is certainly not explicable on the basis of coincidence, if there is, indeed, such a thing as coincidence. Here we have a sim-

ilar experience to déjà vu, except that it is the reverse—
the confirmation follows the impression that it has already
happened.

Ilsa Brown is a librarian in Mansfield, Ohio. All her
life she has been having psychic experiences. When she
went to boarding school in her native Germany, in Dres-
den, she went to the so-called English garden, where she
had never been before. Immediately upon arriving at the
garden, she knew her way around and knew that she had
been there before; yet she was unable to pinpoint the time
or occasion. Since then, she has had many experiences in
which she would arrive at a town or place only to recognize the place as something she had seen before. In her
case, certain smells seem to evoke certain memories. In
other cases, it is sound, or a pictorial impression, that
seems to stimulate the faculty of recalling an earlier
impression.

Recurring dreams may be an indication of both genuine reincarnation memories and déjà vu. Since the dream
state is merely the opposite of the wakeful state, it stands
to reason that various types of psychic experiences can
take place in either one of these two states. Recurring
dreams, however, are usually psychic rather than psychological, and indicate some form of ESP communication.
The majority of recurring dream cases I am familiar with
seem to indicate strongly that they represent partial or
incomplete reincarnation memories. Frequently, these are
accompanied by strong feelings of fear, and often represent memories of one's final moments or some great emotional crisis.

Betty Fiocco, of Los Angeles, is a housewife with many
years of psychic experiences. She has now read a great
deal on ESP and other forms of psychic consciousness,
but in previous years, when the bulk of her experiences
took place, she had no knowledge of parapsychology and
was stumped by the things that happened to her. Of
interest here is an incident that occurred to her in a German restaurant in La Jolla, California. The restaurant had
been open only a few years when Betty Fiocco and her
husband paid it a visit. Upon seeing the German owner of
the place, whose name is Ernie, she instantly felt that she
had known him before, and he felt the same way about

her. Now, to be sure, this was not a matter of romantic connotation at all. They glanced at each other casually, and they knew each other. This went on for several visits that the Fioccos paid the restaurant afterward. The entire thing troubled her so much that she tried time and again to figure out where she had met him. At the same time, he was trying to figure out where he had met the strange lady before. Finally, she had enough nerve to go over to him and ask, "Where have I ever met you before?" and it developed that they had, indeed, never met. He had come from Europe recently and gone on to Chicago and from there to his present place. There had been no place that their paths had crossed, but whatever it was that they had experienced together, perhaps in a previous lifetime, never came to the surface. Was it reincarnation, or was it simply a case of déjà vu?

Finally, there are cases that seem to hint at reincarnation, but are, in effect, only cases of involuntary mediumship. A typical case in point occurred during recent years to Mrs. Joanne Van Hook, of Georgia. She and her husband are in the habit of investigating different landmarks on the trips they take in and around southern states. In August of 1968 they took one of their trips to Tennessee. They packed a picnic bag and took off to a camping site between Townsend, Tennessee, and Gatlinburg. They ate by a nearby stream and then decided to go on an excursion. Just below the campground were a school and church built in the late 1800s. As they approached the building, Mrs. Van Hook had the strange feeling that she had been there before. They got out of the car, and her husband remarked that she looked different, as if her personality had suddenly changed. Out in front of the school was a graveyard. They went inside the school and stood there for about fifteen minutes. Her husband remarked that he felt another "presence" besides them. As they came out of the school, Mrs. Van Hook went straight to the graveyard. She almost seemed to float in, and then went from one grave to another, as if she were hunting for something. She tried to persuade her husband to join her, but he refused. After about ten minutes of this, she came out of the graveyard completely unaware of what she had done, and remembered absolutely nothing of the event. A few weeks later they decided to go again and see what would happen. This time, nothing out of the ordinary happened.

Now, it appears to me that Mrs. Van Hook was being used as a medium by some presence in the area requiring her service. That service may have been looking for a certain gravestone, or expressing an unfulfilled desire. The fact that she remembered nothing afterward, and that it did not reoccur on the second visit, seems strongly to point to such an explanation. Also, neither before nor after did she have any flashes hinting at having been there before.

During World War II, a soldier found himself in Belgium. While his buddies were wondering how to enter a certain house in a particular small town in Belgium, he showed them the way in and went ahead of them up the stairs, explaining, as he went up, where each and every room was. When he was questioned after this about having been there before, he denied ever having left his home in America, and he spoke the truth. He could not explain how he had suddenly found himself possessed of knowledge he did not have in his normal condition. This again may be a case of déjà vu, or it may be reincarnation.

My wife, Catherine, and I were standing in the living room of Pamela Mason, in Hollywood, not long ago. Mrs. Mason had arranged a dinner party for us to meet certain friends of hers. All of a sudden Catherine turned to me and said, "Hans, I have a funny feeling that all this has happened before. I remember having said before what I am saying now, and the people we are meeting now, somehow I remember all of this from a previous occasion, and yet, this is the first time it is happening to us. What does it mean?" Well, of course, Catherine was having a genuine déjà vu experience. Certainly no reincarnation element was involved here. The "I have seen it all and heard it all before" kind of feeling was indeed one of a previous psychic impression, later realized.

Many cases of memories belonging to another person or to another lifetime are, indeed, nothing more than such déjà vu experiences. Others may be due to ESP abilities on the part of the participant. Only cases clearly eliminating ESP or déjà vu as possible explanations, not to mention ordinary causes, will be considered reincarnation cases in this book. Even so, there is a great deal of material, and much of it is impressive.

IV
Apparently Genuine Cases That Cannot Be Fully Proved

In writing about cases involving reincarnation, an author should not rest with the presentation of his story alone, but should try to verify at least a substantial amount of the material obtained, either in flashes of conscious knowledge or through hypnosis. When the story is presented without the proper verification, it becomes nothing more than an interesting account. Such, in my opinion, is the case with much of the material in *Here and Hereafter*, by Ruth Montgomery.

A different slant is taken by Joan Grant's account of her research, especially when it involves ancient Egypt. Here we must consider Miss Grant's own involvement with Egyptian archeology, and the possibility of material having risen from her own unconscious mind. But if this were not so, the need to verify some of the material involving Egyptian archeology is very great and, in my opinion, entirely capable of producing information, data, details, that could be considered genuine only if they were indeed stemming from the communicator, or from the previous incarnation claimed. Surely, in delving into the mystery of a previous lifetime, one is allowed to ask certain test questions in order to establish identity beyond a shadow of a doubt. If such questions are not asked, and if the proper research is not undertaken, then the case becomes weak and, while it may be genuine, lacks the necessary convincing elements.

The cases I am presenting in this chapter are not lacking in research, where research was possible, but are incomplete in other ways. Either there is not enough material available on the case in point, or the material is of a kind that rings true but cannot be verified, no matter how much one would like, due to lack of research sources or to other technical reasons. Even though in these cases I was unable to present a completely convincing picture, all the cases here discussed are incapable of alternative explanations, and therefore fit in with the concept of reincarnation memories as I have established it earlier. In some cases, additional sessions with the person involved might indeed yield additional results, but this is not always possible. Reincarnation is not a matter of life or death to the one to whom the memories occur, and a researcher such as I is not always free to travel to distant cities to follow up on each and every case, much as he would like to.

I am presenting these partial or fractional cases here to show how common among all of us is the fleeting glimpse into a previous lifetime, that it is not a freak experience that happens to a few, but is indeed far more common than is realized by most researchers, let alone the ordinary man in the street.

Whenever people have flashes of memories pertaining to earlier lives, they are generally brief, often confused and out of context, and it is sometimes years before they realize that what appears to them as either waking visions or strong dreams is actually part of an earlier lifetime. Frequently the puzzle doesn't seem to work out, and the pieces do not fall into place, but occasionally people do realize that what appears to them in this form has some meaning and is not merely a figment of their imagination or just another dream.

It is rare, however, that a person can recollect large segments of an earlier existence in the physical world, and it is even rarer that they recollect their earlier lives from the beginning—that is to say, from birth onward. Occasionally there are examples of a recollection in which the person does actually recall his or her own birth. In general, average people may remember as far back as their early school years. I, myself, have exceptionally good recall, but I cannot remember anything before my third birthday. Although there is a dim memory of having been to kindergarten, and having just turned three, this is not a continuous memory at all, but merely a tiny flash in which I see myself in this existence. Now, this is not a reincarnation memory, but represents a good memory such as many people possess in the normal course of their lives.

Ordinarily, people do not recall details of their own lives before such an early age. I am not aware of any case in which a person recalls his own birth, except, of course, the one I am about to relate, but I am sure there must be others of a similar nature in the annals of psychic research.

Mrs. Nancy Anglin comes from Alabama. She is twenty-six years old, is married to a professional musician, and is a licensed practical nurse. They have one son and live in one of the cities of the state of Alabama. Her interests are normal—music, the arts. They have an interest in reading books, but there has never been any particularly strong interest in the occult or in psychic research. This is the more amazing, as Mrs. Anglin has had, all her life, incidents of extrasensory perception, mediumship, and clairvoyance. She has taken these events in her stride without undue anxiety or extraordinary stress. Her ability to foresee the future and recall her impressions will be recorded elsewhere. Here I wish to concern myself solely with the amazing reincarnation memories she has had.

As a matter of fact, calling them reincarnation memories is technically incorrect, since in this case, I believe we are not dealing with an earlier lifetime, but with the beginning of this incarnation. Ever since she was a small child and able to speak, Mrs. Anglin had insisted to her mother that she did recall the moment of her birth into this world. She vividly described the day she was brought home from the hospital, a sixteen-day-old baby. I questioned Mrs. Anglin about the details of this extraordinary memory.

"My birth memories consist of an awareness of being blasted into a place where extremely bright lights and what seemed like the resounding echoes of human voices were imposed on my small person," she explained. "I vaguely seem to remember a detached observance of this affair, including blurred visions of figures clothed with masks and caps. The day I was brought home I remember riding snuggled in the arms of a woman with light brown hair and a prominent nose, arriving at a house where my Aunt Jeff and sixteen-month-old brother were coming out the front door, onto the front porch, I suppose to greet my mother and me. I do remember it was the first time I had seen trees, and was impressed by them. More clear than anything is my memory of observing my mother, and in the thought language of the newborn, wondering, Who is she? What am I, and who are those people standing on the porch? Since I have been a young child I have always had the feeling of total detachment from myself and others, as if I were on the outside looking in."

Now, one might argue that Mrs. Anglin manufactured these impressions of her own birth at a later date, either consciously or, perhaps, unconsciously, from her normal knowledge of what births are like, but this is not so in this case, for we do know that her remarks concerning her birth go back to a very early time in her life, when, being a small child, she had no access to this kind of information. Also, her impressions and descriptions of her own birth are so vivid and so detailed that they seem to indicate an authentic personal experience.

Ordinary memories fade in time, and so it is not surprising that reincarnation memories might also fade as time goes on. It is therefore rather interesting to study the cases of young children having such memories, which in later life will disappear from their conscious minds. A good case in point was brought to my attention recently by a Mrs. Carole Hardin, in Montana. Mrs. Hardin lives with her husband, who works in one of the local mines. She is an art student by correspondence, and they are people in the middle-income bracket—ordinary people, I would say, living in an eight-year-old country house.

They have four children—nine, seven, four, and three years old—and are representative of an average middle-class family. Mrs. Hardin has a crippling condition that prevents her from writing in longhand. Other than that, there really isn't anything extraordinary about them. There is, however, a great deal to be said about one of their children, Brenda, aged four.

Nothing very special happened with little Brenda until Good Friday of 1969. On that day, Brenda sat up, awaking from a sound sleep, and started to talk about a previous life. She had spent the night in the home of Mrs. Hardin's sister, Mrs. Perry.

"I have lived in the country once," the little girl said, "in the South, in a big, white house." She then went on to describe it as having had a big porch with white pillars and a big, green lawn. She referred to a pet horse named Hooper John she seemed rather fond of. Her aunt asked her if there were any other children. "Yes," the little girl said, "a lot of little darkies." She spoke with a strong accent, apparently French, and even gave her name, which was also a French name. Her aunt couldn't even pronounce it. Finally, the little girl added, "But I died." Her aunt thought she had misunderstood her and asked what she had said. "I died," the little girl repeated somewhat impatiently. "I fell off my horse, Hooper John, when I was sixteen, and died." She then lay back down and went back to sleep. The little girl's uncle, Mr. Perry, who was present throughout this amazing conversation, attributed it all to the child's lively imagination, but the following morning the aunt again spoke to little Brenda when she awoke.

Present this time was her daughter Sharon, aged fourteen. Together the two questioned the little girl further: Did she live on a farm when she lived down South? "Of course not," the little girl said; "it was a plantation." She then went on to describe how they raised tobacco, speaking of cutting the tobacco, and sheaves. When asked what it looked like, she said, "You know, like crimped tobacco." Brenda then repeated the same account she had told for the first time the previous night. She spoke of a fire wagon, described a firebox and the purpose it served, but as the day wore on she forgot about this, being, after all, only four years old. By evening she had completely forgotten the incident. However, a few days later she referred to a toy horse as "Hooper John" for just a moment, finally saying, "Oh no, you're not my Hooper John." She put the toy down and has not spoken of it ever since.

Now, this is an extraordinary thing for a four-year-old girl, that is to say, to use phrases, language, and information rarely, if ever, possessed by someone that young; especially so as Brenda had had no occasion to visit the South or to learn about the tobacco business. At age four children do not read books, nor has Mrs. Hardin read any such stories to her at any time. She wondered whether I might hypnotize the little girl and discover additional information, but I hesitated to put someone so young in a hypnotic trance. Hopefully, other snatches of memory might come to her naturally. However, it is quite conceivable that they will not, and that something within her triggered this one-time occurrence. Perhaps a lively dream caused a deep layer of the unconscious to yield buried information from a past incarnation. Four-year-old children are very difficult to question, and as far as Brenda is concerned, the entire incident has no significance whatsoever.

In a number of cases there seems to be a relationship between psychic ability and reincarnation memories, although this does not mean that only those who have ESP have reincarnation flashes, or that those who have reincarnation flashes are also psychic, but there are a number of cases in which both abilities coexist.

A case in point concerns Mrs. Lois Smith of Arkansas. She is married and has five children, one of whom is deceased. Their eight-room house is in the country, and she leads an ordinary, middle-class life, and yet, since age five or six, strange things have happened to her that seem to be beyond the reach of a five-year-old. She would say things that were out of context for her age and surroundings, which amazed her elders. Ever since then, she has developed precognition to a high degree, has been able to foretell future events, and has practiced extrasensory perception in many other forms. There are witnesses to every

one of her predictions, but I am not concerned here with
her psychic experiences as such.

There are two dreams she has had repeatedly. The first
recurring dream concerns an event in which she sees
herself alone in bed at night, and she then sees a man
come in and stab her with a knife in the left side. At this
precise moment she feels exactly where the knife goes in.
It stings her and there is much pain after that, for she
is dying. This dream has come to her many times.

Another dream is more detailed. In this she sees herself
on a ship she describes as a clipper ship. Mrs. Smith has
no knowledge of boats or ships, but the ship she saw in
these recurring dreams seems to be of an earlier age. She
remembers men wearing ruffles, and she remembers a
number of children, and turmoil. She has the feeling of a
robbery and an exchange of riches for the lives of these
children. One of the children reminds her of her own
five-year-old daughter, Linda, but she's not sure of the
resemblance. She sees the child playing under a blanket
with his head covered. She describes the riches as being
in brown or gray bags, and very heavy. A passage on this
ship is quite vivid in her memory. She describes it in great
detail, including even the wooden paneling.

"The placed seemed quite roomy and comfortable,"
she explains. "It was lit by some sort of light enclosed
in a glass globe that hung on the walls here and there, but
mostly it was dimly lit, which led me to believe it were
nighttime. The color was amber, because it reflected off
the wood of the ship. This gave the wood a soft, reddish
color. At shoulder height, there were strips of wood going around the boat's walls. The children," she explained,
"were in another place on the same ship." This was located near a doorway. They seemed happy and con-
tented and unafraid. She remembered having to stoop a
little when entering through a curtain. She didn't feel
frightened, and she remembered only being annoyed at
having to be there at all. The strange thing was that she
didn't feel as if she were participating in this event, but
rather that she was watching it, as if she were outside.

There were men coming into the ship from her left. An
exchange was made, and the men were forming some kind
of relay with the heavy sacks. They wore ruffles on their

sleeves, while others were in odd clothing, and she recalls thinking that they were peasants because of this and their very bad smell. They smelled of fish and oil. One of the men had a long knife stuck through his belt. The belt was like nothing she had even seen before. It was more like a piece of material tied around the waist, and the knife was stuck through it. It was a curving knife with twine around the handle—very big, perhaps thirty inches long. It shone brightly, and she remembers being fascinated with the shine. She also recalls being repelled by the dirty appearance of the man who wore the belt and knife. He was bald, and the shine of his head was almost equal to that of the knife.

She recalls that the robbery was very quiet, and she had a feeling that the entire transaction had the co-operation of someone aboard the ship. Finally, she recalls that the men taking the heavy sacks upstairs were all wearing gray cloths wrapped around their heads—not Turkish style, but so that they had a bald look at the top of their heads.

Now, Mrs. Smith has had no interest in pirate stories or ships, or anything pertaining to the events depicted in her recurrent dreams. The vivid impression left, each time she dreamt this—and she dreamt it many times in exactly the same fashion—did not fade as time went on. She got to wondering what it all meant. Eventually she read books dealing with extrasensory perception, and eventually also she thought that it might indicate some kind of reincarnation memory. Only then did she decide to read books dealing with the subject of reincarnation, and she has since then read several. But, at the time when the dreams occurred to her, there was no knowledge of the field or what it might mean to her.

Rosemary Benoit is a twenty-eight-year-old housewife in Massachusetts. She remembers far back, even as far as when she was only one year old. Today she wonders whether she has lived before. Often she would sit knitting a sweater, which is a job needing some concentration, when suddenly there was a quick flash, and before her eyes, before her mind's eyes, she saw a vision of two girls coming home from school—a driveway of a house—a house she had never seen before except in these visions. All of a sudden she remembered this as if it were a dream from long ago. She didn't know where this place was, but she knew that she had been there.

What she saw involved a black car parked on a hill. A man was in the driver's seat, a man she instinctively knew to be her father. She hugged him, and it was nighttime. The car was standing on a dirt road. There was a large pine tree just next to where the car was parked, and a log cabin below. They were waiting for someone. Her father wasn't the father she has in this lifetime. He was a strange man and, yet, she knew he was her father. She, herself, was in the back seat as her father got out of the car. Next she saw herself out of the car also, playing with the bark of a tree—peeling it. Then someone called to her, and she ran down the hill behind some older children. The name Edwina flashed through her mind. Consciously she does not know this name, yet in the vision she felt she had been there—that she was young, and that it was she who ran down that hill. She clearly saw this girl running last among the children—a girl with long hair, in a plain dress with a ruffled hem and a ruffled bodice. The hem was just above the ankle, the dress had some red and white on it, and she also wore long white stockings.

She began to wonder, Who was Edwina? The name sounded strange to her. Of course, she felt that perhaps this was something from her own childhood memory. She thought about it consciously, and she asked questions of her relatives. The name Edwina did not occur in her family. No such scene had ever taken place in her own lifetime, and yet she is possessed of an extraordinary memory going back to age one.

When I questioned her about details of this vision, she recalled that the car was one of those that were in style perhaps in the 1920s or early '30s. She remembered seeing similar cars in old movies or on television, especially those dealing with Al Capone and his days. The windshield had a bar in the center; the interior was brown, perhaps leather or suede. Beyond that, she cannot recall any details, but there is a haunting feeling that she was Edwina running down a hill in another lifetime.

Ouija boards are the least likely tools to obtain verifiable information in psychic research, as I have often pointed out, and yet, once in a while a Ouija board can be useful in research. Now, a Ouija board is nothing more than a piece of wood inscribed with the letters of the alphabet, numerals, and a few simple words like "yes," "no," and "maybe." Upon it is placed a wooden contraption called the indicator, usually very light weight, sometimes made of glass instead of wood. Upon this indicator rest the hands of two or more people participating in the experiment. These hands must be applied lightly. Naturally, the movements of the indicator across the board are not due to any spirit action per se, but due to the muscular action of the hands, or rather the persons whose hands are placed upon the indicator, but the motivation in moving the indicator to certain letters and thus spelling words and sentences may be due to another control than that of the person operating the board.

I have already pointed out in many of my books that I do not like the use of Ouija boards by the average person, because it presents certain dangers to those who have deep trance mediumship and are not aware of it at the time when they first use such a board. But I do feel that occasionally this board may be an instrument of tapping the unconscious in a verifiable manner.

A strange case in point is the case of Mr. and Mrs. Atta, who live in Columbus, Ohio. Fascinated with extrasensory perception for some time, the couple had acquired a Ouija board and were trying to communicate through it with alleged deceased entities. Having considered it merely a toy at first, the Attas took their board somewhat more seriously when it started to give them information pertaining to the husband.

It all started one evening in 1968, when they had used the board to amuse some of their guests. After the guests had left, Mrs. Atta and her husband sat down alone and tried the board again. This time the communicator, whoever it was, had immediate reference to the husband. The communicator in this case was a woman named Rochelle, who claimed to have been the wife of Mrs. Atta's husband in a previous incarnation. "Did you know Pete in his lifetime?" Mrs. Atta asked. The board indicated assent. "How long ago?" "One hundred and five years ago," said the board without a moment's hesitation. Stimulated by this exchange, Mrs. Atta then pursued the question. It developed that her husband, Pete, had been known as Robert Hinis and that he had lived during the Civil War. Rochelle claimed to have been his wife at the time. At the time of his death, the board explained, Mr. Hinis had been twenty-five years old.

"Where was your home?" asked Mrs. Atta.

"Blacksburg, Virginia," came the answer.

"Where was Rob born?"

"Patascala, Virginia."

"Where were you born?"

"Blacksburg."

"What year was Rob born?"

" '38."

"What year were you born?"

" '38."

"How old were you when you died?"

"Twenty-four."

Mrs. Atta stopped the board and did a quick bit of arithmetic. If Rob had been born in 1838 and died at the age of twenty-five, he had died in the year 1863. Now, Rochelle said she had known him a hundred and five years ago, which also gets us back to 1863. The Civil War lasted from 1861 to 1865. It would be very difficult to do such quick arithmetic without time to think. Besides this, Mrs. Atta knew that her husband was not making this up or trying to play a practical joke on her, and as far as she was concerned, she certainly had no knowledge of either the character of Robert Hinis, nor of the dates mentioned by his alleged wife, Rochelle. She questioned the communicator further.

How had her husband died? It turned out that he had been shot. He had been a scout and a colonel at the same time. This threw Mrs. Atta off, for she could not conceive of a scout being a colonel also. However, there were scout regiments in the Civil War with all the necessary ranks among their officers. A scout, in terms of Civil War history, does not mean a boy scout, but simply a regiment of advance troops.

It developed further that Rochelle and her children had all died together in a fire, and that this fire had been due to war action. Pete, as Rob in his previous lifetime, had killed many men in defense of the United States government. The Confederate soldiers had burned down their house. Somehow the attachment Rochelle had had for her husband, Robert, in the nineteenth century had carried over to his new incarnation as Pete, and she felt she still should help him and his new wife get on as best they could.

After the sessions with the Ouija board, Mrs. Atta felt sort of foolish about the whole thing. She really did not believe that the communication was genuine, but to assure herself that there was nothing to it and to end the matter once and for all, she did write some letters about the period and people involved to what she considered the proper sources of information. These included the Attorney General's department in Roanoke, Virginia; the General Services Administration, at the National Archives, in Washington, D.C.; the Clerk of the County Court House of Montgomery County in Christianburg, Virginia; and the Clerk and Treasurer at Blacksburg, Virginia, a Mrs. Rochelle Brown. She managed to find that there was, indeed, a Blacksburg, Virginia, in existence, although she could not locate Patascala, Virginia. However, she found there was a Palasky near Blacksburg, and wondered if the communicator on the Ouija board had misspelled the word, as she had misspelled many other words. This, Mrs. Atta soon found out, is par for the course when you deal with a Ouija board. Strangely, she could not get anything else out of the communicator, who had called herself Rochelle, beyond this material; at any rate, nothing that proved to be of much value.

When replies came to her inquiries, she felt differently about the matter, however. There was a Robert Hinis from Christianburg County, Virginia, who had died in the Civil War at about the time the Robert Hinis whom the communicator, Rochelle, had spoken of, had died.

Possibly this case might be put down to extrasensory perception, in which Mrs. Atta would have been the medium, but she has not had other psychic experiences, either prior to or after the Ouija board sessions. This remains one of those cases that seem to point toward reincarnation and yet are not fully capable of verification in the true sense.

Reincarnation flashes are really far more numerous

than most people realize, and they are not in any way restricted to any particular nationality, economic group, age group, or other classification. Incomplete reincarnation memories are especially common.

Sally Sarnoskie is a housewife in Pennsylvania. She has had various psychic experiences all her life, mainly precognitions. But the most disturbing event in her life is a recurrent dream that used to occur to her many times as a child, all through high school. Eventually it faded away and has not come back to her since. To this day, she does not understand its true meaning.

The dream always started out in the same way. She saw herself as a small girl, running, full of terror, down a red brick road. She knew that this little girl was herself. As the girl looked behind her, she saw a man swinging a rope with a noose on the end. He was chasing her, and she ran and ran and finally came to a bush. The bush had no leaves at all. The little girl could see straight through it. She hid behind the bush and the man kept coming after her. When he came upon her and was ready to put the rope on her, Mrs. Sarnoskie would wake up. Was she reliving death at the hands of an evil person? Every time this dream occurred to her, she found herself in a state of absolute terror upon awakening. It would be easier to dismiss this as merely a symbolic dream capable of the usual psychoanalytical interpretation were it not for the fact that all her other dreams were totally dissimilar to this one.

Recurrent dreams that happen in precisely the same manner time and again are not very common. It has been my conviction and the conviction of many other parapsychologists that such dream material is unusual and indicative of some form of paranormal experience. It is quite possible that Mrs. Sarnoskie did indeed recall a terrifying experience from the past, but until something further happens to jolt her or to jog her memory into yielding still more evidential material from past lives, we will have to accept her testimony as one of the many cases indicative of possible reincarnation but not fully verifiable at this time.

People can go on for years without ever encountering anything having to do with the supernormal or reincarnation, but then all of a sudden something happens to change their lives and their outlook. Mrs. Loretta Sohmer is a housewife; she used to be a hairdresser, and she's married to a man working as an IBM supervisor. In July of 1967 something happened that made her wonder about having lived before.

"We were on our way to New York," she explained, "when we stopped at Cooperstown to see the Hall of Fame. Upon entering the city limits, the scenery became very familiar to me. When we reached the Hall of Fame I felt depressed and upset. I correctly directed my husband to a street I knew well, and named a bridge with water running under it. The name of the street, which I believed was Brook, turned out to be Brookside. Also the name Sherman kept running through my mind, and we searched a cemetery that was familiar also, but did not find anyone of that name. By this time our children grew tired and we had to go on our way. Since that time, I am determined to go back and see what else will turn up. I feel certain I have lived there before. I have had two dreams also that were giving me further leads to follow, but of course, they were just dreams."

In dealing with these phenomena one must always be careful to eliminate obviously normal reasons for having such experiences. In the case of Mrs. Sohmer there certainly doesn't seem to be any reason why she should suddenly remember street names or be familiar with city streets or parts of a place she had never seen before in her lifetime. But not all reincarnation-type dreams are recurrent. Sometimes a single dream experience can be so shattering and so strong that it leaves an indelible imprint upon the consciousness of an individual.

Lucy is a fourteen-year-old girl living in the state of Georgia. Recently she experienced a dream that was so unusual that it forced her to contact me, wondering whether perhaps it indicated some form of previous life. Lucy is a high school sophomore who has had no outstanding psychic experiences. In fact, the dream was her first and only such experience, and she had no interest in the occult nor does she read a great deal about it, but she does have rather high intuition and sometimes feels things before they actually happen. Yet she never takes her feelings seriously, and considered them just part of her character.

"The dream began," she reports, "in a bedroom furnished in either late 19th or very early 20th century style. There was a rocking chair and one straight-backed chair. There was also a heavy iron bed, and a night stand on which was placed a kerosene lamp and a pitcher and washbasin. The walls and floor were all bare hardwood, and there was one open window, which was screenless and opened onto a bare yard and a white picket fence. Beyond that was a green field, and in the distance a group of trees. I was in the dream, but not as myself. I was in the person of a young woman whose name I don't remember. I do remember lying on the brass bed because the young woman was in childbirth. Now, I assure you that before that dream I had no idea of what childbirth is like, but when I explained the feeling to my mother, she assured me that I had accurately described labor pains. Also, I remember that there was an older woman dressed in a gray dress and a small gray cap. She acted as a midwife. I somehow had the impression that she was my mother-in-law, although I am not sure. The dream broke off here, although I remember three short flashes.

"In one, I remember looking out the window of the same bedroom to check on a baby girl who was playing in the bare yard. Her name was Christina, and she was the child whose birth I had experienced earlier.

"In another scene I saw this same child playing near the water on a deserted beach, while the young woman, who was holding a younger child—a boy named Barry—and her husband, looked on.

"The third and last scene was one in which the girl and her husband were walking down the street in some city. Both were dressed in clothes that were in style around the turn of the century. There was also a gas lamp near the sidewalk, something I believe was common in that time period. So ended my dream. It seemed to me that the dream went from the young married life, which seemed to be a poor time financially, to later and more prosperous years."

For a fourteen-year-old, Lucy sounds very rational and composed. Could it be, then, that she has been given an insight into a previous existence? Could it be that her adult approach to life is partially a holdover of an unfulfilled earlier lifetime?

That advancing years do diminish the memory of a previous lifetime seems to be sure to me. Take, for instance, the case of a young lady of Baltimore, Maryland. When she was four years old, she would talk intelligently about driving a truck. She would not only know technical details of how to drive a truck, but she would also speak freely of the cities she had visited while a truck driver. She could be questioned about this and come up with immediate and intelligent answers that amazed her elders and confounded her parents. Unfortunately, this ability did not last. Realizing that she was different from other children, she became shy and started to clam up. Today she is married and quite mature. During a recent discussion of her childhood ability, she admitted that she always knew that in another lifetime she drove a truck. It doesn't really interest her any longer, since the stories have faded into the background, and her busy life, this lifetime that is, has taken up all her time and energies.

Allen Lopatin is a nineteen-year-old college student living on Long Island, New York. He has been having psychic experiences for many years. Frequently he feels that a mind other than his own is speaking through him. After such impressions he usually finds himself very tired, and frequently must lie down and sleep.

"I often try," he explained, "after such an experience to remember what words have come into my mind, but I find it impossible to do so. In an attempt to overcome this, I have tried to have pencil and paper available so as to write down the words. On a few occasions I have had paper close at hand, and I have written down some series of words. I find that these words are totally unfamiliar to me—the very opposite of what they seem to be when in my mind. In one case I found that I had written three words: crossroads, Emily, Oliver. While writing the words I seemed to be hearing, 'I am at the crossroads with Emily and her father.' I am positive that these words came from someone of about my own age who lived about the turn of the century. During the experience I had the feeling that it had been myself saying these words. I, however, have never known anyone named Emily, nor would I use the word 'crossroads' in normal conversation. After I had written these words down I was certain that the same words had come to my mind previously. Afterwards, besides the always present headache, I had strong feelings of depression and guilt.

"On other occasions, when I am able to write, I find that I have written a series of words, usually five to ten, that include names—last names that are wholly unfamiliar to me. On one occasion I wrote a list of names that I felt were men that I had been with and knew well. While I was writing I felt that I was in the Midwest about the time of the American Civil War."

Robert Wiemer, with whom I have produced two films, came to psychic experiences totally uncommitted, and yet, over the years, he himself has had experiences that have convinced him of the reality of these phenomena.

On March 5, 1968, he and an associate, Richard Berman, were en route to New Orleans between 10:00 A.M. and 1:00 P.M. They were stopping in the town of Hagerstown, Maryland, when Bob glanced up at a second-story Chinese restaurant on one of Hagerstown's largest streets. There was a sudden halt in his movements—a gasp. His mouth flew wide open. Unable to speak for about fifteen seconds, Bob then told of having been to such a place as a small child. To be sure, it was not this Chinese restaurant, but it reminded him of a second-floor Chinese restaurant very much like it. He saw himself in it, not as a patron, but as some sort of resident. His view was that seen from under a table, playing under the table, seeing waiters' legs walking by. He remembers that there were buttons under the table to summon the waiter. Bob had a definite sensation of having lived in such a place and that the place was in Chicago. The impression lasted for a full hour but kept on being on his mind for at least four more days. Despite systematic reasoning, Bob could find no clues to this feeling of having lived in such a place as a Chinese restaurant.

It is perfectly true that one might go through life without ever remembering anything from an alleged previous lifetime until something starts one to thinking. Frequently these are parallels to what one might have experienced in a previous incarnation, and it is the similarity between the two events or places that causes the recall.

Mrs. Betty James is a horse breeder in Pennsylvania. She is in her late thirties, the mother of two lovely daughters, and college educated. Her interests in life are varied. In addition to caring for her family she does volunteer work for the Red Cross, works with the handicapped in nursing homes, and is generally active in the community.

Early in her childhood she had frequently had the feeling that something, or rather someone, was missing in her life. Although she was happy with her parents and her many friends, the feeling persisted. She often felt out of place among her own, somehow vaguely searching for someone who wasn't there.

About a year ago, some friends of hers were having difficulty in caring for their aged father. Since her oldest girl was in college, she decided to spend two days each week with them in order to care for this elderly gentleman until he passed away. For some strange reason she could not understand, there was a change in her attitude toward her own family. Whenever she left in the evening to come home to her own family, whom she dearly loves, she felt as if she were leaving her true home to spend the night and the remainder of the week with strangers. Every day when she returned to the home of the aged man for whom she was now caring, she felt as if she were coming home to her own house. As soon as she crossed the threshold of this man's house, she felt complete—like a whole person. No longer did she have the feeling that someone was absent, but a sense of peace and serenity came over her just as soon as she entered the old man's house.

What confused the matter was the fact that she had several dreams while sleeping in the house. In one of them, the deceased wife of the old man took her on a tour of her home in another town. Afterward, she asked his children whether the descriptions she had of their mother and their childhood residence were correct. To her amazement she was informed that they were.

In another dream, she saw this woman whom she had never met in life, and when her son showed her a picture of her, she almost fainted, for it was the woman she had seen in her dreams. Could it be, then, that this old gentleman, so near death, was thinking of his earlier life and in some way his thoughts had become transferred to her? she argued. But this would not explain the reason for the deep sense of fulfillment she had every time she set foot into his house.

Life has been good to Mrs. James in many ways. She has been happy all her life, and yet the peace and the feeling of having come home that she experienced when going to the old man's house was something beyond her comprehension. After the period of caring for the old man had ended, she felt more miserable and discontented than she had ever been in her life. Returning to her own home, she had lost that precious sense of fulfillment and contentment she had had for a short time in someone else's home. Now Mrs. James cannot help feeling that she knew this man in a previous lifetime and that, perhaps, she was discharging some form of karma.

The case Ellen Seligsohn is particularly interesting, because this lady in her early twenties is about as far removed from any interests in psychic research or the occult as a young lady might be. For one thing, her upbringing in a middle-class Brooklyn home under the guidance of a no-nonsense mother and father would militate against any form of knowledge of or interest in psychic research. Her father is in the ice-cream business. Her mother used to be a dressmaker, but now works with her husband in the ice-cream store.

Ellen was born in New York City and now lives with her parents in Garden City, Long Island.

In 1963 she had an experience involving an earthbound spirit, or ghost. This was in a house the family was then living in in Brooklyn. The experience was rather frightening for the young girl, as it involved being touched by an unseen but very tangible human hand while at the same time not seeing anyone to whom this hand might conceivably belong. She had just retired to bed, leaving her parents in the living room watching television. About fifteen minutes later she felt someone grasp her arm rather strongly, but she did not open her eyes. When the feeling stopped, she finally did look and found that no one was in the room with her. A few weeks later she felt the pillow of her bed go down as if under pressure, as if someone were leaning on the bed, looking at her. Again, without opening her eyes, she saw the vision of a man of about thirty-five years of age leaning over her. A few seconds later the vision left, as did the pressure on her bed. She mentioned these experiences to her parents and friends, but received only ridicule.

Shortly after, the family moved to Garden City, Long Island. To her surprise, her parents then told her the history of the apartment in Brooklyn. It would appear that a woman had been deliberately driven insane by her husband, and another occupant had committed suicide there. Evidently Ellen had picked up the impression left behind by these tragic events, or, more likely, had encountered the surviving ghost of one or both of these unhappy entities. But her psychic side is not what interested me particularly in investigating her experiences.

After the family moved to the house in Garden City, Ellen had no further psychic experiences of the kind that had troubled her in Brooklyn, but there was something else that made her wonder whether she might not have some special gift, some special side of her personality that she didn't fully understand.

When Ellen was ten years old, she became aware of another young girl, who appeared to her in visions and daydreams. Somehow she knew that the young girl used to be herself, even though she did not look like Ellen. A certain scene kept impressing itself upon her mind over and over. In this scene, the young girl was riding a horse, and the horse jumped a hurdle and fell, and when the girl fell off the horse she died.

She saw very clearly how the little girl was dressed. She wore a red jacket and riding pants. There were large tracts of land around, and she had the feeling that this was somewhere in the United States. She also felt that this was in an earlier century, and at one point got the feeling that it was around 1881. The girl had dark hair and didn't look like the present Ellen at all. There were other scenes: she would see this girl in a kind of library wearing a long dress—a dress going down to the ankles—and the library was lit by big, white, bubbling lights. By bubbling lights Ellen described clusters of what she thought were bulblike crystal containers. She wasn't sure whether they were gaslights or electric lights. In this scene the girl was reading a book. The book was open in her hands, and then the scene just faded out. Somehow Ellen felt very emotional about this other girl. Somehow she felt she liked her and felt sorry for her. She had a strong feeling of emotional attachment for this other girl—a feeling as if she knew her.

Over the years these two scenes stayed with her. The last time she had experienced these daydreams was only a few months before she met me. Then, a few weeks before she came to seek my help, she had a terrifying experience. She woke up in the middle of the night, sat bolt upright in bed, and started talking, and yet she felt as if it wasn't she talking at all, but some other person speaking through her. All the time, she heard every word she was saying, unable to control what came out of her mouth. By this time, she was fully awake and realized what she had said. What she had spoken, was one sentence: "Clara J. Wiston, Clara J. Wiston is coming for me."

She was surprised at herself. She had never heard that name before. What did it mean? Who was Clara Wiston? At that moment she was fully awake and thought it was all nonsense and foolishness. For a while she entertained the notion of looking up whether there was a Clara Wiston somewhere, but she really didn't know where to begin to look, so she dropped it, and the matter was of no further interest to her. Then she read one of my books and decided to question me about it. When she came to see me, we went over the entire incident carefully.

It developed that she wasn't sure of the girl's age. Perhaps she saw her at various times of her life; that is to say, first a child of ten and then later as an adolescent. I sent her home with the request to try to return, as it were, in her daydreaming or even in the nocturnal dream state to the period in which Clara Wiston lived, and to try to get additional information. On the night of July 3, 1967, she started to work on herself. "Who is Clara Wiston and where was she born?"

That night she had a dream, and although she could not remember all its details, she was able to write down quite a bit on awakening. In her dream, the girl was talking socially to a gathering of people, and kept mentioning two places—Creskill, or Crestmont, and another place called Crow something. (She couldn't quite get the word that followed Crow.) Subsequently, research in local libraries yielded some results.

There isn't a Creskill or Crestmont anywhere in New York State, including Long Island, but there is a Crown Point, which dates back to 1755. It is located near Ticonderoga, on the neck of land connecting Lake George and Lake Champlain. During the Revolutionary War this was a location of some importance, as it fell to the American troops in 1775. Of course, the place might also have been Croton-on-Hudson, or any name beginning with a syllable like Crow.

What interested me more was the name Clara Wiston. Wiston seemed to me a very uncommon name, and so it turned out to be. My own research in genealogical sources confirmed my suspicion that the name Wiston was indeed a rare name, but finally I discovered in a book called *The Pioneers of Massachusetts,* by Charles H. Pope, published in Boston in 1900, that a Wiston family did indeed exist in New England as early as 1665. John Wiston, father of Joseph Wiston, lived in Scituate, Massachusetts, in that year. Evidently the name is of New England origin, for I also discovered in *Massachusetts Soldiers and Sailors of the Revolutionary War,* Boston, 1908, on page 660, that one Edmond Wiston lived in 1778, a Joseph Wiston also in 1778, and a Simon Wiston in 1776. Was Clara Wiston a descendant of that New England family?

Ellen Seligsohn doesn't really care any longer. Apparently having brought this reincarnation memory to the surface of her conscious mind, something within her was satisfied, for I haven't heard from her lately. Perhaps the personality of Clara Wiston has merged with that of Ellen Seligsohn, forgetting her fatal spill from the horse back in the 1860s. I was disappointed in not being able to prove the existence of Clara Wiston through historical records, but the material contained in local libraries is not always complete. Perhaps with years of patience and additional research, Clara Wiston might be identified. In the meantime, her memory lingers on, albeit in the unconscious of Ellen Seligsohn.

Dorothy Wofford of St. Louis is, by background, one of the working class, according to her own estimate; by status, a housewife who writes a great deal, not always for publication; and by my estimate (for I have had correspondence with the lady for a number of years), a prolific intellectual, who needs only to discipline herself to accomplish a great deal. Mrs. Wofford is also an amateur genealogist who delights in tracing her own and other people's family trees. She has a fairly good educational background, but I would not consider her well read in the true sense of the word, or as an expert in matters literary. Her favorite hobby is the study of astrology, which she pursues to a point few amateurs do. With all these interests in unusual subjects, she has never given reincarnation any thought whatsoever, perhaps because she was too preoccupied with other matters or perhaps because it simply did not occur to her. All her writing is in prose, and she has never had any particular interest in poetry or been able to write any. She does have a great deal of extrasensory perceptual ability, however, and throughout her life she has been able to foretell events or intuitively feel things at a distance.

So it was with a feeling of still another ESP experience that she accepted a number of most unusual occurrences in her life. That is to say, at first she thought it must be all due to ESP and nothing else. There were several instances of her writing certain phrases that seemed to be lines from poetry—lines she was writing without conscious knowledge of why she was putting down those exact words. One of the first quotations of this type was of words she was writing to a teen-age friend of her daughter's by the name of Carolyn. Since she liked this girl almost as much as her own daughter, she felt she should help cheer her up when the young lady was down in spirits.

"Never curse the winter, for who can appreciate to the fullest the spring if he has not experienced the full blast of winter," she wrote.

Three days later, Mrs. Wofford's daughter, Pat, stopped off at the local library, and since Pat was aware of her mother's great interest in New England, she decided to bring home a book of pictures of New England taken by Samuel Chamberlain. Mrs. Wofford opened the book, and one of the first pages of the book drew her attention to it immediately. Underneath the picture were almost the identical words she had written to her daughter's friend just a few days before. This aroused her curiosity, and she checked who had written those words originally. To her amazement she found that they were words of a poetess by the name of Anne Bradstreet, who had lived around 1612 in New England. Mrs. Wofford had never heard of Anne Bradstreet, and the incident would have been forgotten if it weren't for some other events that took place shortly after it.

Always the writer, Mrs. Wofford wrote a prose piece to her husband. A few days after having written to her husband, she bought an LP recording of the American History series. In it was contained a reading of Anne Bradstreet's poem to her own husband, expressing practically the same thought and content. This came as somewhat of a shock to Mrs. Wofford, who had taken no interest whatsoever, at this point, in the life, times, and work of Anne Bradstreet. But the strange "coincidences" continued.

Oftentimes, Mrs. Wofford would write something, considering it her own original thoughts, only to discover that Anne Bradstreet had written the exact phrase before, three hundred years ago. At this point, Mrs. Wofford decided to find out all she could about Anne Bradstreet, and she studied and researched the life and time of the New England poetess.

Until the first phrases had come to her, she had had no knowledge of Anne Bradstreet, or her existence, or any details of her life. Now she discovered that the incessant desire of her own to return "home" to New England was not entirely at variance with Anne Bradstreet's desire, for the poetess had lived in New England and loved the country dearly. Suddenly Mrs. Wofford realized that some of the strange quirks of her character, which she had not been able to place or explain for some time, fell into place when compared to the character of Anne Bradstreet. For instance, Mrs. Wofford had had strong feelings about having lived in New England, and for Elizabethan music, which always arouses her to a depth and intensity that is, as she says, "almost beyond bearing." To be sure, she has

fought this feeling; she has fought the idea of being reincarnated, because to her logical mind the reincarnation of
a romantic poetess in a working-class woman of St. Louis
doesn't make sense.

For many years Mrs. Wofford had a feeling that, before
she died, she must get to Salem, Massachusetts. Finally she
went there, in 1960, and started to search the old burying
grounds when she learned from local sources that Anne
Bradstreet's husband, Simon, is buried in Salem.

Dorothy Wofford states flatly that she does not consider
herself a reincarnated poetess, for she does not consider
the proof adequate, scientifically speaking, and yet she
wonders about this—and so do I.

The difficulty, in some cases, is to distinguish between
extrasensory perception or communication from a dead
entity on the other side of life, and true reincarnation
memories; for it is entirely conceivable that a person might
be a medium, receiving information from a deceased person. Frequently, deceased entities wish to express themselves through living persons on this side of the veil and
make them do their bidding, or work through them, perhaps inspire them if they are artists or writers, and, in
general, to continue physical existence through the medium
of present-day persons. Of this I have written elsewhere
in greater detail, for I am convinced that such a relationship is possible and reasonably common.

It therefore requires a great deal of skill and caution
when investigating reincarnation memories to decide what
is a true reincarnation and what is merely an interesting
case of mediumship.

Dr. Ian Stevenson, psychiatrist at the University of
Virginia in Charlottesville, Virginia, wrote a book entitled
Twenty Cases Suggestive of Reincarnation, in which he
put forth the case for the possibility of reincarnation. He
is a cautious scientist and certainly not given to exaggera-
tion, but, in that work and later publications, Dr. Stevenson has come to the conclusion that reincarnation is indeed possible. It would, in his view, explain the early
genius of such great minds as Wolfgang Amadeus Mozart
and Alexander Hamilton—people who displayed knowledge beyond their years.

My good friend Ethel Johnson Meyers, the New York

medium, has told me of a case in which a five-year-old boy, brought to her by his parents, displayed intimate knowledge of the life, technique, and other details concerning a famous musician who had died a long time before the child was born. The child's manner of speech, in fact, was totally incompatible with his age, but wholly natural for an adult musician.

Both Western and Eastern philosophers interested in reincarnation speak of a record, in existence somewhere beyond the veil, often referred to as the Akashic records. It purports to contain information on every individual, and all the cycles of reincarnation that each individual has gone through and is as yet to go through in the future. This record is the key to a person's karmic responsibilities and the discharge of karma according to Eastern philosophy.

Edgar Cayce spoke of this record, and, during his lifetime as a medium, freely quoted from it for those who sought his advice.

Today there are a number of practitioners, who shall remain nameless here, who claim to be able to do the same thing, that is, to read freely from the Akashic records. Unfortunately, I have never been able to find evidence that these readings are based on fact. Granted that it is very difficult to prove someone's earlier existence in a distant culture, sufficient information could be given so that the individual in question might conceivably trace the names, dates, and details of this earlier lifetime through the usual research channels. This has never been the case whenever I have looked into matters brought to my attention. On the other hand, some of these doubtful practitioners demand considerable fees for their "research" work. Inevitably the record indicates that the person has had an interesting and exciting life prior to his own. Occasionally, there are indications of great sufferings, which in turn might explain the person's present troubles. I am not saying that these readings are all necessarily fraudulent, but they woefully lack evidential detail, and at least in some instances are the product of the readers' own fantasies.

Reincarnation flashes or memories are in reality the exceptions from the rule of forgetfulness. There are other unusual conditions, which occur once in a while, that seem to indicate a confused glimpse at reincarnation. I am speaking of cases in which an individual would be convinced that certain psychic impressions pertain to the present, when in fact they are remnants of an earlier lifetime.

If one's earlier lives are contained in one's present personality, very much like underlying layers of consciousness, then it is conceivable that a confusion between the individual layers could occur. It is a little like a magnetic tape recording using an old tape that has not been fully cleaned of previous impressions and here and there contains an original imprint. When this tape is run through the recorder, parts of the earlier impression will be heard along with the new imprint, causing confusion and lack of clarity.

The comparison with magnetic tape recordings is not as farfetched as it might seem at first glance. I am firmly convinced, from my investigations, that life itself is an electromagnetic force, and that what we call human personality is also a unique electromagnetic field encased in an outer layer called the physical body.

In dealing with reincarnation, we are, however, speaking of several layers of consciousness, or several layers of electromagnetic imprints contained within the one physical body at the time. Memories are imprinted onto each layer of consciousness and, on occasion, the time element is not fully understood, or the conscious mind confuses one layer of time with another. What happens then is that the percipient is convinced that something is happening or will happen in his or her own lifetime that, in fact, has already happened in a previous incarnation. But the impression is so vivid and strong that it is difficult for the individual to realize that he is, in fact, reliving something from the past that has already occurred. It is puzzling, frustrating, tantalizing; but unless the individual understands its meaning, it can lead to serious emotional and even mental disorders in the present lifetime.

A case in point concerns a schoolteacher who is now twenty-eight years old. She has had ESP experiences ever since she was eight years old. She is an average individual with good educational background, well balanced, and comes from a good home. There is nothing very special about this young lady, nor has she had any interest in psychic phenomena or the occult. She is still teaching school in New York City and leads a well-adjusted, normal life now.

Her ESP experiences have some bearing on the strange case I am about to relate. After her father's death, in 1950, when she was just eight years old, she began having extrasensory perceptions. Miss C., as I will call her, is the daughter of a businessman who, in turn, had had premonitions in his lifetime. She was able to foretell the exact results of games she and her classmates would watch when she was eleven years old. As so many others possessed of ESP powers, she predicted the assassination of President John F. Kennedy long before it happened. While still in college, she had a vivid dream in which her mother died. At the time, her mother was hale and hearty. Three days later she had a heart attack, was taken to a hospital, and within a week she passed on. But these, and many other minor ESP incidents, were not the reasons why Miss C. came to seek me out for help. Something had happened to her that she could not cope with, something that seemed to transcend ordinary ESP. I asked the young lady to make herself comfortable in my study and to tell me in her own words what it was that had disturbed her so much.

"When I was nineteen years old, I was walking to my college class one morning," she began, "after getting out of the subway. It was during mid-terms, and I had an exam that day and was nervous about it. All of a sudden a voice said to me, 'You are going to marry Mr. M., and you're going to be very happy.' Along with this I saw a vision above me and to the right. I saw myself standing at a sink, probably doing dishes. Next to the sink was a refrigerator, and over the sink was a large window. The sun was streaming through the window. It was incredible. It looked like liquid gold. When it was over, my fast reaction was, 'Now, where did that come from?' I had not been thinking about him, and I had been worrying only about my exam."

"Whose voice was it?" I interrupted her. "Did you recognize the voice?"

"It was a male voice," Miss C. answered. "It could have been my father's, but I'm not sure."

"Was your father dead at the time?"

"Yes, he was."

"Go on," I said. "What about this Mr. M?"

"Mr. M. was one of my professors in my freshman year. Like almost all the other girls, I had a crush on him. He was a likable and sweet man, but I had not seen him in one whole year, and neither had I thought about him. From then on, many times I would get an ESP feeling about him.

"About a year after the initial vision, I had a feeling I was going to see him. A few days later I was on a bus on Long Island, and I looked down and there he was, driving in his car alongside. Once the voice said to me, when I was skipping down the stairs after class, 'Go this way.' I did, and there he was. Now, I believe this vision with all my heart. It became the most important thing in my life. I wanted to marry him then, but not until I had finished school. I wanted to become perfect for him, and I was trying with all my heart to improve and do well in everything.

"I was now twenty-one years old. One day I was sitting in the school library trying to study. I had a bad cold and felt miserable. I hadn't seen Mr. M. for a year or so, but all of a sudden I couldn't get him out of my mind. It was useless to try and study, because I was just too sick, so I decided to go out for a walk.

"I was walking through the park, and I felt thought waves of him so strongly I was sure I was going to run into him. I didn't want to see him, because I felt sick and was sure I looked miserable. I decided to go back to the school building to avoid him. I walked into the school building and was standing in front of the elevator, waiting for it, and reading the school newspaper.

"Now, there were a number of reasons why I didn't want to see him. I had the vague feeling that he was engaged. It was not a blinding ESP flash—only a vague feeling. Someone else was waiting for the elevator too, but I did not look at him, but then I felt someone staring at me, and I finally looked up.

"I did not recognize him at first. I remember thinking, 'Why is this man staring at me? He looks as if he loves me more than I've ever been loved in my life,' and then I realized it was Mr. M. We said, 'Hello.'

"I'm afraid I was very cold to him; I can't really say why, for I had no proof he was engaged, but suddenly such anger welled up in me, I could barely control it, and I was very cold and barely spoke to him. He got confused and sort of fell out at his floor. Then it began to happen again.

"I would get the feeling I would see him, and there he would be. I kept getting strong, happy thought waves which seemed to concern him. Then all of a sudden it went away. I knew he was getting married. No one ever told me. I never heard any news about him from anyone; only through ESP I knew he was getting married, but I didn't want to believe it.

"Then in June, on a Sunday, I read the announcement of the marriage in the newspaper. The world seemed to crash in around me. I walked out into the kitchen, crying in my mind, 'Why, why?' and the voice said then, 'God, in his wisdom, is infinite.' Nothing has been right since.

"Once, I was in class and something told me to go home and not stay for the next class, but I stayed anyway. Afterwards, as I was walking home, I was passing a bar and I happened to look in the window, and there he was in there, staring out at me. I just walked on, but seeing him upset me very much. For years it was difficult just to keep my mind on an even keel. In all these years I haven't even come close to understanding what it all means, and it is poisoning my life. It is now exactly seven years since the first vision. He has been married for five years and no longer lives in this city. I have graduated from college and am teaching elementary school. I love my work, and I feel I am doing something worth while. Now, it may very well be that I am just a frustrated female and this is what caused the whole thing, or it may still be true. I don't know, but I must find the answer."

For a moment, I sat silently opposite the young lady, pondering what she had just told me. Then I promised to check it all out as best I could. I did. Apparently, what she had told me was true. If Mr. M. has had any feelings of a similar nature about Miss C., he will not speak of it, but my feeling is that he did not, or at best, had a vague sense of puzzlement about the whole thing and his relationship with the young lady. It is entirely possible that

Miss C. somehow slipped through the curtain of time and experienced something that had happened in a previous lifetime, but that Mr. M. is not aware of it. It is, of course, also possible that the inner voice telling her of her future relationship with this man was mistaken, or perhaps hallucinatory, but my own conviction is that what has happened here does have a relationship with reincarnation, and I have so informed Miss C. The young teacher has since accepted this, and now lives a harmonious, full life of her own.

Whittier, California, broke into the news as the place from which President Nixon hails. Of more immediate interest to me, Whittier is the town where Mildred Corkran grew up.

Mrs. Corkran is a lady in her late sixties. Her father was an oil man who traveled a great deal. He had been to India and Australia, and he had been around the world, so that he was able to give his children somewhat more of a background than the average Californian might.

The Corkrans—Mildred, both parents, a brother, and a sister—came from Ohio in 1901 and settled in southern California. Mildred was born in that state. She says she was a lonely child despite her brother and sister—always playing alone or being with animals. She married the first time at eighteen and had three children—two boys and a girl—but her husband passed on in 1931. Later she married again, but that marriage did not work out, and she has been divorced for the past twelve years. Her husband held the rank of major in the Air Force.

Of average height, she has dark brown hair and sparkling blue eyes. She is far livelier than her years would call for, but all in all, is a typical upper-middle-class lady with average interests.

"My main problem is an inferiority complex," she explained to me, "which I have fought for years. People say they never really get to know me, although I seem to know *them* well." If Mrs. Corkran has, indeed, an inferiority complex, I noticed none of it.

We met in San Francisco not long ago. I had asked her to come so that we could discuss her most amazing experiences.

At the time she retired, she had worked as a psychiatric

technician in a hospital. Prior to that, she had also been working for a film exchange in northern California. Her children are grown up now. Her youngest son is an industrial engineer, and her daughter's husband a municipal judge in southern California. She has neither frustrations nor great ambitions and leads a happy, if sedate, life in a small town in California.

The event that amazed, if it didn't upset, Mrs. Corkran, happened in July of 1956. At that time, she was living in Modesto. That afternoon, Mrs. Corkran decided to go shopping to Stockton, which is about thirty miles away. She asked a friend by the name of Greta Boytel to come along for the ride. Her friend readily agreed. To make the shopping expedition more interesting, she asked her friend whether she had ever seen the University of the Pacific. Her friend said she hadn't, so they decided to drive past it to look at it.

It was just about four o'clock in the afternoon, and the two ladies were talking of nothing in particular, and laughing, "for we were both in a very relaxed mood. Shopping does bring out the best in women sometimes." They were winding their way through the afternoon traffic, when all of a sudden Mrs. Corkran felt very strange.

"I had the oddest feeling, as if something had washed over me," she said.

All of a sudden she was no longer on the road, driving her car through the city of Stockton. Instead, she seemed to be in a different place. She saw a path in front of her, flanked on both sides by several large, white, old-fashioned houses with trees. The houses were two stories high and were set back from the street a little bit with picket fences, and there were no sidewalks in front of them—only a kind of dirt path and rows of trees out on what she knew was the parkway.

Suddenly she noticed a woman walking up the pathway, with her back toward her so that she could not observe the woman's face. The woman then stepped to the left and walked off the side of the road. At this instant, Mrs. Corkran knew that this woman was *herself*. Although she did not know the age or period this woman lived in, she seemed grown up.

Then, ahead of that alter ego of hers, Mrs. Corkran

noticed a fence and a small hill. The woman kept walking
toward that hill with a picket fence around it, and then
the whole vision vanished. Mrs. Corkran found herself
back in her driver's seat. The car was still running through
traffic, and she felt rather strange, as if she had just been
deflated.

"Is there anything wrong with you?" her friend asked,
worry in her voice. Apparently Mrs. Corkran had suddenly become very quiet and looked odd. Her friend
thought she had been taken ill. The odd feeling stayed
with Mrs. Corkran for about an hour, and then it slowly
went away. Yet, the impression was so vivid she could
never forget it. She thought about it many times, realizing
full well that she had never been to this place in her life.
To her, it did not look like California, but some place
"back East." Although the incident felt as if it had taken
a long time, it was actually only a second or two. She had
never lost control of the car.

I questioned Mrs. Corkran about the appearance of the
woman she had seen in her vision. "She had on a light
skirt, and it was down to here," she said, indicating her
ankles, "and either a jacket or loose top, but that is about
all I can remember." She is equally sure that the houses
she saw were not of a kind that have ever been built in
California, but reminded her of houses in the eastern part
of the United States. No further visions of this kind ever
occurred to her.

Mild incidents involving ESP, such as knowing who
might be calling before the telephone rings, or a feeling
that a dead relative was present in what used to be his
house, contributed somewhat to her understanding, if not
acceptance, of psychic phenomena. The only other incident tying in with her amazing experience in Stockton
happened in the summer of 1967.

Not far from her present home is the old capital of California, Columbia. One afternoon she decided to take a
ride up there with her dog. She had been there before,
many times, and she had a feeling of belonging there.
This time it was particularly strong.

Columbia is a small gold-mining town, which the state
has turned into a national park. Mrs. Corkran was walking along the main street and looking at the restored build-

ings when all of a sudden it seemed to her as if there weren't any buildings there at all, and again she saw a woman walking ahead of her. The woman was the same person she had seen before in traffic at Stockton, when her first vision overcame her, but this time she wore different clothes. The old-fashioned clothes this woman was wearing were not the kind the people in Columbia put on for tourists. The woman walking ahead of her wore dark gray clothes, a big bonnet, and some very high, heavy shoes, but, even more interestingly, she seemed to be floating ahead of her rather than walking on the ground. All at once Mrs. Corkran realized it was herself that was walking ahead of her in the road, and that she saw a vision of something that had happened in the past—*her* past.

Again the woman did not turn around, so she could not see her face, but the certainty that she was looking at an earlier incarnation of herself remained with her. The feeling did not leave her for several hours. Although Mrs. Corkran was sure that the woman she had seen was herself, there was no physical resemblance between the apparition and her present appearance. But as she grows older, a vague and yet persistent feeling comes back to her again and again. She sees, in her mind's eye, trees, a stream, a quiet place somewhere in the country, and she knows at the same time that she has been there. Every day she yearns more for it, wishing she could be there again.

Mrs. Corkran had indicated an interest in being regressed hypnotically, and so we proceeded to do this. She went under rather quickly and proved to be a good subject for me.

I sent her back hypnotically to meet someone she had known before her birthdate. At first she reported experiencing only darkness, but when I told her to go back a hundred and fifty years or so beyond the threshold of birth, she seemed to observe some people. "Do you see yourself?"

"Sort of shadowy," she replied, with uncertainty in her voice.

I ordered her to go closer until she could see herself

more clearly, and then asked whether the person she saw was indeed herself.

"I think so," she replied.

"What does the woman look like?"

"She's young."

"Describe her," I ordered the hypnotized Mrs. Corkran.

"Rather pretty face, laughing. She just laughs with me. She's got a bonnet in her hand. She's about seventeen, or eighteen or nineteen."

"What is her name?"

"Alice, and her father is there. He's got gray hair. He's busy doing something. This is on the river. He is pulling a net of fishes, or something like it."

"What year is this?" I asked.

"I don't know, except I can see seventeen . . . 1752."

"Are we in America?"

Mrs. Corkran seemed to be hesitant at this point, so I suggested that we advance the period by ten years.

Ten years later Alice was twenty-seven years old. I asked Mrs. Corkran again to describe the woman she saw. This time she was able to get the entire name.

"Alice Mayberry."

"What is the name of the town she lives in?" I inquired.

It turned out to be Exeter in England.

Did she wish to talk to me directly, through Mrs. Corkran? Mrs. Corkran did not think so. The girl seemed unhappy now, and looked older. When I asked her her husband's name, Mrs. Corkran informed me that she didn't have one. I then decided to advance the experiment by another ten years.

"Alice is now thirty-seven years old. Has she got a husband?"

"She has children," Mrs. Corkran said now.

I asked for the children's names.

"Philip, David Mayberry. The husband's name is Silas, and he's dead," she said, and her words were somewhat faltering.

I asked who ruled the country, and without hesitation she said, "The king."

I then inquired what county we were in.

"Sussex . . . I don't know . . . Sussex."

Now, Exeter is not in Sussex, but in Devonshire, but Devonshire does border on Sussex, and for all I know there might be a tiny village, or might have been a tiny village, named Exeter in Sussex as well, but it really doesn't matter because that kind of knowledge can be obtained quite easily by simply looking at a map or post office index of settlements in Great Britain. It is hardly evidential as such.

I now decided to advance the experiment by another ten years, and suggested that Alice was now forty-seven years old, and then fifty-seven years old. What did she look like now?

"She's old."

"Sixty-seven years," I said.

"She is still alive at sixty-seven, but I see the children alone now."

"When does she die? What year does she die in?" I asked.

"Seventeen eighty-seven. I see that on a stone. The stone is on a hill. It is kind of broken down . . . well, kind of old."

I pressed on for information about Philip Mayberry, the son. It would appear that he was a farmer. He had a wife, and it was he who had buried his father, but I could not get anything beyond that.

Mrs. Corkran now exhibited signs of weariness, and in view of her advanced years, I felt I should bring her out of trance. After a suggestion that she would awaken fully refreshed, not remembering anything of our conversation, I brought her out into the conscious state again. She remembered absolutely nothing of the Mayberry incident, or of what she had told me while hypnotically regressed. I considered the experiment successful, even though I could not elicit as much information about her previous incarnation, if indeed there was one, as I had hoped to.

Since I was unable to obtain church affiliation or the name of the cemetery where Mr. Mayberry lies buried, or where Alice might have found her final resting place, checking out a common name like Mayberry presented almost insurmountable difficulties. Unless a church affiliation is known, it is difficult to trace the name of an ordinary citizen. There are no eighteenth-century directories such as we have today, but it is noteworthy that Mrs. Corkran did not manufacture a glamorous image of a former self. Her prior incarnation, if it is indeed that, is a rather ordinary woman, living a rather ordinary life in England. The part of England she refers to does have a great deal of farming and fishing, and the styles she describes would fit the period in question.

What, then, caused her two visions, or triggered the sudden switch from twentieth-century California to eighteenth-century England? I can only surmise that in the case of seeing the old buildings of Columbia, some parallel mechanism was triggered in her unconscious mind, causing it to go back into a prior lifetime. But in the case of the "wave" that washed over her while in the midst of bucking traffic, the matter does not seem quite so simple. There is no question in my mind that she did not relive something from an earlier period in Stockton or Columbia. She did not drive into the past as it were, as others have done; rather did she suddenly leave the present and return into her own past in a different part of the world. There seem to be two factors accounting for this:

1. She was probably very relaxed driving along on a warm afternoon, chatting with a friend, and generally feeling in a good mood. In the relaxed state she was in, her conscious self could have been separated momentarily from her unconscious personality, allowing a memory from the past to come up to the surface and be noticed. But Mrs. Corkran remembers driving past the buildings of the university, explaining as she went along that one of her sons had gone to school there.

2. Could it not be that something in the building itself caused the memory to go back to the earlier lifetime? We know practically nothing about the trigger mechanism that causes people to recall reincarnation memories from the past.

In studying these reactions, we learn a great deal about the results, without, however, really getting to know the techniques involved as fully as we would wish. Further studies may indeed explain how an ordinary housewife like Mrs. Corkran, who has never been to England and who has no particular interest in psychic subjects, can suddenly find herself in the very center of an experience that indicates an earlier existence far away from everything she knows, or has known, in this life.

V
The Strange Case
of Ruth MacGuire

In some empirical sciences, the ability to repeat a certain experience is of importance. To some scientists, it proves that the original experiment or the original experience is authentic. Repeatability, then, becomes the earmark of authenticity.

In psychic research, we often come face to face with situations that ring true, that is to say, that have all the earmarks of an authentic case. Even though one might be convinced that the case happened without benefit of fraud, self-delusion, or other alternate explanation, an outsider unfamiliar with the stringent techniques employed by the conscientious researcher often cries "fraud." To him, the fact that one *could* have faked the results is far more important than the details of the case itself.

When we are dealing with reincarnation memories, it is sometimes possible to assume that the subject might have obtained information by reading up on the subject at hand, or by unconsciously absorbing the matter in his or her childhood without being aware of it. Since it is impossible to prove with one-hundred-per-cent certainty that no outside influences came into play in this particular case, we then must prove the absence of motive, and the likelihood of its having been an authentic case. Ability to defraud is not the same as actual fraud. We must always keep in mind that accusation of a crime is not the same as conviction of a crime. A person is not guilty of murder if he has not committed one, despite the fact that he might have tendencies to do so. Nothing ever takes the place of an overt act, and the likelihood of fakery must be established with just as many good arguments as the probability of genuineness.

After exhaustive research, and having obtained intimate knowledge of my subject, I am firmly convinced that the strange case of Ruth MacGuire is a case of natural reincarnation memories. At no time did Miss MacGuire ask me to investigate her reincarnation flashes. I, myself, found out about them in the course of questioning her about some ESP experiences.

Being a writer herself, she could have seen no advantage in being written about by another author. No money passed between us. Miss MacGuire does not possess an extensive library and is not terribly well-read, even though there is a lending library in one of the nearby towns. She has never left this country, except for a brief period in Canada, and is unfamiliar with the intricacies of European history and geography. On the conscious level, her education is average, although her intelligence is certainly far above it.

Ruth MacGuire contacted me for the first time on May 10, 1967. She had read two of my books and was fascinated by her own ability to foretell future events, which she has had through most of her adult life. She felt that she wanted to communicate them to me for what they were worth and perhaps obtain some information as to how she could develop her own mediumship in the process. I asked her to return a report to me in which she would state briefly all that she considered of an ESP nature throughout her life.

The report came neatly typed, and it contained some remarkable incidents of psychic insight, or premonitions, and of communications with the dead. All of them had witnesses to attest to their genuineness, but it is not Ruth's psychic life, remarkable though it is, that I wish to go into here.

Ruth MacGuire lives in a former inn on one of Connecticut's busier highways. She shares this inn, built in the 1930s, with her three teen-agers and an assortment of cats and dogs and occasional stray friends who drop in to partake of her hospitality, which apparently is boundless. This is the more remarkable, as Ruth is far from affluent. Separated from her husband and now divorced, Ruth lives the life of a Connecticut gypsy, not the least bit worried about tomorrow or financial problems, knowing, somehow, that everything will be all right in the end.

Since her letter was cheerful and her place not far from the route I often take to visit my friends in New England, I proposed that we meet somewhere to discuss her psychic experiences. The prospect of "sitting with me" apparently made her happy, and she invited my wife and me to come up and spend some time at her inn, partaking of such hospitality as she could offer us.

One sentence in her letter made me sit up, and gave me a vague feeling that this visit might be something more than a routine checkup on someone who has had psychic experiences in the past. Wondering if I had ever done any studies in the field of reincarnation, such as Edgar Cayce had done, she reported, "I have a strange memory of England in the last century which has obsessed me since childhood, and although my ancestors were English, Irish, and Danish, and I was born here, as were my parents, I find that when I'm very tired, that I always use the English spelling as in honor, with honour and theatre. I don't do this when I'm aware of what I'm writing, but only when extremely fatigued."

How could I resist such an interesting sentence? That and the name of her place, The Old Chestnut Inn, were enough to make our trip come about earlier than I had hoped. I offered to regress her hypnotically on the occasion of my visit, and she accepted gladly, for there seems to be nothing more exciting to most of us than to find out about ourselves, even about a self that existed in an earlier lifetime. Ruth MacGuire explained that she ordinarily would not accede to a request to be hypnotized, but somehow I had instilled confidence in her. "I must admit," she wrote, "that I usually push back these things because I dread going off the deep end; and because I have had emotional difficulties, I cling very hard to practical, everyday things. I do not want to lose my grip of things."

Making a precarious living from her earnings as a writer and from what her husband sent her, Ruth did indeed live a most difficult life. The Old Chestnut Inn had long ceased to be a tourist attraction, although the pond behind it and a row of cabins farther back indicated that it had once been the kind of inn tourists do stop at. Now, however, it was merely the colorful home of a colorful woman and her brood.

In early August of 1967 my wife and I finally drove up to Kent, Connecticut. We were met at the door of the inn by Ruth MacGuire and two of her teen-age daughters and some friends. Eve Horner, an Austrian-born textile artist and a good friend of Ruth's, had also come up from New York to assist in whatever might be taking place that night. Present also was Paul Kenny, a young friend of one of Ruth's daughters, and my sister-in-law, Marie Rose Buxhoeveden, came along for the ride and whatever she might learn in the process. Ruth MacGuire received us cordially and frankly, and there was immediately a sense of rapport among us all. We were given the best rooms upstairs and proceeded to make ourselves at home. We had dinner, and as the evening wore on, we became very relaxed. That, precisely, was the state I wanted my subject to be in so I could proceed with the most important part of our visit, the regression experiment.

When everyone was sufficiently relaxed, we repaired to the downstairs living room, and Ruth MacGuire made herself comfortable on the couch, while the others sat somewhat apart so as not to disturb her. It was pleasant and not too warm, and just about as quiet as a house in the country can be. There were very few cars passing by outside now, and the most prominent noise, really, was of frogs making merry in the pond outside. As I usually do when I regress an individual, I discussed with my subject whatever conscious flashes or memories she might possess. This is separate from whatever material might come through during the hypnotic session itself, which can then be compared to what was present in the conscious mind.

"You mentioned some form of reincarnation memories," I began when everyone had settled down. "Can you tell me when this first started?"

"I have always remembered my early years," Ruth began, "and so it wasn't much of a surprise that I could see places at an early age that other children could not. When I was four years old, I had the very distinct impression that I knew a fourteenth-century garden somewhere in France. There wasn't much else, just the picture of the garden. Then, when I was six years old, I had the impression that I had lived in seventeenth-century Holland. It was a feeling of having lived at Leyden as a Puritan expatriate in poor health and disgusted with the robust Dutch revelings in the inn where I lived. I remember an early death. When I was seven, I had a very strange longing to dance around a Greek temple in the moonlight, wearing a flowing robe. I put this down to sheer romanticism, but for a seven-year-old this seemed to be rather a passionate longing. I have always had a longing for Greek things ever since, and the feeling for the white temple has persisted in me strongly since that time. Around the same time, I developed a strong feeling for England, and I gradually turned into an Anglophile, which I still am.

"My whole life became oriented toward England; that is to say, the England of the last century. So much so, that I was convinced that it still existed somewhere."

"Can you give me any details of these past lives?" I inquired.

"It was always as a woman," Ruth replied. "Once I drowned. I know what it is like to feel the suffocating water close over one's face and to slip down into the darkness. I also know what it is like to lie in an open coffin and to listen to comments, or to try to raise your arm, to tell onlookers that you are conscious, only to find the arm like iron, utterly immovable. The awareness of these experiences, the drowning and death, came to me in a vivid dream when I was nine.

"Now, I must admit to having a phenomenal memory, which goes back to one year of life. My aunt and my mother often used to say, 'But you can't remember that.

You were only eighteen months old.' Yet I would describe a kimono my aunt wore, or the lighting fixtures in an apartment, and both turned out to be correct.

"I also have a vivid imagination, which is one reason I try to hold myself in check. There is also another strange thing. I can on occasion reach feats of accomplishment which do not have any relationship to my ordinary capabilities, almost as if I did not do these things. Once I came home from a movie, and although I play very badly, if at all, I was able to play a concerto by Max Steiner on the piano, as if I knew it.

"Another time I painted a seascape because I had to see the sea. I had never before painted in oil. I am not a painter. I have danced a Hindu folk dance, made Danish pastry, and recently acted with an amateur drama group, and have been accused of professional status in all these endeavors. No wonder I feel like an impostor."

After a moment of silence, I continued questioning her. "Have you at any time had a definite impression of being in a place where you could identify people or the names of towns or anything like that, perhaps?"

"I have very strong feelings about the year 1857 in India. I feel that that was a tremendously traumatic year for me. I have a feeling that my life ended in 1857. When I was just a child I picked up a ten-cent piece dated 1857. As I looked at the date on the coin, I felt terribly depressed, and my body was seized with trembling. Somehow the date meant something to me."

"You mentioned memories of having lived in England, India, and Holland. Have you ever been to these places?"

"No, unfortunately not. I was born in New York City; both my parents were born in New York City, and except for a brief visit to Canada, I have never left this country."

"Have you ever had any recurrent dreams?"

"Yes, when I was a small child I often dreamt of a scene in which I saw some flat land and two women who were with me. The dream always ended in sheer panic. In the midst of the flat land there were some dark, cylindrical objects which seemed to frighten me. When I was in Canada, and stood on flat land with tall buildings in the distance, there was a vague feeling of recognition, as if the tall objects were some forms of buildings, but gradually I realized that what I was seeing were windmills in the Dutch landscape, which, of course, is very flat.

"Gradually I became aware of the fact that there was a terrible sense of pressure and hurrying and trying to escape, and it tied up with another dream I had had all through my childhood, of running down steps—flights after flights of steps, with someone in pursuit. I used to wake up in terror, absolutely unable to breathe, so real was the experience. I had the distinct impression that I was running for my life. Somehow the two dreams interconnected."

"Did you see the person who was pursuing you?"

"No, I only knew there were people. I could hear the footsteps. I seemed to feel that they were some kind of guards or soldiers, but I couldn't see them. I saw swords. The atmosphere was that of the middle sixteen hundreds. Glimpses of boots on the stairs; high boots and a cloak, but not really the person. I felt it was in Holland."

"How long did this last?"

"I'd say for about ten years, and then it gradually faded away. It didn't occur any longer. The dreams were almost identical all those years. It never came back, but in the 1940s I had a terrible sense of terror again when I saw a Dutch plate with a windmill on it. Somehow it reawakened forgotten memories in me."

"Did you see yourself in these visions and dreams?" I asked.

"Yes."

"How did you look?"

"Very much the same as I look now, except that my hair was darker and I think I had brown eyes; I'm not sure. The face was very similar, the nose a bit sharper, pointed upward, and slender. I have also seen myself in another incarnation as an Englishwoman, one who died at age twenty-seven, I believe."

"Do you ever get any names?"

"No, I'm sorry. I didn't get any names, just a strong sense of identity."

"Do you ever get any feelings about locations, places?" I asked.

"I get Lucknow, in India. I have a feeling about that, but not as an Indian, rather as an Anglican living in

India. I've always had a very strong pull toward India, mixed feelings of fascination and loathing at the same time."

"You mentioned the year 1857 and India before. Is there any connection between that and the memory of India and Lucknow, which you have just mentioned?" I asked.

"It could be. There is a feeling of terror, and yet a great love of Indian music, and then there is a great fear of a dark-skinned man. I don't know what it is."

"Consciously speaking, and logically, does the year 1857 mean anything to you?"

"Well, the only thing I can think of is my grandmother. She was born in 1857, but that hardly seems important."

"Have you ever had dreams where you seem to be falling from great heights?"

"Yes, something to do with the stairs. When I was being pursued I would touch the top of a long flight of marble steps, touch it with my foot and fly and touch the bottom step with my foot, as if I were taking giant strides. I had a terrible sensation of pain in the pit of my stomach, much as one feels when the elevator misses the floor slightly and pulls up."

"Was there any continuance of the picture?"

"I just kept on going. It was as if, if I stopped, something terrible would happen to me, but I never knew quite what it was. I never stopped running."

"How did you get out after you fell down the stairs? How did you see yourself get out?"

"I didn't really fall, I just sort of touched. It was miraculous the way I took those stairs."

"How were you dressed?"

"I had a cloak and long skirt. That's all I can see—lots of petticoats and long skirts."

"What period would you say they belonged to?"

"I'd say the early 1600s, perhaps 1630 or 1640."

"During your meetings with mediums or psychics in connection with your interest in ESP, did you ever discuss your visions and dreams?"

"No, I really have never discussed it with them. Many psychics have told me that I, too, was psychic, but I didn't

feel like discussing this, as I was afraid of being laughed
at. I didn't want people to think I was too imaginative."

"Have you ever been hypnotized?"

"No."

"Do you think you would make a good subject?"

"I think so, because I have a very co-operative nature."

I then proceeded to suggest to her that she should relax
completely and told her that I would take her back ten
years at a time.

When she was ten years old (by suggestion, that is),
I asked her where she lived.

"In Manhattan, 3852 Nagel Avenue."

"What is your father's name?"

"Thomas Francis Raymond."

"What is your mother's name?"

"Charlotte MacGuire."

"Where do you go to school?"

"P.S. 52."

"What is your favorite teacher's name?"

"Miss MacLoughlin."

"What does she teach you?"

"Poetry; she proclaims poetry."

"What is your homeroom teacher's name?"

"She was. She taught me everything. She wore black
chiffon to school with beads. She said, 'I wish children
would be neater. I get a very clear picture of the kind of
home they come from, and I know if I went to Ruth
MacGuire's home everything would be lovely. Everything
would be very neat and perfect, because that is the impression that she gives,' and I was very much chagrined,
because the other children laughed."

I then regressed her to age seven and asked her again
where she lived.

"2339 Davidson Avenue in the Bronx."

"Where do you go to school?"

"St. Nicholas of Tolentine Parochial School."

"What is your favorite teacher's name?"

"She was a nun, Sister Bonaventura."

I proceeded to take her back further, year by year.
Then I crossed the threshold of birth and suggested that
she go back to minus five, minus ten, minus twenty years.

"What do you see now? Look around."

"It's all vapors, big thick clouds and vapors, and it's cold, very cold."

I suggested she go back even further and told her to go back to one hundred years before her birth.

"Where are you now?"

"I'm in England—Sussex."

"Where in Sussex?"

"I don't know yet—wait, there is a house and a lawn and my sister."

"What is your sister's name?"

"Ann."

"What is your name?"

"Martha."

"What is your father's name?"

"George."

"What is the family name, his entire name?"

"Andrews."

"What does he do?"

"A lawyer."

"Where does he live? What town?"

"Buck . . . Buck . . . no, Stokeley. Something to do with Stokeley and Buckminster. I don't know. He's not here all the time. He goes away."

"Where is the house?"

"It's in the country, but he has to go to the city sometimes."

"What town is the house in?"

"Two names—Stokeley on Bow . . . no."

"What county is it in?"

"Stokeley on Bow in Sussex . . . something like that."

Later I checked up on these places. It was most unlikely for Ruth MacGuire to have any intimate knowledge of villages and obscure little towns in England, having never gone there nor having studied English geography to any extent. There is no Stokeley in England. However, I found a Stockesley in Yorkshire. There is also a Stockesby, and as for Buckminster, it does exist. Buckminster is on the border between Leicestershire and Lincolnshire, and as I looked at a detail map of the area, I discovered that very close to Buckminster there are two other villages which might conceivably be the "Stokeley" the entranced Ruth MacGuire was talking about. There is a Stonesby west of Buckminster, and there is a Stokerochford north of Buckminster. Both of these villages are very close to Buckminster. As for the word Bow, there is a village named Bow in Cornwall, but I doubt that there is any connection between Cornwall and Yorkshire in this instance. There is no Stokeley on Bow in Sussex. In fact, none of the places here mentioned are in Sussex, which is much farther south. Why the entranced subject confused the counties, I do not know, but I find it rather remarkable that she came up with the name Buckminster, a village or small town of which I have never heard and which I found only by consulting the detailed map of British counties I have in my possession. Meanwhile I continued my questioning.

"What year are we in now?"

"1809."

"What is your mother's name?"

"My mother isn't there. She is dead."

I insisted on her mother's name.

"Mabel."

"What was she before she married your father?"

"Mabel Breen."

"When did she die?"

"She died when I was two years old, in 1800 I think."

"Where did you go to school?"

"I didn't."

"Where did you go to church?"

"The Parish Church . . . Saint something. I didn't like the minister."

"What was his name, and what was the name of the church?"

"He had two names, Holly Benton, and he spit when he preached."

"Do you remember the name of the church?"

"Yes, St. Hildegard."

"Where was it located?"

"In the village. We walked, and I had such a pretty hat."

"Where was your house?"

"Just outside the village. Oh, it was a pretty little house. It had dormer windows. It was of stone . . . no, brick, and big, wide windows and a green lawn, and such lovely roses in the garden, and they took very good care of the garden. Mrs. Benton . . . Mrs. Benton was the house-keeper."

"Did you live there, or did you leave town?" I asked.

"I lived there until I got married."

"Whom did you marry?"

"An officer in the service."

"What was his name?"

"Ronald Whiting."

"What branch of the service was he in?"

"Her Majesty's Troops Dragoons. I hated it."

"Do you remember what number the regiment was?"

"Number 67, I think."

"Who was the colonel of the regiment? Do you remember the commanding officer's name?"

"Oh, him. I didn't like him at all."

"But, what was his name?"

"Edgeworth."

"Do you remember any other officers in the regiment?"

"No, I wasn't very well, and I went sometimes to the regimental affairs, but I didn't like them very much. I hated the military."

"After you were married, where did you go to live?"

"I always dreaded being sent away . . . sent to places so far away."

"What do you mean, 'so far away'? Where were you sent?"

"We went to India."

"Where in India?"

"Calcutta, and then another place where there was an uprising."

"Where was the uprising? Was it a town, a fort?"

"Not a big city, like Calcutta. I think it was a town— Mysore, if there is such a place."

When I nodded that there was indeed such a place, she continued.

"My husband was very angry because I didn't like that kind of living . . . always on the move. I wanted to go back to England. It was so hot. Sometimes it was so dirty, and the natives distressed me while they fascinated me, and I couldn't cope with the whole problem in India. I wanted to do something about it and I couldn't. I just

fumed and fretted. I felt it was all wrong. I couldn't see
why we had to be there, and then he would go away. He
would always go away leaving me with the servants. There
were plenty of servants. There was nothing for me to do,
of course."

"Was that in Mysore?"

"Both in Calcutta and Mysore and then this other
place."

She seemed to have trouble remembering the other
place, so I asked, "What year are we in now?"

"1852 we went there. We had to stay there for five
years before we could be sent anywhere else, and there
was this terrible day when he wasn't there. He had gone
away."

"Where had he gone to?"

"Oh, he had to go away. They had to go away. They
thought trouble was coming."

"Who was making trouble? Who were the people that
were making the trouble?"

"The natives were very angry. They didn't want us
there."

"Were these the native Indians?"

"Yes."

"Were they civilians?"

"Oh, they were civilians, and there were some army
Sikhs and they came in one day like a dam breaking . . .
came in, the bodies screaming, shouting, pillaging, raping.
I ran and hid. The children, they got it, it was terrible . . .
all the bloodshed and the wickedness, and there was no
place to run . . . nowhere. I was so soiled . . . so deeply
crushed. They spared nobody. They were frenzied, wild,
with bloodshot eyes, angry, rioting."

"What year was that in?"

"We went to India in 1852, and we stayed there five
years."

"It was 1857, then?"

"Yes."

"And what happened after that? Did you leave India?"

"Well, yes we did. I had to leave, but it was the end
of everything for me. Well, I wasn't killed. It would have
been better if I had been."

"What about your husband?"

"He wasn't there. He had been sent on this other, foolish chase. They thought trouble was coming."

"Where from?"

"The other end. The other end, two miles away, and then they came and nothing was sacred, absolutely nothing . . . the children killed and wounded, stomped upon."

"Where was that?"

"In Lucknow. Yes, in Lucknow, at the officers' quarters. It was terrible, and this Indian came. He was very tall, very menacing, very dark. I thought he was going to strangle me, but he raped me. Isn't that awful? I never knew why there had to be an empire. Just that little green island would have been enough. Why did we have to go out there in the first place?"

"Where was your husband at the time?"

"He had been sent with the troops to the other end, where they had suspected there would be trouble, and while they were gone, the men came, wild, a flood of human hatred, and, oh, there was no appeal. There was nothing that could reach them. This large, menacing man, with large, aquiline nose, pinned me to the wall. He had a stare, and I hoped that he was going to kiss me, but he didn't. He was disgusting, fascinating, but it was awful, because some of us didn't die. We had to live with that memory."

"You went back to England then?"

"I never got there."

"What happened to you?"

"I fell."

"Where did you fall?"

"On the ship. I don't know whether I fell, or whether I was pushed. I was so unhappy."

"Where did the ship go to?"

"It was going back to England. My husband was furious."

"Why was he furious?"

"He was very unreasonable. I think that he wished that I had been killed instead of raped. He said I was . . . well, having been touched by a native, was unclean. He wouldn't even talk to me."

"And when you fell on the ship, what happened then to you?"

"I drowned. I could feel the water closing over my face and I didn't care, and it was frightening. For a moment I struggled, and then a strange feeling of happiness came over me. I had tried to breathe, but I couldn't, and so I gave up the struggle."

"What was the next thing that happened to you then?"

"I fainted. I just breathed in the water, and I don't remember anything. Yes, I remember being dead. They must have got my body. I remember being in a coffin. They must have retrieved it, because it was in a coffin, and they were making the kind of remarks that people do."

"Did you see yourself in the coffin?"

"Yes. I must have been on shipboard. I saw the coffin and the people passing by, and I wanted to tell them, 'I hear what you are saying. I hear,' and I tried to move my arm. I tried, and it was like lead. I couldn't move. I couldn't wiggle. I couldn't even move my nose . . . couldn't even indicate that I was there and I was listening."

"And after that?"

"Nothing after that . . . nothing."

Later I researched this amazing account of her presence in another lifetime during the Indian rebellion. To begin with, Ruth MacGuire is not a student of Indian history. If she had any general knowledge of British Imperial policies in India during the nineteenth century, it would not include specifics as to where battles and sieges took place. But I questioned Ruth thoroughly, and I am convinced that she did not even have that much knowledge about British India during the time of Queen Victoria, nor did she, indeed, show any interest in this period, except for what happened to her in another life.

If Ronald Whiting was a member of the 67th Dragoons, he could have been in British India at the critical moment. The rebellion took place in 1857. The Sikhs did indeed play a role in it, although at various times they supported the British colonial effort and not always that of the rebels.

A little later, I asked the entranced Ruth to go back into her Indian past, and to answer a few questions.

"What is a sepoy?"

Without a moment's hesitation, she answered, "A sepoy . . . it's a kind of a native."

"What does he do? What does a sepoy do professionally?"

"He's with the troops, isn't he?"

I very much doubt Ruth MacGuire would have had the knowledge to describe correctly the meaning of the word "sepoy." The fact that she did not use this term does not mean that she did not know it. I deliberately tried it on her to see what her reaction would be.

She spoke of Lucknow, and the terrible things that happened there. It is a historical fact that the compound at Lucknow was under siege by the rebel troops, and that thousands were actually killed during that period both at Lucknow and at Delhi. Delhi had been in the hands of the rebels but was finally besieged and taken back by the British colonial troops, at which time a great bloodbath took place. Lucknow was then free, and the women and children and the remnants of the garrison left. It is also true that many, if not most, of the women, were shipped home to England after the two years of terror they had been through during the rebellion in India.

Ruth MacGuire, still deeply in trance, seemed to be reliving the terror of her last moments on earth as the wife of a British officer. I decided to pursue my inquiry into what happened after her death.

"What was the next sensation that followed?" I asked.

"Nothing," she replied softly. "Just this dark mist, and then there were people, shadows and presences, and people I didn't know, but my mother was there, and I saw her."

"What did she look like to you?"

"She was comfortable and pleasant."

"Were you anywhere near the ship then?"

"No, it was on a misty plane. I saw my mother, and there was a comfortable feeling that I had found her at last. Then there was a little child that had died at birth. That was all. We seemed to be moving very slowly, almost as if we were not walking . . . just as if we were moving on a ribbon."

"Like gliding?" I suggested.

"Yes," Ruth replied.

"And then there was a great light. I went towards the light, but it was so intense, and my mother was sort of half pushing. I felt as if I had no power of my own to move, but she seemed to have, and someone else, a presence I couldn't quite tell what or who it was, but there was a power that just impelled me on, and I moved on this floating ribbon of light towards the light."

"Did you see anyone else you know?"

"There was someone else . . . a grandfather, and he was very kind and told me not to be frightened, that he had been there for a long time, and he said after I had been there and studied a bit and gone on I'd be in the mauve light, and I thought that was very pretty, because it was like violets."

"And did you study?"

"I don't remember, but I seem to have gained some advantage. I don't remember the details. It was like growing or breathing, or something of that sort, and it just happened to you, and then I continued onwards towards the light."

"When you got to the light, what did you see?"

"This blinding white light, but it wasn't harshly blinding. It was brilliant and beautiful."

"Were there any people in it or near it?"

"It was too blinding to tell. There were people . . . sort of bluish-white figures all around it. There was lovely music, but I don't know where it came from."

"Did anyone speak to you?"

"Not in the sense of speaking. There was some sort of communication, and I remember being told to be good and to be compliant and I would learn why the terrible things had happened to me, and that I must learn that no matter how cruelly I had been treated, or how senselessly, savagely, that I must treat it all with love, love, love. . . . No resentment, no sharp edges, just kind of a soft, lovely, relaxed receptiveness. Yes, receptivity and acceptance, not just a stupid compliance, you understand. They said, if I did that I would grow. I was very frightened when I went over, and I hated my husband for being so stubborn and stupid, and I hated men . . . hated the man who had assaulted me."

"Did you recognize any of the people around the light?"

"I seemed to have found aunts and cousins and some friends."

"How did you leave that place?"

"Well, it was like moving down a river on a boat, very slowly and gradually, as if you weren't really aware of progressing, and yet you knew you were progressing."

"Where were you going then?"

"I wasn't sure where I was going. It was just the thing that people said. There was a wise man. He seemed to be with me . . . an elder of some sort, very gentle, very calm, very detached, and he said, 'Come, child; come, child; hush, child.' "

"Did he tell you anything about your status?" I asked.

"Yes; he said, 'Lose all the resentment you have, you are still holding, for that which has happened to you, because it has only happened so that you may learn to love,' and I said, 'I can't, I can't,' and he said, 'Yes, you will, child. You will. Just come along with me,' and then I seemed to respect him. I wanted his understanding, and I wanted some approval. I wanted to grow, so I went, but I said, 'I haven't gone back to my England . . . my lovely little spot of green in the sea,' and he said, 'Oh, you'll see it again. It won't go anywhere. Don't worry about it. Just come along with me.' He was a dear. He was much nicer than the preacher."

"And when you had been with him, where did you go from there? What was your next stop on the journey?"

"Then I seemed to sort of go into a kind of sleep."

"Where were you sleeping? On what? On a bed?"

"No, there wasn't anything material there, which was something I had to get used to, but I wanted my dress with the ribbons. I used to think about it a lot, but then I learned that, you know, one oughtn't think about clothes. It wasn't very important. But, it wasn't the dress, you understand . . . not woman's vanity . . . not that kind of thing at all. It was just that the dress was so precious to me . . . that I had happy memories with it. I wanted to have the memories."

"When you went to sleep, what happened next?"

"I slept for a while."

"And then what happened?"

"I seemed to be learning things while I was sleeping . . . not really sleeping . . . just lying acquiescent."

"And after you learned these things, did you continue to learn?"

"I stayed with the people for a while, if you call it living ... it is, in a way, but not like on earth. It's different. There were so many things I had to get over. I had felt I was quite a nice lady, you know, the English gentle-woman, making little visits to the poor. That was silly. That isn't being good, you know. You can't just do it that way and stop. You have to start from scratch all the way from the beginning, and it mostly involves *attitudes*. That is what I learned, not just the outer words. And then, I used to be very good with the Bible. I read it every day and I prayed a lot, and I was what you would call a pious person, but when I looked back from over there, I had to laugh at my little vanities. I didn't know any-thing. I just went through the motions. It isn't until you get your inner moves all straightened out that you really know and you've really learned of things."

"Now, when you had been taught the true values, did you stay with them, or did you move on?"

"I stayed with them for a while. I was very happy learning these things, and then they said something about coming back and trying out what I'd learned, and I didn't really want to then, because I was so happy."

"Who said that you had to go back?"

"The elder. The wise man."

"What was his name?"

"I think I called him 'Sir,' but he had a name something like Valentine, but it wasn't Valentine."

"Did he ever tell you who he was?"

"He said he was my teacher."

"But who was he on earth?"

"I never asked him."

"Now, he said you had to go back, and you didn't like to, but you went anyway?"

"Well, I didn't really have any choice, you know. These things are all decided."

"And how did it happen that you went back? Just what happened?"

"Well, he said, 'It's time, now, for you.' He said, 'What you do here, you've learned; you practice, you meditate, you get the right idea, the right attitude, but you can't know if you're going to make it stick until you try it in

the world, and you have to try it in the world before you
know whether you've really got it in your bones.' "

"And how did they make you go back?"

"Oh, they said, 'You have to be a baby,' and I said, 'I
don't want to be a baby. There's nothing dignified in being
a baby. You wet your pants all the time, and I can't bear
it,' and they smiled and they said, 'Well, you just have to.
You'll be a baby and everybody will love you. It's not so
bad,' and I thought it was a great indignity, and they said,
'Pride, pride, pride . . . something you'll have to get
over.' "

"And how did they do it?"

"Oh, then they sort of put me to sleep, I think. I don't
know. I seemed to be going to sleep and then taking some
kind of dive, you know . . . a spin."

"And then?"

"And then that's it. I was back here."

"What is the first thing you remember afterwards?"

"I remember crying . . . crying in my mother's hair. She
had long, beautiful, chestnut hair, and I remember she
used to brush it and it was fun to watch. I was just a
baby, but I was smarter than they thought I was, and it
used to get me crazy."

"Did you know who you were before you became a
baby, when you were a baby?"

"No, I just knew . . . I knew there was a purpose. This
is the difference, you see . . . not just a little glob of Jell-o,
just a baby with dimples and unquestioning thoughts, and
this is what they could never understand. My thoughts
were always questioning. I wanted to know what went on.
I knew what went on. I couldn't explain it, and they
wouldn't have listened had I been able to explain it."

"Who were they? Do you remember their names? Were
they your parents?"

"Yes, my parents in this life. It was a long time ago
—1909—and my aunt and my mother and my grandmother were very important and very good to me."

Since Ruth had spoken of other incarnations when we
discussed her memories in the conscious state, I decided
to take her back even further. I commanded her to go
back beyond India, and to go further back in time.

"It is now three hundred years before your present birth. What do you see?" I asked.

"Smoke in the room. A fireplace. I am in a room in a cottage, and the fireplace is smoking. It burns my throat, and they can't open the window. It's cold and they won't open the door."

"Do you see yourself?"

"Yes."

"How old do you look?"

"About twelve."

"Do you know your name?"

"It's a Biblical name ... Magdalene ... Magdalene Darling."

"In what town are you?"

"Now we are in Holland. We are not in England, but we speak English, and the other people don't."

"What is the year?"

"The year is 1613."

"And what is the town?"

"Leyden."

"Why are you here?"

"Everything gets sort of stupid. My father was there, but he wasn't around very much, and my aunt and my mother are both there, and we have to wait and, and there is something about the new world, in passage."

"On what ship is the passage?"

"We don't know. We are waiting and we have rooms at the inn—this inn in the town."

"Who is sending the ships?"

"Well, you see, we are not very well thought of in England, I am sorry to say. We are very respectable people, really. Perhaps too respectable."

"What faith are you?"

"Oh, we are Puritans."

"Do you remember the name of the company who sends the ships ... the name of the owner of the ships?"

"Well, I didn't pay very much attention to things like that. I wasn't well, you see. I had this cough. My mother and my aunt—they were there. They hated it, and they kept saying that I had to have good courage, strong faith, or, We'd come to the new world ... everything would be different. We wouldn't have to be persecuted and all that, but it seemed so hopeless. We were there so long."

"What town did your people come from in England?"

"My father comes from the North."

"What town does he come from?"

"North Riding on the Moors."

"Where in the North Riding? What village?"

"Horton."

"What is your father's name?"

"John Darling."

"And your mother's name?"

"My mother was Johanna."

"And what was her maiden name before her marriage?"

"Bliss."

"Where did she come from? What town in England?"

"She, too, came from the North . . . Durham. It's near Newcastle somewhere."

Again, my later research established the validity of Ruth's statement. Horton is indeed in Yorkshire, although on present-day maps it is in the West Riding rather than in the North Riding, but it is in the northern part of the West Riding, as this particular area is even now called. Durham is indeed directly south of Newcastle, and also not very far from Horton. Only someone very familiar with English geography would have such knowledge. I have been in the area, and I do not recall these places. The name Darling, incidentally, is quite common in Yorkshire.

In 1612 the Dutch founded New Amsterdam, which is now New York City. Actually, the Puritans who had come to Holland because of persecutions at home in England, emigrated a few years later than the date of 1613 given by Ruth in trance. Most of the émigrés left between 1629 and 1637, but it is entirely possible that some left at an earlier date. There is no doubt that English Puritans did spend time in Holland, which was much more favorably inclined toward their religion. Leyden is the nearest large city toward the coast opposite England. Many Puritans did, indeed, find refuge in seventeenth-century Leyden.

I continued to question Ruth.

"Now you are going with them to the New World?"

"Yes, my aunt, my mother's sister, we are supposed to

go to the Plymouth Colony, but are we ever going to get there? There is never any room on the ships. We have to wait and wait, and disaster after disaster, and mother said I'd end up speaking Dutch, which she didn't particularly want. She said they were . . . oh, she used a word that expressed contempt . . . blubbers. She said they were bear blubbers, but you see, it was at the inn, and these men were quite coarse. Mother was not, of course."

"Do you remember the name of the inn in Leyden?"

"Three Turks, I think."

"And the year is still 1613?"

"Yes, and it's damp and cold, but the fire is always smoking, and then, of course, it's always brighter and warmer downstairs, but we don't want to go down there because those roistering Dutchmen . . . well, my mother doesn't want me to be exposed to them."

"Did you take the ship across?"

"No, I never got there. I died in Leyden."

"How old were you then?"

"Thirteen."

"And your parents returned to England?"

"I don't know what happened to them, really. I had this cough and it was miserable, and I was in bed. I couldn't leave the room, and they kept saying, 'Courage, child. You'll get well,' but I . . ."

"How long did you stay in Holland?"

"Three years."

"Did you always live in the inn?"

"Well, we lived with a family at first, but it was rather crowded, and my father said we were best off at the inn."

"What sort of place did the family have?"

"It was a farm out in the country and I liked that much better, because there were apple trees, and the cows, and windmills, and it was fun to watch them going around."

"Did you like the windmills?"

"Yes, I liked them in the daytime. I loved to watch them, but at night they sort of frightened me because they looked so like giants with seven arms going around and around, waiting to devour. The children were nice, and the Dutch people were nice on the farm, but when we had to go into town, it was different."

"What was the name of the farm in the little village you lived in? Do you remember that?"

"Greck, or something."

"Was it near Leyden?"

"Leyden was the nearest big city to it."

"What province was that in?"

"It began with a U . . . U . . ."

"Was it Utrecht?"

"Yes, that was it—Utrecht, but we didn't pay much attention to where we were then. We were glad to get out of England, and there were lots of things to do—ice skating in the winter, an iceboat, and I loved that, but then when we went to the city it was horrid and not very clean, and then I died in the inn, in the room at the inn."

The hour was growing late. I detected signs of weariness in Ruth and decided to bring her back into the present. This took only a few moments, and then she awoke, none the worse for the hour she had spent in hypnotic trance. She remembered absolutely nothing, and felt refreshed and gay.

The next morning, after a hearty breakfast, we returned to New York City, leaving Ruth happy and calm in the knowledge that she had "spilled the beans" on her reincarnation experiences, and looking forward to my validating some or all of it in the future. She asked no questions . . . wanted to know nothing about what she had said while hypnotized. But she started to read on the subject of reincarnation, and took an interest in books that she had never read before. I felt I could not very well stop her from doing so, since she had told me everything she knew under hypnosis and there was little likelihood of anything further coming through at this time.

The techniques described by Joan Grant and Dr. Dennis Kelsey in their book *Many Lifetimes* impressed her, so she decided to try them on herself. She used a pendulum to evoke her other levels of consciousness. Apparently this method was successful in her case.

In February of 1968 she communicated with me again. She vividly described a market place in Calcutta and then added some details to her frightful experience of going back to England aboard ship. Apparently, she had become pregnant as a result of the experience that she had gone through during the siege of Lucknow. In addition, she had formed some sort of attachment to an Indian officer aboard ship, who had first protected her from the others and then forced his attentions upon her in private. Despite the strong impression, in her own mind she still doubted the validity of these prenatal experiences and made it a point to warn me that she could not prove any of it.

We communicated and corresponded off and on, and met a couple of times for dinner. These occasions were always delightful and festive, but we did not discuss the serious business of reincarnation at such times. Evidently, the visions remained in her subconscious mind, and in some instances became deeper, for in July of 1969 she jotted down some of the most important ones for me.

The vision of a market place in Calcutta was even more vivid now. The colonel's wife is named Dora, and she is in the market to look at brassware, pottery, fabric, and food. Dora wears a green and white plaid dress with a flounced skirt, while Ruth wears a pale, straight muslin. Both women wear bonnets and carry sunshades. A woman squats near a low table on which are arranged some sweets made from apricots. She is nursing an infant, whose head is covered with flies. Dora takes a handkerchief from her bag and gives it to the woman, indicating that she is to wave off the flies with it. The woman smiles her thanks and places the handkerchief on the baby's head. The two women move on.

A second vision concerns a stone church in England with a square tower covered with ivy. Ruth sees herself standing on the steps with her new husband. He is in uniform, while she is wearing a bridal gown and veil and is very nervous. There are friends and villagers at the bottom of the path throwing petals at them. Ruth is embarrassed by this. She wishes they were on the steamer that is to take them to Calcutta. She closes her eyes and knows that she will have to walk through the crowd to get to the carriage, and she dreads it.

The third vision sees her in the compound at Lucknow. All the men have gone except a few who are doing guard duty. The drums have been going for hours, and some of the women are beside themselves with fear but are trying not to show it. Mrs. Jennings' ayah is about to give birth.

Dora is bustling about, preparing for the event. She has commandeered linens from all sources and has unguents and jars in readiness. Someone is burning incense. The ayah's moment has come. Ruth is standing by with a basin of water. She cannot stand the sights and smells, and everything turns dark green and she faints dead away.

The final vision sees her aboard ship, going home to England, but it is not a happy time. She sees herself in the bunk, with the ship pitching and tossing. She is very ill. Dora, however, thinks it is merely seasickness. She is trying to feed her gruel and tea. However, Ruth is sick for another reason. She is pregnant by the sepoy who ravished her. She is defiled. Her husband said so. There is nothing for her to do but turn her face to the wall and die. He said so. When everyone is sleeping, she will go out on deck. She will lean against the flimsy rail. If the ship should lurch and she goes over, who will care? There is nothing but disgrace, and she would be done with this life.

Now, these four visions are, in fact, only repetitions and embellishments of the material Ruth has spoken of consciously in part, and more elaborately under hypnosis, but there are some details not found in the earlier versions. It is, of course, entirely possible that Ruth has embroidered her stories, either consciously or unconsciously, with details that would make them better stories, but I do not think so. She has nothing to gain from this. It is rather an unsavory experience that she is recording, and a less truthful person than Ruth might, in fact, suppress it, or certain details. Apparently, in telling me all her reincarnation memories, Ruth has also relieved herself of the pressures that came with them. She has, I think, accepted these experiences as a legitimate part of her character, and acknowledges the need for her earlier sufferings.

What makes the case of Ruth MacGuire particularly interesting in the annals of reincarnation material, is her total honesty in reporting it, her original reluctance to speak of it, and her specific knowledge of minor geographical details of England and India not compatible with her general state of knowledge. If anything, her case rings true and should be considered a valid case of reincarnation. In particular, I find her description of the in-between stage, following one death and preceding another birth, of interest. It affords us a glimpse into the mechanics of rebirth, even if it does not answer all the questions associated with it. But it seems to indicate that we have very little choice as to whether or not we wish to go back to this vale of tears.

VI
The Lady
from Atlanta

June Volpe was born in a small town in Pennsylvania, the daughter of an average couple who now live in retirement in Florida. When she was only a teen-ager, June married Sam Volpe, a man of Italian extraction. She, herself, was of Dutch-German background. Eventually they moved into a small town in western Pennsylvania, where they bought a house and where Sam followed a career in the glass industry. His work was neither extraordinary nor dull, and June's family was no different from her neighbors.

With four children, her life was always busy, and even when the two older children left home, there was plenty to do around the house. The elder son was in the service, and one daughter is married now. Only the two younger children are still at home. June and Sam lived a pleasant if somewhat uneventful life, far from the mainstream of adventure, far from any big city. To reach Pittsburgh, the nearest big city, requires many hours of driving.

June has been to Long Island and knows some parts of New York State in addition to her own Pennsylvania, but it wasn't until 1959, when she was twenty-nine years old,

119

that June went on her first major trip. In June of that year she undertook her first visit South, to Florida, where her parents then lived.

The first week of her stay in Silver Springs passed uneventfully. It had been raining, and June was somewhat concerned about the lack of good weather. One evening she found herself sitting in the kitchen mending some clothes when her older daughter, who was then living with June's parents, came up to her and said, "Mamma, before you go home, I want you to come and see the haunted house."

June started to laugh, for the very notion of a haunted house was totally alien to her. She just didn't believe in such things, but her daughter insisted.

"No, really, Mamma. They say it's haunted by the lady who used to live there."

June is a practical-minded person, and she was about to dismiss the remark of her fifteen-year-old daughter, when her mother spoke up, suggesting that she go over to the site next morning right after breakfast. June, wanting to end the conversation, agreed halfheartedly to go and have a look at this haunted house. With that, the subject was dropped, and the conversation turned to family matters.

Around eleven-thirty, June went to bed and quickly dropped off to sleep. Suddenly she found herself in a two-seated wagon with a fringed top. Two men sat in front talking, and a large colored woman was at her side, grumbling to herself, and seemingly quite concerned for June's welfare. The strange thing was that June saw *herself* wearing a long, ruffled, full, white dress. Her hair was long, auburn in color. In her hand she held a parasol, which she was moving around with nervous gestures. She wanted to hurry, to go faster, and she felt excitement racing through her body as she pleaded with the driver to go faster.

They drove now through a small town and over a dirt road, past wooden frame and brick homes, shops, and a church, all of them with metal hitching posts, most of black iron with a horse's head or an angel on top, and a metal ring to tie the horses to. Next she saw a little red railroad station and narrow-gauge track, and a pretty fountain with three cherubs blowing little horns, with the water streaming out of them. The streets were lined with palms and large shade trees dripping with moss. A warm, pleasant breeze blew, ruffling her skirt and hair, which was hanging long about her shoulders. Now the carriage reached the end of town and went down a dirt road to her left. On one side she noticed tall, golden wheat swaying in the soft breeze. On the other side of the road there was tall corn. The young man driving the two-horse carriage turned and shouted to her, "There it is. You can see it from here."

"Where, where? Oh, yes, I can see it. Please hurry. Hurry, or I shall get out and run to it by myself."

The man laughed in a teasing way and hurried the horses on a bit faster to the curve at the end of the lane.

A large, white, two-story house stood there, with a circular drive and a large shade tree in front of the porch, which extended across the front of the house. Flowers grew about the yard, and the lawn was a green carpet, spread out as if just for her. The carriage had barely stopped when she stepped down and went up onto the porch and through the front door, into a large hallway. She heard herself screaming with delight as she raced from one room to the next.

"Oh, it's beautiful and I love it, and it's mine, all mine," she heard herself say. She noticed a stairway going up to the right. At the foot of the staircase was a room toward the left. Then, coming through the front door, to the right she noticed a library. A painted mural of a hunting scene was on the left-hand wall, above a red velvet love seat decorated in the Victorian manner. Bookshelves, reaching from floor to ceiling against the wall, were separated by a lovely wood and brick fireplace. The walls were all white throughout the house.

She found herself walking through the house, looking at all the rooms, noticing that there were five bedrooms upstairs, and noticing that each of them had a fireplace and that they were furnished beautifully. An overwhelming feeling of having come home pervaded her, and she was happy and filled to the brim with contentment.

In the dream, she saw herself, yet not looking like herself, but somehow feeling identical with the person going through the house. It looked as if the girl she saw was about eighteen or nineteen years old, possibly a few years older, and not at all like the person June was at the time of the dream. Still, she could not understand how she could be both her present self and also the girl in the dream.

She awoke early with a strange, eerie, almost sickening, feeling. She couldn't understand this, for it had been a lovely dream. Why would it make her feel so bad? The more she tried to shake off the vivid memory of the dream and the strange, unsettled feeling that came with it, the worse she began to feel.

The rain had stopped now, and it was a warm, humid morning. As soon as breakfast and the dishes were finished, June's father reminded her that she had promised to go and have a look at the haunted house. Still under the unsettling influence of her dream, June reluctantly agreed. Her daughter, Lolly, and her son, Mich, came along for the ride. Evidently, her father noticed that she wasn't quite herself. "What's the matter with you this morning, June?" he inquired. She only shook her head. "It's nothing. I just had a bad dream. I'll be all right." Her father nodded, and let the matter rest.

After a while the scene seemed strangely familiar. With mounting excitement, she noticed that she knew the way, yet she also knew that she had never been here before in her life. Soon the car entered a totally deserted "ghost town" called Red Mill. The town was exactly the same as she had seen it in the dream the night before, but now the houses and shops were all crumbling; even the fountain in the middle of town was in shambles. June knew evey part of the place. She knew where her father would have to turn off to get into the lane leading to the house of her dream, and before she knew it, that was exactly what he was doing. It was all very frightening and confusing, yet the excitement was as strong as it had been in her dream.

Her father stopped the car at the entrance to an overgrown lane. The wheat and corn fields of her dream were gone now, and only weeds, tall grass, and underbrush grew. The house was black with age, and falling down. The porch was all but gone. Suddenly she found herself racing as fast as she could go toward the house, with the children in close pursuit. Her father had declined to come along as he had some business to take care of in town. He would be back for them later. Her daughter had been to the house many times before without experiencing anything special. To her, it was just an old house, perhaps with eerie overtones, and fun to play in, but there were no actual psychic overtones, nor was there anything out of the ordinary surrounding the old, broken-down house.

The house was quite empty now, except for some grain that was being stored in the living room by a rental farmer, but June did not see the house as it was. Rather did she experience it, somehow, as it had been when she had known it in another lifetime. She felt a surge of happy contentment, as if she had been away for a long, long time, and had finally returned home.

Room by room, June and her two children went through the house now. She remembered how the lace curtains moved gently over the dining-room windows, but, of course, that was impossible. There were no lace curtains any more. Everything was gone except the faded-out hunting scene painted on the library wall. It was the same scene she had seen in her dream the night before.

"There used to be a desk over there," June heard herself mumble. "And the settee went over there."

"Mamma, how do you know?" her daughter said, somewhat frightened by her mother's strange knowledge of a house she had never seen in her life before.

June did not answer. She wondered about it herself.

On the way over, Lolly had told her mother about a terrible murder that had taken place in this very house. This was the first time that June had heard about Mrs. Simms. Apparently her daughter had picked up some of the local stories concerning the abandoned house. A Mrs. Elizabeth Simms had once lived in it and had been murdered, but the cause of her death and the name of her murderer had never been discovered.

Now June stood in the house that she knew so well, and yet couldn't really know. She followed her chidren up the stairs and heard her daughter say, "Mamma, this is the room that Mrs. Simms was murdered in." Despite the grim words, June felt peaceful in that room. After a while she descended the stairs and returned to the library.

Outside, a thundershower was coming down, and they decided to wait until it stopped. By this time, June's father would have returned, and was probably waiting outside at the top of the lane. While they were waiting, Lolly suddenly said, "I wonder what the last thing was she did before she went upstairs and was murdered that night."

No sooner had her daughter said this than June felt unseen hands clutch her waist from behind, and she seemed to have no control over her body at all or even over what she was saying. Somehow she was moved first to the fireplace.

"She stood here for a moment, looking at the pictures on the mantel," she heard herself say in a very strange voice. Next she was literally moved across the room, through the doorway and up the stairs. "She held the candle with one hand, and held up her skirt hem with the other. She was very tired and worried about something."

June could hear her daughter say, pleadingly, "Mamma, what's the matter? You look funny, Mamma. You're so white. You're frightening me, Mamma. Don't do that. What's the matter?" But June couldn't really hear her. She couldnt speak. When she reached the second step from the top, she heard loud footsteps hurrying down the hall, coming close to her. Suddenly she panicked and turned. She could not move down the stairs. Something was pushing her back, wanting her to go on up. Desperately, June grabbed onto the railing and, hand over hand, pulled herself to the bottom of the staircase. Her new blouse was ripped up the back. She felt sick to her stomach, and stood on the front porch, or what was still left of the porch, for a while, breathing deeply and with difficulty, the fresh, cool air. Her panic was gone now, and she could vividly remember the impression of human hands on her back. No doubt about it, someone in the house, unseen though that person might have been, wanted her to go up the stairs.

June and her children started to leave, but she kept hearing someone calling to her from the house, "Come back. Please, come back. Don't go, please." Desperately she fought a battle within herself not to turn and run back to the house and up those stairs. Finally, she turned to look back, and when she did, she saw a young girl in a long white dress, with long brown hair, standing at the window. The girl in the window looked a lot like her.

In the car on their way back to Silver Springs the children asked why she had behaved in such a strange manner. "You frightened us, Mamma," her daughter said. June nodded grimly. She was frightened herself. Neither of her children had heard the voice nor seen the apparition at the window, but they had seen her behavior on the stairs and noticed the tearing of her blouse.

That evening she mentioned her experience to her parents. "Well, these things do happen," her father said, and with this remark, the matter was dropped.

As the days went on, June became more and more convinced that the apparition at the window had been merely her exaggerated imagination. For some reason, she thought, she had become agitated, and in the nervous state she was in, due to the strange experience on the stairs, she might have imagined seeing a woman where there was, in reality, no one.

During the rest of her stay in Silver Springs she had no further unusual dreams. When she returned home to Pennsylvania a month later, however, her husband noticed a great change in her. It was almost as if she had become another person. Where her temperament before her trip to Florida had been rather timid and complacent, she now seemed to be much more demanding and sophisticated in her interests. There was a lively enthusiasm, a desire to fight for what she believed in, that had not existed before.

Ever since her strange experience at the crumbling house, she had a strong desire to return, and she knew that she would have to go back there some day. From time to time she noticed a southern accent in her speech. The whole incident left her no peace, and eventually she wrote to her father and asked for his help to find out once and for all what it all meant. Her father suggested that she get in touch with an old gentleman who had been the postmaster when Red Mill was still a going town. He might be a good source of information about the Simms family and that which transpired about a hundred years ago.

After several letters, June finally received an answer. Yes, there had been a Simms family, with seven children, and there was a lot of heartache in that family. There was, first of all, Laura Lee, who had run off and disappeared, and then there was Robert, who was a cripple because he had been run over by a horse and wagon.

When the place at Red Mill was still a thriving plantation, it was one of the best in the area. Apparently, Mr. and Mrs. Simms had married young. They had come from an aristocratic family in Atlanta, Georgia, around 1860. It was just when Florida was beginning to develop.

Allen, the oldest boy, joined the Union forces when the Civil War broke out, despite his father, and was immediately disowned. He was killed in Atlanta, Georgia, trying to protect his grandparents from being killed when the Union troops moved into their plantation. The plantation itself was burned, looted, and destroyed.

Another son served in the Confederate Army at the dispatcher's headquarters. After Robert had died in an accident in the swamps, the mother was left alone, for Robert the elder had died of a stroke due to the sudden death of his favorite son.

When the war was over, Mrs. Simms decided to open a small store, not so much for financial gain as to keep herself busy. It was a grocery and supply store. At the time June had visited the house for the first and only time, she had found some yellow ledgers and notebooks in the house. They pertained mainly to the running of the grocery store. She had picked them up and kept them in her possession. There were also some letters, and it appeared from them that there was another son, James.

Mrs. Simms was eighty-nine at the time of her death. Apparently, she was brushing her hair in the bedroom, when she was shot in the back with a shotgun and killed instantly. The story goes, according to the former postmaster, that James had become a traitor to the Southern cause toward the end of the war. Having gambled heavily, he was in great need of funds. For that reason, he worked with Union spies, selling them Southern secrets, but the Confederate espionage apparatus got wind of it and he

escaped by the skin of his teeth. James then became a
fugitive, always careful of Confederate agents. Even after
the war, James was afraid for his life. No one knows
whether James's mother was killed for some sort of revenge, or by mistake, but the killer was never found.
Apparently, the tragedy happened in 1896. The ledger,
which June had discovered in the house, gave entries all
the way up to 1913, so it is probable that the son still
lived at that date.

A year ago her father informed June that he had heard
that the place had been torn down, that there was nothing
left to remind her of the once-proud plantation. Despite
this, June's longing for the place was as strong as ever.
In her mind's eye she would see it as it was, and she
could hardly resist the desire to return to "her old home."

In addition to the house, she saw another scene time
and again, a creek with lots of stones and water ripples
around it, and on one side a big tree with Spanish moss
hanging down from it, touching the water. The scene was
peaceful and quiet, but she had never been to such a place,
nor had she ever seen a similar picture.

As if her strange experiences, her change of personality,
and her overwhelming desire to return to a place she
hardly knew weren't enough to upset June, there was
something else.

Gradually she had become aware of another experience
somewhere in the dim, dark past of her existence. This
was a memory of a girl with soft, brown hair who looked
a lot like her. This girl arrived home with three other
women, two older ones and one her own age. They were
traveling in a buggy of sorts, drawn by two horses. The
driver wore a black suit, and something told her that this
happened about 1693.

As the scene unrolled, she saw them stop in front of
a long brick building and felt instinctively that this was
not in America, but in Germany. She noticed that the girl
pulled back the curtain and stepped down from the buggy,
and that she was followed into the house by the others.
The girl was of slender build and about twenty years old,
wearing a long, dark, hooded coat wrapped tightly about
her.

June felt that they had returned home from visiting a

Dutch relative. The relative lived in a wooden, shingled house of two stories, with a water wheel connected with it. There was a quiet, red-faced, heavily built man sitting in front of the mill, and June seemed to hear some conversation in a language she thought to be Dutch. Then June suddenly felt that it was she entering the kitchen of the house. A large, heavily built woman stood fussing in the kitchen, and welcomed her. That night she slept in a large, straw-filled, "swinging" bed on the second floor. There were three people to a bed because it is warmer that way, and the beds were very wide.

Since June is of German-Dutch descent, she assumed that this scene had something to do with her ancestry. She did understand some Dutch and German, although she could not speak either. Still, the memory was more than just a fading scene from the past. It was something that was also very strong, though not as compelling as the identification with the unhappy woman in the Florida plantation house.

Her memories of what appear to be previous lifetimes were not like some of the ordinary memories of things she did in her past. Somehow, they were much more vivid, and they disturbed June. At one point she decided to discuss the matter with her priest. The good father listened patiently and seriously, and when June asked him whether he thought there was something wrong with her, he shook his head. "No," he said. "There is nothing wrong with you, my dear, except perhaps that you are too sensitive for your own good," and with that, he dismissed her. But June was not satisfied with such bland advice. She went to a clinic in Ridgeway, Pennsylvania, and subjected herself to every conceivable psychiatric test. Dr. John Dickerson, the resident psychiatrist, eventually sent her home with the remark that she was probably mentally healthier than he was, and that there was nothing wrong with her at all.

Since June had always rejected the possibility of the supernatural, it disturbed her to have dreamed of the Simms home before she had ever laid eyes upon it. The memory of the girl in the carriage in Germany had actually been with her for a long time before the visit to Florida.

But she had never paid it any heed. Now, however, in the light of the Florida adventure, it took on new dimensions.

All these matters were on her mind when she turned on her television set one fine morning, and watched me discuss psychic phenomena with Marie Torre on Pittsburgh television. All of a sudden she knew whom she could ask about her strange memories. When she got in contact with me, I immediately wrote back asking her to come to meet me the next time I was in Pittsburgh.

Unfortunately, however, June was not allowed to travel much. One valve of her heart is completely blocked. She therefore doesn't travel very much and must avoid strain. Her town is over one hundred miles from Pittsburgh. Regretfully, June declined to meet me, and instead issued an invitation to come and meet her at home. Then other doubts arose in my mind. If she had such a heart defect, could I safely hypnotize her? I asked her to check the entire matter with her physician before I could go any further. Then, too, I wanted her to check with her husband whether there were any objections to my starting to work with June, since it might entail a considerable amount of time and research.

If her reincarnation memories proved to be evidential, I felt that we might have to continue for a considerable length of time with hypnosis, and I wanted to make sure I would not be interrupted halfway to my goal.

On March 20, 1968, I received a most cordial letter from June. Both her personal physician and the doctor at the clinic had encouraged her to proceed with the experiment. I was told only to avoid fatiguing her, and this I readily agreed to. Her husband, Sam, also put nothing in our way, so I made arrangements for June to meet me in Pittsburgh on the first of May. Despite my offer to have her flown in from her little town in western Pennsylvania, she came by bus, and was none the worse for it.

Even our first meeting in person was rather strange. My plane had been delayed, and I had begun to worry that Mrs. Volpe might find waiting uncomfortable. Mentally, perhaps, I may have sent out some thoughts that reached her mind. After all, she had had ESP all through her life. When I reached the hotel at which she was staying, I picked up the house phone and asked for her room. At that precise moment she stepped up from behind me. She had been in her room and had suddenly gotten an intuition to go down to the lobby to greet me. Thus we met and returned immediately upstairs to begin our first hypnosis session as soon as possible.

After I had put her under, I suggested that she was getting younger. Physically her face slackened, and when I suggested that she was just six years old, you could almost see the little girl. Then she became a baby before my eyes, and finally I sent her back across the threshold of birth, and suggested that the time now was fifty years before her birth as June. Another personality now seemed to possess her body.

I asked quietly, "What is your name?"

"Mary Elizabeth."

"Where do you live?"

"I live in Georgia."

"What is your mother's name?"

"Catherine."

"What is your father's name?"

"Frank."

"Where do you live in Georgia?"

"On our plantation."

"What is it called? What town is it in?"

"Atlanta—Atlanta, Georgia."

"And what's your family's name?"

"Tibbits."

"Do you have any brothers and sisters?"

"I have a brother."

"What's his name ?"

"Melvin."

"How old is he?"

"Twenty-three."

"How old are you?"

"I'm eighteen."

"Where were you born?"

"Right here."

"In Atlanta?"

"Ahuh, in that little room up there at the top of the stairs."

"Where's the house? What street is the house on? The plantation, where is it? In Atlanta?"

"We have one of the largest plantations here in Atlanta, Georgia, that you'd ever want to see."

"Where did you go to school?"

"We had private tutors come in, taught, my brother and I, in the library."

"What church did you go to?"

"White Baptist Church."

"Where is it located?"

"Down the lane."

"What's your grandfather's name?"

"He's dead."

"What was his name?"

"Gordon."

"Does your father serve in the Army?"

"No, Pop's too old."

"Does he have a brother in the Army?"

"No, they keep talking all the time about the Army and carpetbaggers and high taxes."

"What year is this now?"

"It's 18 . . . 18 . . . I don't know."

"What's the president's name?"

"Jackson."

"Tell me a little bit about yourself. What do you do all day?"

"Go to teas."

"Do you have any friends?"

"Robert."

"Robert what?"

"Simms."

"How old is he?"

"Twenty-two."

"What does he do? Where does he live?"

"His family lives the next plantation over."

"How far away?"

"Across the creek. Over the lane."

"Are you going to marry him?"

"Oh, yes, if I could only get him to tell me he wants to marry me. I know he wants to marry me. I don't know . . . He doesn't want to get married yet."

"Why, is he too young?"

"No, something about new land."

"New land where?"

"Florida, I guess they call it."

"He wants to go there?"

"Yes. I don't know why he wants to leave Georgia. This is the most beautiful state in the whole world. He makes me so mad. We could be so happy."

"Would you go with him?"

"Yes, I'd go anywhere with him, if he'd just ask me to marry him."

"What do your parents think about him?"

"Our families have been friends for a long, long, long time—way before we were ever born."

"Elizabeth, you are now twenty-eight years old. It's ten years later. What is your name now, Elizabeth?"

"I'm Elizabeth Simms."

"Where do you live?"

"Red Mill, Florida."

"What is your husband's name?"

"Robert Simms."

"Do you like it in Red Mill?"

"Yes, it's my home."

"Do you have any children?"

"Yes."

"How many?"

"Five. The baby's just small. She's a little doll. I called her Mary Jane."

"You are now ten, twenty, thirty years . . . you are becoming older now. The children are grown. The children have left the house. You are now a very old lady, Elizabeth. Do you see yourself in the house?"

"Yes."

"You are alone in the house now. What's happening in the house?"

"I'm sad."

"What are you doing?"

"Looking at the pictures on the mantel."

"How old are you now?"

"Eighty-nine years old."

"And you're all by yourself?"

"No, poor Daisy."

"Who is with you?"

"Daisy, the colored maid. Ninety . . . she's gone to bed."

"Then what happens?"

"I'm not well."

"Something happens."

"I'm so tired."

"One day you stand in front of the mirror and someone hurts you. Who is it? Do you remember? Now we can talk about it. Its all over. No one can hurt you again."

"My baby."

"Your baby? What is he doing? Which one of your babies?"

"James."

"What is he doing?"

"Rifle."

"What does he do?"

"Catch his button . . ."

"And what happens then?"

"Ohh!"

"You're all right. You can't be hurt any more. Do you remember what happens then?"

"Everyone, everyone's gone."

"What do you do? Where do you stay?"

"Here. This is my home."

"Is there a difference now? Do you look different?"

"Yes."

"Now, after he shoots, what happens?"

"I don't care."

"You don't care for what?"

"Don't punish him. It was an accident."

"You mean, he didn't mean to?"

"No, his jacket . . . the button . . ."

"But why was he pointing it at you?"

"We'd been having trouble with prowlers. My niece and the maid had been seeing . . . seeing dark shadows of a man prowling around the house, and he tried to get in and they had a shotgun in the hall, by the hall window, leaning up against the wall by my room."

"What did he do?"

"James had come home unexpectedly, come upstairs, and I was brushing my hair. I always took great pride in my hair. It was still pretty."

"I'm sure it was."

"James picked up the rifle. He was wondering what it was doing there, and he tucked it under his arm. I saw him in the mirror, over my shoulder. As he greeted me, the trigger caught in the button of his jacket pocket."

"And it hurt you."

"Yes, it hurt me."

"And then what happened? What did you do then? Did you see yourself after that?"

"Yes."

"How did you look?"

"Crumpled on the floor."

"But you were not really on the floor, were you . . . you, yourself?"

"I stood looking at myself."

"Then where did you go?"

"Wandered."

"Did you meet anyone you knew?"

"No, I was all alone."

"In the house?"

"In the house."

"How long did you stay that way?"

"For a long time."

"What was the next thing that happened to you after that?"

"A young girl came to the house one day, with two young children. She was so much like I was when I was that age. A sweet little girl."

"So what did you do?"

"She seemed to like my house, my home."

"Did you know her?"

"No."

"Did you communicate with her before she came to the house?"

"I showed her my house."

"How did you know where to find her?"

"*I don't know*. I showed her my house and when she came . . . when she came it was like living again. She made me happy."

"Are you her? Is she you? Or are you two different people?"

"I don't know."

"When you were in the house, floating around for a while, did you at any time disappear from it, or not remember anything?"

"Yes, there was a time when I seemed to rest. There was nothing."

"And then what?"

"Just darkness, and then I showed this young girl my home."

"In between, did anybody talk to you?"

"No."

"Nobody came to talk to you before that young girl came?"

"No. In the house, people came. They wanted to look about the house . . . curious."

"But not to talk to you?"

"This little girl was different."

"Do you remember being a child again? After the darkness, the period when everything was dark and you rested, after that, do you remember being a child?"

"Yes, yes."

"How was it? How did you become a child from the darkness? How did you go from the dark period of rest to become a child again?"

"Baby."

"You remember a baby?"

"A baby was playing on a porch with a clothesline and some clothespins."

"What was the first thing you remember when you woke up as a baby?"

"A woman came out and picked me up and carried me indoors."

"And the years went by, and then you grew up, and then one day you told this girl about your old home, is that it?"

"Yes."

"Why did you suddenly think of your home? What made it happen?"

"She was so much like I was. Not her temperament. She was so, so pure and good, I guess you could say."

"So you decided you would want to remember."

"I wanted her to live in my house. It was our house together."

"Did you know that the house has since been torn down to make way for another house? Time has gone on. Are you aware of that?"

"No, they can't take my home away."

"You still own it?"

"Yes."

"And this girl who is now you, are you her? Are you going to live in her mind with her, as her?"

"I must. She gives me purpose."

"Did you know someone who was a postmaster when you lived in Red Mill?"

"There was a young man who wanted to be postmaster for a long time."

"What was his name?"

"Jeremy McDonald."

"Do you remember any of the people in Red Mill who were in the Army?"

"There were many, many of our boys."

"Any officers that you can recall by name?"

"My son was an officer."

"Which one?"

"One fought for the Union forces against his father's wishes."

"What regiment was he in?"

"Cavalry, Persing . . . Persing of Cavalry."

"Anyone in the Southern armies?"

"My son."

"Which one?"

"Allen."

"What regiment? What rank?"

"He was lieutenant, Confederate Forces."

"But in which branch of the forces?"

"He was Lee's dispatcher. He was a fine, loyal officer, wounded three times."

"He was a lieutenant, cavalry or infantry?"

"Cavalry."

I decided to bring June out of her hypnotic state. After all, it was our first session together, and I did not wish to overtire her. There would be time for another session the following morning.

When June awoke, she remembered absolutely nothing. She felt as if she had just had a nice, long nap. I immediately questioned her about any knowledge she might possess, either consciously or unconsciously, about the Simms family, but it appeared that she knew nothing more

than what she had already told me. "The only thing
I know is what the old postmaster told me," June explained. She could not *now* recall the postmaster's name.
She did not know what name Mrs. Simms was known
under prior to her marriage.

I don't think June lied to me. She answered my
questions immediately and without reflecting, in a straight-
forward manner. There was no particular reward in her
coming to Pittsburgh to see me, nor would there be any
publicity for a long time to come. June had nothing to
expect in a material way from our working together, and
I do not believe that her makeup was such that she would
have enjoyed telling tall tales. When she denied any
knowledge of the Simms family, beyond what the old
postmaster had told her, I took her at face value. I hon-
estly had no reason to feel otherwise.

I questioned her now somewhat more closely about
her own background. Married at fifteen and now the
mother of four children, she had lived in only three
places: in western Pennsylvania; in East Hempstead,
Long Island; and again in western Pennsylvania. At no
time had she taken any interest in the South, or in Southern history. None of her grandparents, or other members
of either her or her husband's family are from the South,
nor have they anything to do with the state of Georgia.
She has never been to Atlanta. Yet June has always
shown a great interest in the history of the War Between
the States. She doesn't know why the Civil War period
attracts her so much, but it all started when she was
about eighteen years old. She read some books dealing
with the period, without ever studying it formally. Her
education ended at the high-school level. But she took
night classes in such diverse subjects as interior decorating, psychology, history, and writing.

It was getting late, and I suggested that June get some
rest.

The following morning we met again. This time she
went under even more easily than the night before, which
is not surprising, since the second or third session does
go easier in hypnosis than the initial effort. I quickly took
her back to her own birth, and then fifty years before it.
Once again we established that her name was Elizabeth.

Then I reminded her that we had talked before and that
we would continue our conversation about Georgia now.

"Tell me, Elizabeth, what street do you live on in Atlanta?"

"We don't live on a street."

"Do you live in the country?"

"Yes."

"What's the name of your place?"

"On a large plantation."

"What is it called?"

"Hill Place."

"Who are your neighbors?"

"Our neighbors are quite far away—across the creek."

"What's the nearest place to you?"

"The Simms plantation."

"How far are you from Atlanta?"

"Oh, that all depends on, if it's a hot day it seems
longer."

"How do you go to Atlanta? By what conveyance?"

"Papa always says, 'Jacob, bring around the buggy.' "

"What sort of church do you go to on Sunday?"

"The Baptist Church."

"Has it got a name?"

"Just the Baptist Church."

"It doesn't have a special name?"

"No."

"What's the minister's name?"

"Reverend Harold Clements."

"Do you know the mayor?"

"Yes, I like to tease him."

"What's his name?"

"I call him Tubby."

"Why do you call him Tubby?"

"Because he's so round."

"Well, that's a good enough reason; but what do the
people call him? What's his real name?"

"Judge Boland."

"What is his first name?"

"I don't think I know."

"Boland, huh? Has he been mayor very long?"

"Yes, for a long, long time."

"What party does he belong to?"

"Women of the South, sir, do not indulge in politics."

"You do know who's President of the United States."

"Of course."

"Who is? Who is the president now? Every school child must know that, and you're an educated young lady. Surely you know who is now President. You've read about him. What kind of a man is the President?"

"A great man."

"What does he look like?"

"He's tall and handsome. A distinguished, young man."

"Where does he come from, North or South?"

"From the South, sir."

"Is he a military man or a civilian man?"

"He was a military man of great distinction."

"What's the color of his hair?"

"A light blond color."

"What's your papa's favorite newspaper?"

"Georgia . . ."

"The Georgia what?"

"Tribune."

"Talk to me about some of your fine friends in Atlanta. The people that come to your father's house—who are they? I know that you're interested in Mr. Simms, but you must have other friends, and your father must have some friends. Has he any friends who are in the Senate or in the House?"

"There are men who are much confused about our government and the way our country is being handled. They join my father in the drawing room twice a week."

"What are they talking about?"

"I don't know."

"What do they think they ought to do about the government?"

"I don't know. Something drastic must be done."

"Do you know any of the names of these people that come to see your father?"

"Generally, before they arrive, the womenfolk are allowed to retire."

"Do you know who the Senator is from your state, in Congress?"

"Yes."

"What is his name?"

"I'd rather not say."

"Why? Don't you like him?"

"Not particularly. Last year he asked my father for my hand in marriage. I will not marry a man I do not love!"

"When you went to Atlanta, did you do any shopping, buying goods and things, and finery?"

"We went to Atlanta, Mamma and I, and my cousin."

"What is the cousin's name?"

"Alice Jenkins. She lives in Virginia."

"Where in Virginia?"

"Norfolk."

"Do they have a house there?"

"Yes."

"What did her father do?"

"He was a bookkeeper."

"For whom?"

"Munitions firm."

"What is their name?"

"Jenkins."

"Is he an owner of it?"

"No, in the family some way, I guess."

"So your cousin and your mother and you went shopping in Atlanta. Where did you go? Where did you do the shopping? What place, what store? Tell me about it."

"In a big department store. The last time we went, Mamma scolded me."

"Why did she scold you?"

"You know the cute little stools where you sit down to relax? I whirled around them, and Mamma said it wasn't dignified at all."

"What's the name of the store? Do you remember?"

"Harry Millin's . . . on Main Street."

"Did you see any other stores?"

"Confectionery store."

"Do you remember the name of the place?"

"Mr. Willike's. He was always nice to me. He used to save two little pieces just for me."

"Did you have anyone living in Atlanta, any friends or relatives?"

"Mamma had many friends."

"Do you remember any of them? Did you ever visit any of them?"

"Yes, sir."

"Like who?"

"Mrs. McDennis."

"What's her first name, or her husband's first name?"

"I'm not sure. I was always instructed to call people by their last name."

"Mrs. McDennis. What does her husband do?"

"Foreman."

"In what?"

"On a plantation."

"Any girl friends?"

"Some of them are like cats. You ought to hear the way they talk about the new colt that Papa just gave me."

"Where did he get it?"

"It was born to Mr. Silver Black."

"Who is Mr. Silver Black?"

"He's a horse."

"Did your father have an attorney, a lawyer, to take care of his business?"

"Yes, sir."

"Do you remember what his name was?"

"Gaylord Linholm."

"And your father was Franklin Tibbits. You're eighteen now, right?"

"Yes, sir."

"What year were you born?"

"Eighteen two."

"You were born in 1802?"

"Yes, sir."

"What is your birthday? When do you celebrate your birthday?"

"August second. My mother says that's why I have such a violent temper, because I was born in August, when it was so hot."

"How long has the plantation been in the family now?"

"My great grandfather built it."

"What was his name?"

"Harrison."

"Harrison Tibbits?"

"Yes."

"What was your great grandmother's name?"

"Marie."

"Marie, and then their son would be your grandfather?"

"Yes, sir."

"What was his name?"

"I think my grandfather's name was Franklin."

"Your father is Frank, and your mother is . . ."

"Catherine."

"With a C or a K?"

"With a C. Father likes to tease her. He calls her Katie. It makes Mamma mad, but she doesn't stay mad at Papa."

"You were baptized in the same church that you always go to now in Atlanta?"

"Oh, yes, sir. It has been a great tradition in our family."

"Now, today, think of today now. People are talking. Do you think there'll be a war? What do you hear?"

"There is great unrest. Everyone is a little afraid to say things openly. Men are angry. They demand that something be done soon."

"Done about what?"

"Our taxes. The government is trying to force, they say because of the slaves, they have raised . . . they have raised all the taxes, put a heavy levy on everything. The plantation businessmen are up in arms about it. They are trying to drain our blood from us."

"Have you ever been to a place called Red Mill?"

"No, sir."

"Never heard of it?"

"No, sir."

"Now, you know this boy, Simms, real well?"

"Yes, sir."

"Do you like him?"

"I love him, sir."

"And he loves you?"

"Yes, sir. He declared his love."

"How do your parents feel about him?"

"They are most pleased, sir."

"Do you think the two of you are going to get married?"

"Oh, yes."

"How soon?"

"I want to get married now."

"Mmm, but you're only eighteen."

"It makes no difference. Robert wants to wait until he has a home to take me to."

"When will that be, do you think?"

"I don't know. Soon, I hope."

"And have you met Mr. Simms?"

"Oh, yes, sir."

"What is Mr. Simms' first name?"

"John."

"John. You mean, Robert's father is named John Simms."

"Yes, sir."

"Mr. Simms has just one son—Robert?"

"Yes, sir."

"Are there any other children?"

"A daughter, Evelyn."

"How old is she?"

"Twelve."

"And Robert is twenty?"

"Twenty-two."

"Have you met any other people at the Simms house, from town?"

"At teas."

"Like what?"

"The women from the women's group at the church."

"Did you ever meet any officers?"

"One very handsome young man."

"What's his name?"

"Lieutenant Colonel Michael Wrinceson."

"That's an unusual name, isn't it?"

"Yes, it is."

"What's he in charge of?"

"He works in an office."

"In Atlanta?"

"Georgia."

"Cavalry or infantry?"

"Cavalry, sir."

"You've met him?"

"He came to the house one time. Papa was most pleased to see him, and they both hurried into the library."

"Have you ever met any doctors?"

"No, sir."

"Well, when somebody is sick, who do you call?"

"Daisy always takes care of us if we're sick."

"Have you ever seen any boats or ships?"

"We went for a ride on the Mississippi on a big paddle boat."

"What was it called?"

"The *Lilly Belle*."

"Where did you go on her?"

"Up the river."

"To what town?"

"We went to Louisiana."

"What did you do in New Orleans?"

"We went to a big ball there."

"Who gave the ball?"

"Mr. and Mrs. Thornton."

"Do you speak French?"

"A little."

"Did you meet anyone in New Orleans, other than the Thorntons?"

"Handsome officers."

"Like who?"

"Paul . . . I remember their faces and their first names."

"Did you meet the Governor?"

"Yes."

"What was his name?"

"I don't know. I suppose I forgot it because I didn't like him. He was a fussy old man, not one bit of fun."

"But you know the Governor of Georgia. Surely you know him, in Atlanta. Have you ever seen him?"

"Yes, sir."

"What's his name?"

"I'd rather not say."

"Why, do you have anything against him?"

"No, sir. He comes to those meetings. We are not allowed to discuss who comes."

"You can talk to me."

"Papa says not to trust anybody. There are spies everywhere."

"I'm on your side."

"They have imprisoned quite a few of our men."

"Who has?"

"The government."

"Why would they do that?"

"They were trying to overthrow the government. The meetings are secret."

"Who would want to overthrow the government? Who is the leader who would want to do that? Is there someone in Washington who says that?"

"Mr. Seward. He's in the Cabinet."

"Your father doesn't like Mr. Seward?"

"No, sir."

"Are there any other cousins on your father's side?"

"There is a disturbance in the family."

"What happened?"

"The brothers . . . the plantation was left to my father. They don't correspond any more."

"Where did they go off to?"

"I don't know. They're not spoken about in our family."

"I see. Do you remember any other relatives in Atlanta, or in Georgia?"

"Aunt Genevieve Jenkins."

"Where does she live?"

"In Georgia, in the main part of town."

"And what does her husband do?"

"She's a widow, sir."

"What did he do before he passed on?"

"He was a boat captain, sir. He was lost in a storm at sea before Alice was born."

"When was Alice born? Is she younger than you, or older than you?"

"A year older."

"So she was born in 1801 if you were born in 1802, and he was lost before she was born?"

"Yes, sir."

"How is the Norfolk Jenkins related to Alice Jenkins?"

"Cousins, somehow."

It was time to bring June out of her hypnotic state. When she awoke, she felt fine and was ready to go home to her little town in western Pennsylvania. A few days later, I heard from her again. There was nothing special to report, really, except a certain unrest she kept feeling, and a continuing, strong emphasis on a personality change that had begun after her return from Florida, and that somehow was becoming more pronounced as time went on. Moreover, June found herself saying and doing things that were completely out of character with her usual identity. Even her parents noticed this on the occasion when they were together.

Principally, June, that is to say, the old June, was somewhat timid, and not likely to say anything without first thinking it over very carefully. The new personality was the exact opposite—tactful, but sometimes painfully truthful, and if one didn't like what she had to say, that was just too bad. Many a family fight erupted because of pronounced opinions on this or that, expressed by the "new" June personality.

Gradually, however, Sam has gotten used to the changes in his wife, for he truly loves her. There are things that he doesn't understand, nor does he wish to understand them any further. He accepts them, and has learned to live with them.

Whereas the old June was simply dedicated to her domestic chores, the new personality suddenly developed an interest in the arts—music, amateur theatrics, all these things became a part of her new interests, and despite the fact that June lives in a small town, far away from the mainstream of cultural activities, she is trying to read whatever she can get her hands on, and keep up with the most sophisticated world outside. To her husband, this is all right, even though he himself does not have such ambitions.

As time went on, the personality of the alleged Mrs. Simms, and of the "old" June began to merge into one new personality in which, however, the elusive spirit of the plantation owner's widow was dominant, or became more and more dominant as time went on. To be sure, June neither encouraged nor sought this change, but to the contrary, found it upsetting. In order to allay her fears, I briefly explained that I suspected a factual reincarnation memory, and, without telling her of any verifications, presented the matter merely as a possible hypothesis. I also assured her that there was no danger involved, and that if she wished to suppress the personality of Mrs.

Simms in her character, she could do so by merely asking me to suggest this in one of our next sessions with hypnosis.

This June did not choose to do. Somehow she felt that it was her destiny to live with her prenatal memory, and to make the best of it. Then, too, it intrigued her, and in a life as placid and ordinary as hers, any form of excitement was welcome. With all her tragedies, the life of Mrs. Simms seemed a better thing to contemplate than the secure existence of June, the housewife in western Pennsylvania. If she could have the best of both worlds, so much the better.

I asked June to do no more checking into the subject of hypnosis or reincarnation, and to avoid any books on the subject. I promised her to look into all the material at the earliest possible time, and when it was all finished, to tell her who she was, who she had been, and what the future of both personalities might be. This seemed to satisfy June, and from that time on I told her nothing beyond casual conversation on the subject in general. As soon as possible, I would come and visit her in her little town in western Pennsylvania, to continue my search for additional evidence dealing with the two lives June had apparently led in previous times.

I heard from her again in early June. What had puzzled me all along was the possibility of June's experiences being attributable only to ESP, perhaps through precognition, as in the case of her dream prior to seeing the ghost town of Red Mill. I wanted to make sure that extrasensory perception could not answer all the questions.

One night early in June she had retired and somehow could not sleep. The clock struck two as she felt a strange loosening of the bonds between her body and spirit, and she had the feeling that she was floating apart from her body. Looking down upon the bed, she saw herself lying on it. The filmy part of herself then faded away, and all at once she found herself standing in her parents' trailer.

Her parents then, and now, have lived in a trailer at Brookville, Florida, a considerable distance from western Pennsylvania. June had never been to this particular trailer. She stood there for a moment in what appeared to be a living room, and then went straight down the hall to her mother's room, and as she passed her father's room she could actually hear him snoring. She then stepped inside, to her mother's bed, bent down, and kissed her on the forehead, at the same time touching her mother's soft, wrinkled hand. At this precise moment, her mother opened her eyes, looked up, and said, "Junie, what are you doing here?" With that, June just faded away again and found herself back in her own house.

The next morning she passed it all off as a dream, thinking that perhaps her unconscious was trying to tell her she should write to her mother. Three days later she received a letter from her mother. In the letter, her mother described a dream she had had in which she has seen June standing by her bed the night before, and then suddenly fading away. This had frightened her, because she knew about June's heart condition. "And it was so real," she added.

June's mother uses a particular bath powder, with a certain aroma. That morning, June's daughter, Cynthia, came into her room, and immediately remarked that her mother smelled particularly good this morning. Had her father bought her some new bath powder for Mother's Day? But June had not used any bath powder or perfume that night at all.

Her mother, on the other hand, had gotten up after June had faded away from her bedside, and made herself a cup of coffee in the kitchen. When she looked at the clock it was exactly 2:20 A.M.

I was not too surprised to hear of June's astral projection experience. Oftentimes, psychic people tend to have stronger prenatal memories than ordinary people. This doesn't mean that ESP is necessary to have prenatal memories, but that the two faculties frequently go hand in hand. I suspect it has to do with the greater degree of sensitivity encountered in psychic people.

It was time to visit June and her family in her little town in western Pennsylvania, and I began to make all the arrangements. It meant changing planes in Pittsburgh, and then being picked up at the little airport by June and her husband, but they were most eager to do so and invited us to spend the night at their home, since it would be impossible to return before the following day.

On July 30, 1968, we arrived after a somewhat bumpy flight from Pittsburgh. The little airport was exactly as I had imagined it, just large enough to accommodate small planes and the country around it was rolling hillsides, wide open and inviting in its own, peaceful way.

Sam and June drove us to their town, which was about a half hour distant. Their white house sat back from the road somewhat, surrounded by shady, tall maple trees. In back of the house there was a hillside lot rising up to the edge of the woods. The two-story house is twenty years old, and it has a pleasant downstairs parlor, kitchen, and several bedrooms upstairs. We were given the best room in the house, and found it indeed comfortable and quiet.

Later, when we made the rounds of the little town, we realized that this was far removed from the mainstream of city activity such as we had come from, but nevertheless, this was a busy little town, wrapped up in its own problems. Perhaps these problems were enlarged by the people who created or solved them, but to them, matters involving a charity affair or the latest scandal were about the only things that created excitement, and excitement is what the American countryside lacks most.

June had very carefully concealed her own case of excitement from her neighbors, for she did not want them nosing in when her guests from New York arrived. Thus, it was entirely unnecessary for me to have warned her not to talk to local newspapermen, for she had guarded our secret well. About the only thing June had ever done with the Florida experience was a fictional account of the Simms murder case such as she knew it, based entirely on the skimpy story told her by the old postmaster in Florida. I read her notes for that story, and found that they contained nothing we had not already discussed. There was nothing in them about reincarnation, of course, or about Atlanta, or Georgia, only an extended account of the Simms family and, particularly, of how Mrs. Simms died, by hands unknown.

June has for years tried to write professionally, and she has even used the services of a New York literary agent, but she has sold very little, unfortunately. It is amazing that someone who writes as colorfully as she does and who has a flair for poetry, nevertheless is unable to spell even the simplest words. This, however, does not deter her from continuing with a would-be literary career, even though she realizes that the chances for publication of her stories are slim. Truly creative in her own way, she finds the greatest joy in writing them, and does not worry too much whether they will eventually be accepted or not.

I had asked June to contact her father in Florida, requesting him to authenticate the existence of Red Mill, if possible. I felt that this type of information would not harm whatever we might obtain through hypnosis, since we had already discussed it consciously.

June's father, a total skeptic concerning matters of this nature, had done a pretty thorough job, and the results were somewhat distressing to June. It appeared that the old Simms place was located at the village of Anthony, in Marion County, Florida, two miles north of Oak, on Old Route U.S. 301, about seven miles north of Ocala. This village was founded prior to the Civil War and named after Susan B. Anthony, the famous supporter of woman suffrage.

The village today is partially in ruins. There are still some people living there, but it is only a matter of time until they, too, will go elsewhere. Thus, what appeared as a ghost town to June many years ago, is again becoming a ghost town.

The area is in north-central Florida, and perhaps best known for the tourist attraction of Silver Springs. The Chamber of Commerce in Ocala has no records of a village called Red Mill. As far as they are concerned, there never was a ghost town by that name. June would have believed that her experience was nothing more than a vision or a dream had it not been for the fact that her father had taken her and her children there. She remembers distinctly seeing a faded sign reading RED MILL hanging on the still-standing little red station, but there's little doubt in June's mind that Anthony and Red Mill are one and the same place.

Depressed by the discrepancies in what she remembers as facts, and what her father was able to obtain, she decided to leave the corroboration of her experiences entirely to me. She really didn't care whether it was all her imagination or reality. All she wanted to know was what it meant to her and her future and her family, and as long as it would not hurt anyone, she was perfectly content to accept my verdict, whatever it might be.

Shortly after we had arrived and settled down comfortably at June and Sam's house, I asked Sam for his own impression concerning the changes that had come over June after her return from Florida. He acknowledged that there had been a major change in her personality. For one thing, her sudden interest in the local community theater was out of character. She wasn't the kind of person who wanted to be an actress, but all of a sudden she wanted to partake in the stage plays put on by the little theater.

"Before her visit to Florida, she wasn't interested in anything, as a matter of fact. After she got back, she was interested in politics, something she never cared for before, and in archeology, and other things that didn't interest her at all."

Sam works as a laboratory technician at the local glass factory. He himself has had some psychic experiences, and is not hostile to the idea of ESP itself. His father had psychic experiences before him, so perhaps there is a tradition in the family about that sort of thing. He himself had been born in the little town, and his father had come there as a child. His outside interests include forestry and the preservation of animal life in the surrounding area, which includes a large state park. Sam is not particularly concerned with such things as reincarnation memories, and he really hasn't thought about the results of Mrs. Simms' influencing the character of his wife. He takes it all in his stride.

It had gotten late, and we decided to go to bed. The following morning, right after breakfast, I decided to have my first hypnosis session with June. The children were sent to play outside, Sam was at work, and my wife, Catherine, was still upstairs, asleep. Except for an occasional bird chirping outside, it was very quiet. Quickly June was under hypnosis, slipping back to her previous existence as Elizabeth Simms. This time June seemed particularly agitated by something. I asked if there was anything wrong.

"I'm afraid."

"Why are you afraid?"

"There is so much fighting."

"Who is fighting?"

"Robert and Michael, my son and my husband. Always arguing."

"What are they arguing about?"

"The plantation. Robert wants Michael to settle down, take over his responsibilities, and he won't. He hates the plantation. He loves his horses. He raises thoroughbreds."

"Tell me about the plantation. What is it called?"

"We don't have a name for it."

"How far is it from Atlanta?"

"Quite a ways."

"How many miles? How long does it take to go there?"

"A day and a half."

"Do you remember your father's plantation in Atlanta? What was that called?"

"Hill Place."

"How far was it *from* Atlanta?"

"Oh, about two hours' drive by buggy."

"Do you think that there will be a war?"

"Yes, sir."

"Between whom?"

"The states."

"Why do you think there will be a war?"

"It has to come eventually."

"You're thirty-five years old. You are living on the plantation. You are Elizabeth Simms. You are married. Tell me, is there a war on now?"

"Yes, sir."

"What kind of a war is it?"

"Between the North and the South."

"And how old are you?"

"I'm thirty-six."

"The war has been on for how long?"

"A year."

"Who is the governor of this state?"

"A southern woman does not discuss politics, sir."

"Whom would you like to see governor?"

"Our main interest, sir, is who shall become our President."

"Well, who should be?"

"Thomas Jefferson . . . there's someone coming."

"Who is coming?"

"Cavalry men . . . they have to go into the glades. A prisoner escaped . . . a very important prisoner . . . a Yankee."

"Then what year are we in now?"

"Eighteen sixty-one."

"You are eighteen years old. You are Mary Elizabeth Tibbits. What does the town look like? How much of a town is it?"

"There's not much of it. It's just a small town."

"How many people?"

"About a thousand, I'd say."

"What do they call the place?"

"Atlanta, sir. It's not a very big place."

After I had brought June out of her hypnotic state I began to question her concerning any knowledge she might have of life in nineteenth-century Georgia. I threw the name Tibbits at her. It made no impression. She thought she had heard it somewhere before, but really didn't know for sure. I tried Hill Place. No reaction. I said, "Jenkins, Linholm, Boland." All I received in reply was a firm "No." June's face showed absolutely no sign of recognition. Now I tried Seward. This seemed to ring a bell. "The only Seward that I would know anything about would be in history, something to do with politics," she said. How far, did she think, did Atlanta go back? "I haven't the slightest idea when it was settled," she replied firmly.

"After you came back from that Florida trip, did you discover any change in you?" I asked. "It was just as if I had been asleep for a long, long time, and I woke up, and I had a lot of living to catch up with."

Where she had been a conformist prior to her trip to Florida, she had turned into a freethinker after her return. In the six years since then, she had never gone back, however. That one and only visit to the house lasted for about an hour and a half. During her stay in the house, she had found time also to scan some of the yellowed papers in an old trunk in the house. Unfortunately, she had not taken anything along with her except a few of the ledgers, which she had showed me during our first visit in Pittsburgh.

"Was there any difference in the way you would cook, or in the way you would do certain chores?" I asked.

"Yes, as far as sewing is concerned, and then there was this urge to sort of feather my nest better, and I took a course in interior decorating, and things like that, but I seemed to know automatically how to make drapes, slip covers, even my own clothing, which I didn't do before."

Even though June's great grandfather had been a sharp-shooter with the Union forces, there had always been a sense of sympathy for the South in her makeup. This existed even before her visit to Florida. She somehow felt bad that the South had lost.

Another strange thing concerned June's liking of clocks. Since her return from Florida she had become increasingly conscious of time, and had installed clocks in every room of her house.

It was time for lunch now, so we called the session. That afternoon, after June had rested somewhat, I put her again under hypnosis. I had not forgotten that she had also spoken of another lifetime abroad, in an earlier period, and I wanted to delve into that particular memory at this time. She went under quickly and without difficulty. I sent her back several hundred years, until she was able to see the girl she had briefly described earlier.

We quickly established that girl had brown hair, was of medium build, and looked about nineteen or twenty years of age. Her eyes resembled June's; other than that, there was no resemblance.

"Describe her clothes."

"She has a long dress. It seems to have little, round buttons from the waist up. The dress comes down in sort of a peak in the front of the bodice."

"I want you to go around and look at them until you find out where you are. Look for some indication of the place and the time."

"The one woman, the aunt, wears a shawl . . . dark, crocheted shawl around her shoulders. They all have long dresses. The room is not a bright room."

"Can you see yourself in this scene?"

"Just the girl that looks similar to me. Gloria Heimier, I think it is."

"What is the name of the town or the village, or whatever the place is?"

"Düsseldorf."

"What is the year we are in?"

"Seventeen sixty-eight, I think."

"Seventeen sixty-eight. How old is the girl, as you look at her?"

"Eighteen."

"Then she was born in 1750. Was she born here, in this town?"

"Yes."

"What are her parents' names?"

"Franz Heimier . . . Anna."

"What does her father do for a living?"

"He had a little shop . . . little store."

"Is she married?"

"No."

"Is she an only child? Are there any brothers and sisters?"

"No, she seems to be the only one."

"What church does she go to?"

"Catholic, I believe."

"What is the name of her church, or her parish church, where she worships?"

"Sacred Flower, something like that."

"Ask her who rules the country she lives in."

"I don't see a name. I just see a face."

"What does it look like?"

"It has a . . . like a funny kind of a helmet or hat on, with a plume. The man has a full face, heavy brows, a large man. He has a heavy mustache. He's a ruler, I believe . . . Emperor, something like that."

"Now, this girl is eighteen years old. How old was she when she died?"

"Twenty-two."

"What does she die of?"

"Fever."

"You see her at eighteen, in 1768. She died in 1772 at twenty-two. What happens as you see this scene?"

"She's pouring tea."

"For whom?"

"For her aunt and, I believe, her mother."

"In what way is this scene important? What is the occasion?"

"She feels like a servant in the home."

"Is she unhappy?"

"Yes, yes, she's very quiet, aloof."

"Well, why at this moment? Why not at any other moment?"

"Something to do with what the women are talking about."

"What are they talking about?"

"Family gossip."

"Do you think there's a link between yourself and her?"

"Yes."

"What is it that you have to do that she couldn't do? What is unfinished?"

"To be able to stand on my own two feet, to say no."

"To say no to whom?"

"When things aren't right, to say no to anyone. Not to be afraid of being rebuked, hurt."

"Where is she buried?"

"I see a small, round tombstone. GLORIA HEIMIER, AGE 22, BORN 1750—DIED 1772."

"Anything else?"

"There's a little bunch of flowers on the grave."

"Is there anyone else under that grave, or just her?"

"There's lots of tombstones close by all around."

"Any others with the name Heimier?"

"There are several."

"Can you read any of them?"

"Seventeen o five."

"Born 1705 or died 1705?"

"Born."

"Any first names?"

"Maria, Franz, born 1700 and died 1752."

"And all this is still in Düsseldorf?"

"Outside the town."

"All right, now, I want you to come away from there with me. I want you to slowly walk backwards towards the present. I want you to come up."

"I can't."

"Why not? Why do you want to stay?"

"Because, she's holding onto my hand. She wants me to stay. She needs someone who understands. I've got to help her."

"Help her in what?"

"Escape from the kind of life she's living."

"Well, then tell her to come with us."

"She won't come. She has to make a trip to the country."

"All right, then bid her good-by and come with me now. I want you to come forward into the present.

"You are now back in another incarnation. You are Mary Elizabeth Simms. You are fifty years old. You live on a plantation. You are Mrs. Simms. Do you know the instrument through whom you are speaking? Why did you come and seek her out?"

"So everyone would know."

"What?"

"That my home was a family home and a happy one."

"Is there anything that you want done to make you happier?"

"No, not right now."

"Are you planning to stay with her?"

"Yes."

"What was the town in which you lived in 1820 when you were eighteen years old? What was the name of the place? Was it Atlanta?"

"People called it that, yes, sir."

"In 1820?"

"Yes, sir."

"That's very strange, because the records do not show this. Are you sure it was Atlanta?"

"The other plantation owners called it Atlanta, because of a legend. They hoped that the day would come when it would become the Golden City that once sank to the bottom of the sea."

"At the time, when you were eighteen years old, there wasn't any city yet, was there?"

"No, sir."

"What was it then, farm land?"

"Yes, sir."

"How how many people lived around there?"

"There are quite a few plantations."

"Were there any Indians around?"

"No, sir."

"Where had the Indians gone?"

"They had been driven back into the marsh."

"Were they civilized, or were they wild?"

"There are no civilized Indians, sir."

"You remember the name of the county in which all this was situated? The part of the territory?"

"County Claire."

"What was the main village, or main town, in that county?"

"There was a place where we could go to do our shopping, about two miles away."

"What was it called?"

"Well, it was called Atlanta."

"Were there any other towns further away that you can remember?"

"You could travel for miles, and see just plantation land."

"How did people get there?"

"They came by carriage from Georgia . . . by paddle-wheel boats."

"On what river?"

"Generally down the Mississippi, and then over across land."

"Wasn't there any railroad?"

"Not yet."

"When the railroad came, where did it end?"

"It went from Atlanta down through North Carolina, down through Virginia, all the same line."

"Now, Atlanta, was that the end of the railroad, or did it go further?"

"A little further, down to the tip of Virginia."

"In Georgia, what was the name of that place where the railroad ended? What did they call it?"

"A small town, Billings."

"And how far was that from Atlanta?"

"Not too far."

"Do you remember, sometime during your long life in that part of the world, any names of governors, or of the mayors? Any of them?"

"There was a Calhoun."

"What was his rank?"

"Senator, I think."

"How about any of the people around the city of Atlanta, mayors, governors?"

"Well, there was Tubby."

"What was Tubby's name, real name, I mean, in the books, in history?"

"I'm so tired."

"Was he the first mayor of Atlanta, or were there any others before him?"

"I believe Tubby was the second or third."

"How old were you at the time?"

"Eighteen or nineteen."

"You are living in Atlanta. It is 1849. How old are you now?"

"I'm thirty-nine."

"Tell me, who was the mayor in 1849?"

"Why are these things so important?"

I noticed an unwillingness to answer my questions, so I decided it was time to bring June out of hypnosis. She awoke apparently fully refreshed, and again having no conscious memory whatever as to what had transpired during the half hour or so she had been under hypnosis.

Although I had not done any detailed research concerning the material that had come through her in the earlier sessions, I did read the history of Atlanta to some degree to see whether I might pick up some clues, which, in turn, would lead to better questioning. Quite obviously, there were discrepancies in what she had told me under hypnosis, and in what history has recorded. How would I be able to reconcile these differences? Further research might be the answer.

I had hardly gotten back to New York City when I received an urgent letter from June. Under the influence of a sedative given to her by a doctor to relieve some pain she was having in connection with an infection, she had had a strange dream experience.

The girl in the carriage was with her, and she had a good chance to look at her again. She was still wearing the long, brown, hooded cape, which she dropped and let fall at her feet. She then held out her arm, and June saw herself take it. She felt that the girl was pleading with her to help her. Large tears rolled down her face, which was thin and pale.

At the same time, a few words impressed themselves on June's unconscious mind. They were "Jägerndorf," "Frederick," and "war," and finally, "1768." She begged June to go with her, but June hesitated. Apparently she had hesitated too long, for as she finally edged closer to the apparition in her dream, the girl seemed to melt away in a foglike, swirling mass around them, and was gone.

June awoke still feeling the girl's hand, bony and small as it had been, in her own. There were tears streaming down June's face as she was crying out, "Wait, wait, I want to go with you. Don't leave me."

That day June kept smelling flowers in her bedroom, although there were none in the house. She didn't wish to discuss it with Sam out of fear he might think she was still ill. Had the sedative caused the strange experience, June wondered? But, of course, the clarity of the words she remembered afterward seemed to militate against such an interpretation.

June tried to recollect anything else the girl might have said in the dream. The only other snatch of a phrase that came back to her mind was what the girl had said when she had first seen her, "Good morrow, Missie," she had said in a sweet voice, as if the two of them had been good friends and thought a lot of each other. Other than that, nothing seemed to come back.

I was highly impressed by the few words June had managed to remember. I instantly recognized the word "Jägerndorf" as the name of a medium-sized town in Bohemian Silesia. I doubt very much that June had known this on her own.

I requested that she observe all her dreams from now on, and to send me transcripts of anything unusual in that line. She was to write them down immediately upon awakening, and to do no research and make no inquiries whatever.

On January 31, 1969, June again visited with her earlier incarnation in Georgia. This time, she recalled the name of a politician visiting her father's home: Quincy Cabot. There seemed to have been some connection between this man and a foreign government, June felt. There was also additional material concerning Gloria. The only thing she saw was a tombstone of a very old kind. June felt that what she saw was a tomb of a relative of Gloria's named Marie, and the date 1683.

Gloria keeps beckoning to her in her dreams, but June is afraid to go with her now. She has the feeling that if she did give in and follow Gloria, she might never come back as June. There are vague impressions of cobblestone streets without sidewalks, and once, as June sat by the window, looking out at the heavy snowfall outside her house, she suddenly found herself thinking, Why, it looks just like an Austrian winter. Of course, she wouldn't know. She has never been to Europe in her life.

I heard again from June on February 19, 1969. In a dream/vision, she had seen her father, that is to say, her father in a previous incarnation. She had seen a house with a large, white, wood-and-marble fireplace, and various people standing around, amongst them a twelve-year-old boy clicking his heels in a continental manner. There were some older women in the room also. A name came to her—Marjorie Ashenbach. June felt that a man she saw in the group was Elizabeth Simms' father.

I instructed her not only to watch out for dream impressions, but also for anything that might come to her at odd moments while awake. To facilitate this, June put aside a few minutes a day for regular meditation sessions when she could be alone and relaxed.

During one of these sessions, in April of 1969, she received further information concerning Gloria. June felt that the girl had been in love with a soldier, but that this had been against her mother's wishes and without her knowledge. There was also something about a trial being held in a dark, paneled room with long benches on each side of the room and a little box where the accused stood. She had the feeling that it was the soldier being tried, and that he was a Prussian soldier. She described his hat as being a high hat, somewhat like that of a Pope, and white tight pants. I instantly recognized her description of the soldier's uniform as fitting the outfit a late-eighteenth-century grenadier would have worn in Prussia.

Then, a little later, she had a sudden flashback of the street where Gloria lived. It was in this street that Gloria

held her secret meetings with the soldier. Intermingled
with these impressions of Gloria's life were further scenes
of Elizabeth Simms' Atlanta.

One might argue that June, who liked to write poetry,
was making these scenes up from her own mind, guided
perhaps by her unconscious. Be this as it may, they are
certainly correct for the time and situations given, and
while not evidential in themselves, are interesting in evaluating the entire case.

"When the shutters were closed during the day's heat,"
June wrote down her impressions, "the darkened rooms
were damp and cool with the smell of tree moss. A dull,
flat smell it was. The afternoon nap in the cool, darkened
rooms was a delight. The heat outside was so dry that
even your nostrils felt dry, and the air hung heavy over
the fields, and the men would glance up at the heat of the
sun, beneath their wide-brimmed hats, astride their
mounts in the field, and take scarves that hung around
their necks and wipe the sweat from their necks and faces
and curse the heat. The air in the large rooms seemed to
hang motionless all about us, and the house was quiet.
The quiet footsteps of Daisy and Jacob in the hallway outside the large, white room was the only thing that could be
heard as we dropped gently off to sleep. Our heads rested
against large, soft pillows. Papa called it 'The ladies pan-
taloon time,' shushed by Mamma. By this time we grate-
fully stripped to our pantaloons and undervests. It gave me
a sense of freedom, and I wished I didn't ever have to
wear those long, old dresses again. Mamma fussed and
fumed, and said I was no better than the animals God
had placed on earth, and that they had to wear clothes
He had given them, and theirs was of fur. One time I an-
nounced that some day I was going to wear my pantaloons
riding at midnight, and Papa dropped his dish of mashed
potatoes and Mamma choked on her cup of tea. Daisy
just growled at me and shook her head, but I don't care.
I just want to be free and ride the wild wind about me."

I instructed June to continue watching for any impressions or visions she might have naturally, but not to try
to force any of this material from her subconscious.

Beth, as June now seemed to call her more and more
instead of Elizabeth, was particularly reluctant to yield

any more names or actual information concerning the visitors at her father's place. There seemed to be a sense of endangering people by naming them. Now, one might argue that that is simply a subterfuge, and the June consciously or unconsciously was simply playing a game in order to avoid having to give concrete information. I don't think so, because the character of Beth Simms does indeed fit in with the fear of compromising political names by naming them to me, a stranger.

Far more interesting was the change that was now taking place in June's whole personality. Thirty-nine years old at this moment, she felt far younger. There was a sense of jubilation in being alive within her she had never had before. She felt almost reckless, and searched for something crazy to do. This was totally in contradiction to her "old" character. She felt like writing poetry, and she wrote some pretty good poetry. It was May, and spring was all around the house. Western Pennsylvania can be very beautiful around that time of year, and June lived those days to the fullest.

Impressions came to her all the time now, at irregular intervals. Some of them merely duplicated visions that she had had in September, October, and November of 1968, but they all contained only material that I was already familiar with. Now and again there was something new. The name Joseph Mayo, for instance. She saw him as a short, fat man in a gray suit with a wine-red vest, little hair, and small-rimmed glasses, together with a tall, stately gentleman, who stood on the porch of their large, white colonial house in the South, and they talked.

On another occasion she saw herself halfway up the Simms staircase, wearing a long, wine-red dress with a small, black swirl design all over it. It had long sleeves and white cuffs with small buttons almost to the elbow. She was happy, humming to herself. She saw herself holding up the skirt of her dress just to the proper height. It seemed that she was about thirty-eight years old, with long hair which was wrapped about the top of her head into a soft, large bun. Again, she sees the small, fat man called Joseph, only the name Tubby seems to be associated with him now. She hears someone refer to a waistcoat, and doesn't understand what the word means.

Then there was the word Gwinnett County, and lush, green fields, tall trees, and a Creek Indian squatting down at a rippling creek that flowed on endlessly through the fields and woods, and the Indian drinking the cool, clear water. His horse bends its head to drink of the water, too.

Another scene shows her a group of young girls in long, full dresses, sitting and drinking tea from little cups and laughing and talking. She hears them speaking with a southern accent, and she registers some of their names—Mae Thornton, Anna Blake, Evelyn Simms, Pauline Pendleton, Mary Bawds. Then there is a trip to a department store on Whitehall Street in Atlanta, Georgia, and she somehow knows she is forty-eight years old.

More names rise up from her suppressed subconscious. Friends of her father, smoking cigars and drinking brandy, are seen in a vision in a large library. There are arguments among them, and their voices are loud. She hears some of the names. There is Jefferson Davis, a tall man with shaggy hair, Paul Bragg, Tom Pendleton, Harmon Gilmer, James Herald, Alfred Helm, Talbot Westcut, John Holt, and Jessica Jennings. John Holt seems close to the Tibbits family. He is from Norfolk, Virginia, as is Jessica Jennings. He is a mayor, and the year is 1820. She sees the image of a tall Confederate soldier, Captain Robert M. Simms, born May 18, 1823. He serves on Longstreet's staff.

A scene in Norfolk, Virginia, in a brick-faced colonial house at the corner of Willow Street and Church. President Monroe is being discussed by two men passing by in front of the building. They wear high felt hats, and the year is 1819.

The majority of impressions concerned Mrs. Simms. However, there were some additional ones relating to Gloria Heimier. "There is a beauty about her that is compelling, or maybe haunting is a better word," June wrote of her. "You want to rush to her and help her in some way." She managed to get the dates for Gloria's father, Franz Heimier, born 1700, died at fifty-two years of age in 1752. Gloria herself died in 1772, born 1750.

There is a small church in the valley, but June does not know what denomination. She sees a large steeple with a metal cross at the top. It is a stone, white-wood-trimmed church with a very steep hill directly behind it. What confuses June is the fact that she senses two residences, one in a city and one in a small village, the name of which is Jägerndorf. She feels that Gloria died in the city.

June also received impressions of Gloria's childhood friend, a blond girl named Olga Meyerson. Then there was a sentence in June's report that I found particularly arresting: "The only important person I can see is a Frederick the Great, leading his troops somewhere, and an encounter with his enemies. He rides erect on a shiny, black mount. His dress is black and silver in color."

Then again, she had something more to add to the circle of friends Mrs. Simms had known in Gwinnett County. There was an Agatha Tiffin, who lived on a farm with her parents, Ethel and Paul; her father made wagon wheels. The year was 1833.

As I started to sift all this material and began my research to find as much corroboration of June's impressions as possible, I decided it would be best to have one more hypnotic session with her. Even though a great deal of this knowledge was now in my own subconscious mind, and one could argue the possibility of June's getting it from me, I felt that an additional session might also yield new names that were not known to me at the time. Thus I invited June to join me once again in Pittsburgh, and on June 23, 1969, she did just that. I quickly regressed her to the year 1820 and asked her to describe the place she lived in.

"Was there a city anywhere?"

"No, sir."

"What was the nearest village?"

"There weren't any villages. There was a trading post."

"What did you call the trading post?"

"It was just a trading post. Papa used to go there. He'd tell me a lot of stories when I was a little girl, about his trips."

"Now, if you wanted to buy something in a store, where would you go?"

"To the post or to Virginia."

"Where?"

"Virginia, Norfolk."

"Wasn't that far away?"

"Yes, sir, but my aunt lived there."

"But near the Hill Place, wasn't there anything nearer?"

"There was land as far as you could see, and crops, and green grass."

"What did they call the state?"

"Georgia."

"What was the capital of Georgia?"

"Why do you want to know?"

"Where did the governor of Georgia live?"

"I don't want to talk about it."

"Were there any Indians around?"

"Yes, sir, Creek and Cherokee."

"Were you friendly with any of them?"

"Yes, sir."

"What happened to them?"

"They were forced to leave."

"Who forced them?"

"I don't want to talk about things that aren't happy."

"Where did they go?"

"They were sent away."

"What happened to their land?"

"It was taken over."

"Now, when you were living at Hill Place in those days, did you ever write letters to anyone?"

"My cousin."

"What was her name?"

"Alice Anne Jenkins."

"Have you even been to Norfolk?"

"Yes, sir."

"Did you like it?"

"Yes, sir."

"What did you like most about it?"

"All the fancy balls."

"Who gave those balls?"

"Friends of Papa, and Aunt Jessica."

"Do you remember the music they played?"

"Waltzes."

"How many musicians did they usually have?"

"Six."

"What sort of instruments did they play?"

"There was a harpsichord and a harp, and a violin . . ."

"Do you remember some of the songs they used to sing?"

"One."

"Can you tell me about it?"

"Yellow the Blues."

"How did it go?"

"Yellow the blues, my girl, my girl. Yellow the blues, I love thee true . . ."

"Was there a regiment stationed in Norfolk in those days? Don't tell me what they said to you. Just tell me a couple of the names, all right?"

"There was a Lieutenant Arnold Himbrook."

"Was he in the infantry?"

"Cavalry, sir."

"Oh, and do you remember what regiment he served in?"

"No, a girl never cares about the regiment, only the soldiers."

"Was it a state regiment, or federal?"

"State, sir."

"You went there often?"

"Several times a year."

"What kind of a house was it?"

"It was like a whole block; like a house all on one block, but there were different houses all fastened together, and it was all brick, with a big, white, heavy door and a big, brass knocker."

"Did you ever have any silver coins?"

"I have a penny."

"What did it look like, that penny?"

"Eighteen fifty, a new penny."

"What's on it?"

"It's large, and it's brass."

"What's on the front?"

"I don't know. There's an eagle on the back."

"Is there something on the front?"

"I can't turn it over."

"Is the eagle just sitting there, or does he have anything with him?"

"He has something in his talons."

"Tell me, Norfolk is on the water, isn't it?"

"Yes, sir."

"Did you see any ships?"

"Yes, sir."

"Do you remember any of them?"

"The *Billy White*."

"Was that a civilian ship, or a navy ship?"

"A civilian ship, hauled cotton across the ocean."

"Weren't there any warships in Norfolk?"

"I don't remember them, only the loading of the big bales, four-masters."

"How old were you the first time you went to Atlanta?"

"I'm not sure."

"Were you still a little girl?"

"No."

"You weren't married yet, were you?"

"I think so. It's like looking for something."

"Well, you know Atlanta is a big city, isn't it?"

"Not when I was there."

"What did it look like?"

"There was a train."

"A train?"

"A train in 1848 or 1850."

"And did the train not go any further?"

"No, northeast of Atlanta, I believe."

"What did they call that place? I mean, where the train ended."

"A *junction* of some sort."

"Was it then called Atlanta?"

"When the train went through, yes."

"Before?"

"No, not for a while."

"Did it have another name?"

"Yes, but I can't . . ."

"Who was Uncle Tubby?"

"Joseph Mayo."

"What did he do?"

"He was the mayor."

"The mayor of what?"

"Of Mayo County."

"What year was that?"

"I don't know."

"Was this before Atlanta?"

"Uncle Tubby was the first mayor of Atlanta."

"Did you call your uncle 'Tubby'?"

"Yes, sir."

"What profession did he have before he became mayor?"

"He was a planter of tobacco, and he talked politics with the gentlemen."

"Now, when you went to Florida, how old were you then?"

"I was nineteen."

"And what was Florida called in those days?"

"It was territory that was to become Florida."

"Did you go down there by horse or by coach?"

"We went down by boat, paddle river boat."

"On what river? Or on the sea? How did you go down there? Was it on the sea or the river?"

"I don't remember. I know we docked. It was a river where we docked at in Anthony."

"What was it?"

"Anthony."

"What was the name of the boat?"

"Sue Clarity."

"When you were living in the Hill Place, did your father ever have any friends in?"

"Yes, sir."

"Did you meet any of them?"

"Henry Payne."

"What did he do?"

"A lot of the men were plantation owners all over the South."

"Anyone else?"

"Alfred Helm."

"Did any of them ever have any rank?"

"Jefferson Davis came to the house."

"Why did he come?"

"The gentlemen used to gather for meetings and take turns talking over politics."

"Did Mr. Davis ever talk money with anybody, and finances?"

"Yes."

"Did he have anyone in particular who could help him?"

"Papa's overseer used to help quite a bit."

Beth seemed to tire of the conversation now, and I noticed that it was time to bring June out of her hypnotic state, but since I did not know how soon we could meet again, I discussed Beth's presence in June's body with her. To my amazement, Beth realized very well that she was living vicariously through another person. Even though that other person, in Beth's thinking, was also herself, she wanted to take over. I explained that it was necessary for June to remain herself to the outside world, but that Beth could merge her own character, her own desires and unfulfilled hopes and wishes, with the personality of June. Perhaps a stronger, better personality would then emerge for June. But this wasn't what Beth had in mind at all. She wanted to continue her own life, untrammeled by anyone else's. I made it plain that this could not be, explained patiently that I did, indeed, have the power to send her away from June's unconscious mind forever. In the end we compromised, and Beth promised to help June strengthen her own character, without, however, destroying June's own personality.

After June returned to herself, we discussed briefly whether there was anything she remembered, but as in all the previous sessions, she remembered absolutely nothing of what she had mentioned under hypnosis. The only thing new she could contribute was a strange feeling of suddenly having forgotten her knowledge of English, which had occurred to her a few times in the recent past. For a brief moment she had had the feeling that she was speaking a foreign language, although she could not really express herself in it. English had sounded strange to her ears at that point. Worried about her hearing, she had consulted an ear specialist, only to find that she was in perfectly good health as far as her hearing was concerned.

After June had returned home to western Pennsylvania, a great sadness overtook her. This was not the first time that June had felt depressed. Over the years, she had sometimes toyed with the idea of suicide, for no particular reason, and on one occasion she had taken a few more sleeping pills than necessary, but whenever thoughts of death had come to her, something or someone within her had changed her mind and cheered her up. Now June knew that it was Beth who didn't wish to lose her instrument of expression.

By the fall of 1969, the deep depression left her, and a more mature presence of Beth filled June's being. It was as if the two personalities had finally come to terms.

There was another impression, this time about Gloria. June reported that the soldier's name was Wilhelm and that Gloria had been pregnant, but had died a few hours after a baby son had been born to her. Gloria's lover had been hanged, and June does not know why. It had something to do with the Army in some way, however, she felt. He was hanged in the square early in the morning. There was a morning mist in the air, and other soldiers had prepared him for the hanging.

The trip to the mill that June had seen several times in visions apparently was for Gloria to come to stay with an uncle and aunt until after the baby was born. June does not know what happened to the child. The mother had refused to have anything to do with him, and June hears her words still ringing in her ears: "When it comes, take it to the wheel and be done with it." Wilhelm was hanged in the late fall, before the child was born.

In mid-August of 1969 I received an urgent message from June. Early that morning she had awakened in a cold sweat. Glancing at the clock, she had seen that it was only four-thirty. She had wanted to scream at the top of her lungs, but had fought back the almost overwhelming urge to do so. At the same time, she had heard herself saying a phrase over and over in a language she did not understand. The words stood out strongly in her memory, and so she wrote them down for me. What she had said, in somewhat peculiar German, was, "My good William, no, no, my darling William, not here. Quickly, the children. My darling, my good William."

Clearly, June was reliving some highly traumatic experience in Gloria's life. It might be argued that some ancestral knowledge of German or Pennsylvania Dutch could be responsible for the few words uttered that morning, but these expressions are also compatible with the reincarnation memory concerning Gloria. What I hoped to do now was prove that some of this material was, indeed, factual.

In trying to prove or disprove the accuracy of June's statements, I assumed that any intimate knowledge of early nineteenth-century Atlanta would be unusual for someone of June's background. If, in the process of trying to prove the material to be accurate, I should find erroneous statements as well, I felt that this would not necessarily militate against the authenticity of the case.

I have learned over the years that those on the other side of life frequently find it impossible to remember details of their previous lives, especially when these details are not of an emotional kind. If, however, the percentage of hits were to be considerable, the case itself would, to me, assume the ring of truth, even if there were also misses and omissions. I would, in fact, be very suspicious of any psychic communication that proved to be one hundred per cent accurate. No human being, whether in the flesh or in the world of spirit, is that reliable and exact. Here, then, is the evidence, insofar as I was able to verify it.

Hill Place, the name of the plantation somewhere in Georgia must have belonged to the Hill family at one time, hence the name. The name Hill was prominent in Georgia in the first half of the nineteenth century, and in fact is still prominent in that state. One may only think of Senator Benjamin Hill, but there are many other Hills listed in directories of this area. A William Hill was a member of the Inferior Court in 1823, according to *Atlanta and Environs,* by the celebrated Georgia historian Franklin M. Garrett, published in 1954.

I was unable to locate the exact spot where the Hill Place existed, but if, as June claimed, it took a two-hour buggy ride from what is now Atlanta, then it could have been much further inland than I had at first assumed. There is also a mention of a paddle boat on the river, and if this is the Mississippi River, it would be even further west. I am firmly convinced that many of the data given under hypnosis are correct, but that the sequence may have been different from that given. It may very well be that there existed confusion in the mind of Elizabeth Simms, speaking through June, if indeed she was, causing various names to be attached to different personalities from those to whom they should have been, or transposing the dates. Out of this chaotic condition I tried to get some order.

There is a prominent mention of a Judge Boland. In the earlier sessions he was designated as a mayor of Atlanta. He is also identified as the man whom Elizabeth called "Tubby," but in the later sessions, Tubby is referred to as Joseph Mayo, who was also a mayor. Here, then, are the facts.

The second mayor of Atlanta proper was Dr. Benjamin F. Bomar, according to the Atlanta Public Library librarian, Isabel Erlich. This was in the late 1840s and early 1850s. But there were three generations of well-known physicians bearing the name Boland in Atlanta during the nineteenth century, according to Franklin M. Garrett, Research Director of the Atlanta Historical Society. On the other hand, there was a Judge Bellinger, who died in 1853. He was a legislator, a justice of the Inferior Court, and active in politics between 1820 and 1853, according to *Atlanta and Environs,* Volume I, page 361. But it was customary in those days to call any dignified individual, especially if he was of personal prominence, with the honorific name of "Judge." As a matter of fact, to this very day there are a lot of honorary colonels in Kentucky and other Southern states. Could it be that Mr. Boland was not really a judge, but only given this name as a matter of courtesy, or did the confused mind of Elizabeth Simms confer the title, rightfully belonging to Judge Bellinger, to one of the Boland family?

There was certainly confusion about dates. When the alleged Mrs. Simms speaks of the year 1820 in Atlanta, she must be mistaken, for the city as such came into being only in 1837. The land on which Atlanta now stands was owned and occupied by the Creeks Indians until 1821, and there was no white settlement until then. The town of Atlanta was first called Terminus, because the new railroad, connecting the western part of the South and the Atlantic coast, terminated at this spot, in what was then DeKalb County. Later it was briefly known as Marthasville and eventually became Atlanta, so named after the well-known legend of Atlantis. But it is, of course, possible that, speaking in retrospect, the entity might have confused the dates. I have always found it true that those who have gone onto the other side cannot cope with figures, dates, and other details of time, because there is, apparently, no such thing as time over there.

The description of Indians being driven from their lands is entirely correct. These were mainly Creek and Cherokee Indians. There is a hypnosis reference to a Claire County. The pronunciation isn't too clear, and it may well be that she meant to say Clarke County. This is the more likely, as I have found several members of the Hill family residing in that area in 1827. In the list of land lottery grants made to veterans of the Revolutionary War, published in Atlanta in 1955, there are also a Clay County and a Clayton County in Georgia. Both of these are not too far from present-day Atlanta.

In discussing the coming of the railroad, the entity referred to the date of 1824, and also mentioned two towns—Dancy, North Carolina, and Billings. Neither of these two places was I able to locate, but the records are not very reliable, since small places have often changed names in the course of time. There is, however, mention of a Senator Calhoun. While Miss Erlich did not think that the famed Senator Calhoun was ever active in Atlanta, I find, to the contrary, that he was instrumental in bringing the railroad to Atlanta, or what was then called Terminus. Although the final stages of this railroad were only completed after the Senator died in 1850, he was indeed connected with the fortunes and well-being of the area in and around Atlanta. Reference to this is made in *Atlanta and Environs,* by the aforementioned Franklin M. Garrett.

Since Elizabeth was thirty-six years old in 1861, she could not have been born in 1802 as she had claimed in the very first session we had, but must have been born in 1825. When she spoke of her life as an eighteen-year-old in Atlanta, which would make this 1843, she mentioned that it wasn't much of a town, that it was small and that there were about a thousand people there at that time. This is entirely correct.

In another session she also mentions the Cherokee Indians as being active in the area, which is something the average person wouldn't know. Elizabeth gave Tibbits as her maiden name. I have been unable, to date, to locate a

Franklin Tibbits, but the United States Census of Georgia for 1820 does list a Thomas Tibbits on page 147.

She referred to a Baptist Church as being the one she went to to pray, and the same church she was baptized in. It is true that the First Baptist Church was the most prominent church in Atlanta during the early days of that settlement. In a portion of the tape fraught with difficulties, I find upon replaying that she also mentions a Father Tillis as her teacher. The United States Census of Georgia for 1820 does list a Joseph Tillus, on page 148. She mentioned President Jackson as having been in her house. The fact is that Andrew Jackson did come to Atlanta in connection with the redistribution of land formerly of the Cherokee Nation. This was in 1835, according to Mr. Garrett.

When speaking of the stores and establishments of the city of Atlanta, the entity referred to Harry Millin's Store on Main Street. According to the bulletin of the Atlanta Historical Society, there were an Andrew, James, and Thomas Millican listed in 1833 in DeKalb County.

As for the Simms family, with whom she became later involved, they are listed in various records. This is not surprising, since we know as a matter of fact that Elizabeth Simms did live in the house in Florida until her death. What is important to prove, however, is whether June is the reincarnated Elizabeth Simms. That the original existed is a matter of record. There are Simmses listed for Clarke County, Georgia, between 1820 and 1827. There is a Robert Simms also in the list of land lottery grants made to veterans of the Revolutionary War on page 63, and the United States Census of Georgia for 1820 gives a Robert, Benjamin, and James Simms on page 134.

Although I was unable to connect a Reverend Harold Clements with the Baptist Church as claimed by the subject under hypnosis, there is a Henry Clements listed in the 1820 Census, on page 29. Whether this is the right Clements, I do not know.

Mr. Seward was indeed a prominent Washington politician, but I must discount knowledge of this name, since it is a prominent name that might have been familiar to June from reading books or simply from her school days.

On June 13, 1969, June sent me a typed list of all the

names that clung to her memory in connection with her previous incarnations. I had not discussed any details of my findings with her, of course, and the list actually comprises both her dream/visions and conscious flashes of reincarnation memories. All the names that have occurred during our hypnotic sessions are contained in this list, but there are also a few others.

The name Harmon Gilmer appears. Gilmer is the name of an early governor of Georgia—during the time when Elizabeth might have lived in Atlanta. Among friends of her father's when she lived in Georgia, June mentioned also a certain Talbert Westcut. The Atlanta Historical Society Bulletin for 1931 lists a Tillman Westbrook as living in DeKalb County in 1833. June referred to the Jenkins family as being related to her own. There were many prominent Jenkinses in the register of land lottery grants made to veterans of the Revolutionary War, and they are also listed for 1827, the period under discussion.

The entity referred to a Whitehall Street in the Atlanta she knew. It is a fact that Whitehall Street was and is one of the main streets of Atlanta.

Dr. Benjamin F. Bomar had a store dealing in general merchandise on Whitehall Street in 1849. He was mayor of Atlanta at the same period of his life and also one of the founding fathers of the Baptist Church. These three factors together seem to indicate that perhaps June might have been referring to Dr. Bomar, rather than to Boland, when speaking of her Uncle Tubby, since a mayor can easily be called Judge as a matter of courtesy also. Bomar fits far more neatly into the facts, as brought out under hypnosis, than any other names close to what June had said, but it is entirely possible that she was confusing several persons with each other.

By far one of the most interesting bits of information concerns her naming of Gwinnett County. Franklin Garrett was able to confirm that Gwinnett County was created in 1818 and existed indeed in Georgia at the time when Elizabeth Simms might have been a young girl. How could a Pennsylvania housewife have such intimate knowledge of a state she had never been to? What's more, in her June 13, 1969, roundup of impressions, she says, "Father buys supplies from a trading post in Gwinnett

County, Georgia territory, in 1818." Gwinnett was in existence in 1818 and is now part of metropolitan Atlanta, so it is entirely possible that she confuses in her mind the later name of Atlanta, given to what was then only known as Gwinnett County, Georgia.

In evaluating the material obtained through hypnosis from June, and correlating it with her wakeful visions, one must inevitably come to a conclusion that there are three possibilities explaining her amazing memories of another lifetime. Either she has obtained consciously or unconsciously material from books she may have read and incorporated this material in her own unconscious mind, or it is a fantasy and product of wishful thinking about a romantic South she never saw, or finally, we are faced with paranormal material. After careful consideration, I must reject the first two hypotheses.

As for the paranormal aspects, there, again, we are faced with two possibilities. Conceivably, she might have had a precognitive dream of her visit to the Florida house. Then, upon entering the dilapidated mansion, she might have served as the medium to a resident ghost who, in turn, was able to express herself through her, and in fact, possess her for a considerable length of time both in the waking condition and through dreams.

In that case, her knowledge of a previous lifetime in Georgia would not be the result of prenatal memories, but of information obtained from the entity, Elizabeth Simms herself. June would then be simply the channel, or medium, through whom Elizabeth is reliving a cherished memory. If it were only for the recollection of life in Atlanta a hundred years ago, I might conceivably consider such a possibility, but there is also the other lifetime, in the eighteenth century in what appears to be Germany. It is highly unlikely that June was possessed by two different entities at the same time. Also, I do not know any cases of prolonged possession of a medium by a deceased entity that goes on for a number of years and can be interrupted by everyday living only to return to the possessive state at will.

It was far more difficult to prove the existence of Gloria Heimier. To begin with, we were dealing with a small town in what is now Czechoslovakia and which was then part of the Austrian Empire, although at various times fought over by Prussia as well.

Originally, June had said that Gloria came from Düsseldorf, but later changed this to Jägerndorf. Now, Düsseldorf is a well-known German city, and it is possible that in getting her impressions partially, she might have taken the name to sound like Düsseldorf rather than Jägerndorf. The juxtaposition of Jägerndorf with the date 1768 and the name Frederick is particularly interesting, because Frederick the Great was indeed involved with Jägerndorf in the period mentioned. Silesia was then fought over by Prussia and Austria, and Prussia's king at the time was Frederick the Great. Also, in describing the uniform worn by the soldier named Wilhelm during his trial, she described quite accurately the kind of uniform worn at the time by the grenadiers.

I made contact with the head of the State Archives at Jägerndorf, which is now called Krnov, in northern Czechoslovakia. The director, fortunately, also spoke German, so we corresponded in that language. Mr. Viktor Weiser looked into all the local records, but could not find a Gloria Heimier, 1750 to 1772. At least under this spelling, the name Heimier does not occur in either birth or baptismal registry, nor does it show up in the local burial records. Mr. Weiser confirmed that there is a Church of the Holy Ghost dating back to the fourteenth century, and that said church is still in existence. Could she have confused Sacred Flower with Sacred Spirit?

As far as the events of the year 1768 are concerned, Mr. Weiser remarked that the Prussians occupied Jägerndorf many times during the wars of the eighteenth century, beginning with 1741 and ending with 1779. In the year 1768 there was peace for the moment at least, and there were no Prussian soldiers stationed in town; however, the Prussians returned in 1778, during the War of the Bavarian Succession. In that same year, a major fire devastated large sections of the city, presumably also destroying some of the old records.

It is entirely possible that a Prussian soldier might have been court-martialed for cavorting with an Austrian girl. Jägerndorf was, after all, a border town, and politically a sensitive spot. Could June have invented Gloria and her lifetime? I think not, because the knowledge required to put together 1768, Frederick the Great, and Jägerndorf is not within her character or educational background.

Linguistically, also, both the Southern belle and the Silesian maid were truly in character and the accents perfect. I do not think that June is that great an actress to fake those details, even though she had lately shown an interest in appearing with a local theater group. However, her work with that theater group is mainly with the prop and costume department, and not on stage.

Since she was able to disclose details of her former lives to me, the personalities whose remnants live on in June have become integrated with her own character, and June herself is no longer as restless as she once was. Whether this is due to her logical acceptance of her role, or whether the personalities themselves have come to rest within her is a moot question. The fact is, June is well and adjusted to being just June. She has incorporated all the improvements brought her by the continued presence within her personality of what may very well have been her earlier lives.

One final note to round out the picture: A short time ago, June's niece acquired a place not far from the old Simms house in Anthony, Florida. With her parents, she visited the "ruins" of the Simms house only to find the place still standing, although in shambles.

Thus the report of the house being totally gone was, to paraphrase Mark Twain, grossly exaggerated.

Not that it seems to matter, for Beth now makes her home in a small town in western Pennsylvania anyway.

VII
A Tale of
Two Catharines

"I am not vain enough to claim a queen as a previous incarnation," Mrs. Catharine Warren-Browne said to me. "I could well have been a bawd, a tavern maid, or a nun, but it is strange how certain things have in a way been thrust upon my notice."

Her modesty stood Mrs. Warren-Browne in good stead. A sincere and unassuming woman, she rejected any notions of having been a queen in a previous lifetime as preposterous, and yet the evidence points precisely in that direction.

Catharine was born in Lancashire, England, daughter of a naval commander and descendant of an old Northumbrian family on her mother's side. Many of her paternal ancestors were naval officers, including Admiral Blake, and her family is highly respected in England. Many of her ancestors have sat in Parliament, some are noblemen, and her father was killed at sea in 1939 as a result of the war.

Catharine led an interesting and unusual life while in England. On many occasions, she had psychic experiences ranging from the knowledge of future events to actual ability to see ghosts and experience the uncanny in houses in which her family lived or where she was visiting, but her psychic experiences do not properly belong here, astounding though they are. She had visions of events in the past, experiences with displacements in time that, too, were truly amazing.

The family is Catholic, and she comes from an area of England that is even today predominantly Catholic. Many of her friends have been priests or abbots, and she considers herself a very good Catholic to this day, even though she wonders why the Church does not pay greater attention to the reality of psychic phenomena. She knows only too well that these things are happening and that they are by no means evil or to be feared.

She and her husband had been living in an old priory in 1959, when his father died and left them to cope with estate taxes. Under the present government, English inheritance taxes are staggering; thus, the money left them by Mr. Warren-Browne's father was taxed to the tune of 92 per cent. Under those circumstances they found it impossible to carry on life in England. They had to sell the house and farm, and in 1959 they came to America to start life all over at ages thirty-eight and forty-two.

The Warren-Brownes fit themselves rather astonishingly into the new environment. Perhaps because they had lived in various parts of the world before, perhaps because the sunny climate of California made things so much easier, they found that living in California was by far preferable to living in England.

"We are not well off in the way we used to be, but we have wonderful children all grown up, my husband and I love travel and exploring, especially the Arizona desert, so all is well with us."

When I met the Warren-Brownes in Hollywood in 1968, I found them to be friendly, unassuming people. Mr. Warren-Browne was most interested in his new program of boat-building, a career he had recently started, while Mrs. Warren-Browne was particularly keen on doing a novel about a period that she found herself strangely involved in—sixteenth-century England.

It somehow seemed incongruous to be speaking with these two cultivated English people in the sunny climate of a Hollywood swimming pool, but they had taken their world with them, and though most of their world was in the past, it had given them a sense of fulfillment to the degree that life in California, superficial as it is, meant a great deal more to them than it would have meant had they not had many unusual and amazing adventures in Europe before coming to America.

As a result of our conversations, I later went to England to follow up on some of the things that had happened to Catharine in her earlier years. My wife and I traveled through the area of England around Little Malvern, south of Worcester, to try to envision what it must have been like through the 1920s and '30s.

This part of England is particularly strongly Catholic. It is like a charmed island surrounded by industrial sites and somehow different from any other part of the British Isles. It is predominantly Tudor in architecture, and there are entire villages and towns consisting almost totally of sixteenth-century, and even earlier, buildings in a state of perfection rarely seen elsewhere. It seems almost as if the area abounds in historical sites somehow preserved for the present by a kindly fate, despite wars and destruction and progress.

As I am concerned here only with that part of Catharine's amazing life that has bearing on reincarnation memories, I will skip the extrasensory-perception experiences she has had since age four, when she described a scene that was to take place fully a year later. I will not dwell on her experience of seeing the Roman legions walk upon the Malvern Hills on the very spot where they had fought with Britons and Saxons in the sixth century, nor will I speak here of the ghostly monks she has seen, nor of the time she and her family lived at what turned out to be one of the most haunted houses in Wiltshire. Her involvement here included a tragic ending, for she was seemingly pushed down a flight of stairs by unseen hands, and as a consequence spent considerable time in the hospital and also lost a child. But her spunky character always got her back onto her feet, and, with typical British understatement, she considers this period in her life unfortunate but not tragic.

She has always found great comfort in her Roman

Catholic religion, and when she moved to an old priory of the Knights Templars near Ross-on-Wye, she reopened the chapel with permission of the Church and had priests from nearby Belmont Abbey say Mass there now and again. As a consequence, she received an authentic reliquary from Monsignor Montini, who later became the present Pope. Although she had occasionally discussed the question of reincarnation with her monastic friends, it wasn't of particular interest to her one way or the other.

Now, in retrospect, certain incidents make sense to her, although, at the time, they seemed to be completely out of context and truly strange.

When Catharine was only thirteen years old, the family had a governess by the name of Miss Gant. Catharine's mother liked her very much, because Miss Gant was very learned. The children did not like her, because they found her fanatic and given to holding forth on various subjects in history at the breakfast table.

On one such occasion, the conversation turned to the life of Henry VIII. A book about the king had just been published, and Miss Gant remarked that the king had just been a monster, worse than Caligula. At this, Catharine became suddenly very agitated, and remarked that she was wrong. "Henry was a misunderstood man," she said quietly. Her mother insisted that she apologize to the governess, but ignoring her own mother, Catharine went on to speak of the life Henry VIII as if she had known him intimately.

"The subject is closed," Miss Gant said rather snidely. "He was a very unpleasant man, and God punished him. He died of a very horrible disease." But Catharine's father backed her up at this point and let her have her say.

In quasi-medical terms little Catharine now described Henry VIII's fatal illness, denying that he had ever had syphilis, in the process shocking her mother, and remarking that the king had died of obesity and varicose ulcer in his leg that would not heal due to a high blood-sugar content.

Such knowledge on the part of a thirteen-year-old girl was amazing, but even Catharine thought no more of it at the time. There may have been other incidents bearing on the matter at hand, but Catharine does not recall them.

In 1957, she was very ill, recuperating at a private hospital in Bath, England. Due to a fall, she had had some surgery and was on the critical list when a close friend, the Abbot Alphege Gleason, came to visit her at the hospital. He stepped up to her bed and said, "Poor Catharine, what are they doing to you?" Very sleepily, the patient replied, "Here is good Master Coverdale come to comfort me."

Her visitor was taken aback. "Master Coverdale?" he said. "You are a learned young woman, but I should have thought I might have been taken for Cranmer, whom I'd always admired," he replied with a smile. By now Catharine was fully awake and asked, "Who on earth is Coverdale?" Many years later she discovered that Dr. Coverdale was a preacher friend and protégé of Katharine Parr, one of the queens of Henry VIII.

Mrs. Warren-Browne has had eight pregnancies but, due to a blood factor, has only three living children. On several occasions she would be in good spirits right up to the impending birth. At that point she would break into uncontrollable tears for no apparent reason. On one occasion, she was asked by her physician, Dr. Farr, in Sussex, England, why she felt so depressed at this particular point when all seemed to be going so well. For no apparent reason Mrs. Warren-Browne replied, "She was healthy, too, but she died of puerperal fever." The doctor asked whom she was talking about, and Mrs. Warren-Browne truthfully replied she did not know, nor did she have any idea why she had made the remark. The doctor then proceeded to tell her that this disease no longer presented any threat to mothers because it had been brought under control through modern methods, but that it was indeed a fatal disease centuries ago.

Years later, research established that Katharine Parr did indeed die of that disease.

After Mrs. Warren-Browne's son Giles was born, she became very ill and had what she called waking dreams, in the sense that they were far more realistic than ordinary dreams are. Suddenly she saw herself as a woman almost dead in a great, canopied bed. The woman had long, red-gold hair. Then Mrs. Warren-Browne would come out of this state and feel very depressed and sorry for the woman she had seen in her vision, but she always shrugged it off as a rather fanciful dream.

Ten years went by, and if there were incidents relating to the period of Henry VIII, they escaped Mrs. Warren-Browne's attention in the course of her daily activities.

She has a good education, and her knowledge of history now is equal to that of anyone with her background, but she has never had any particular interest in the period of Henry VIII other than what any Englishwoman might have. As for Katharine Parr, the name meant little to her except that she recalled it from her school days as the name of one of the wives of Henry VIII. Beyond that, there seemed to be no conscious connection.

In September of 1968 she and her husband happened to be in Iowa. He had some business there, and she was working on a book on and off as time permitted. She owned a pack of alphabet cards, and as she went about her work, she kept finding these cards arranged to spell the word Parr. She had not done this, nor was anyone around who could have so arranged the cards. She recognized the name Parr and thought that perhaps it had something to do with an ancestor of her family's on her mother's side. For, a long time back, there had been some connection with the Parr family of Northumberland.

She had no one to discuss this with, but decided to try the method of divining by pendulum. She put her wedding ring on a thread, and to her amazement it worked. There was indeed someone present who wished to communicate with her, and being fully aware of her psychic past, she did not reject this notion out of hand. Instead she decided it would be more practical to have an alphabet to work with, so she got out her Ouija board, and despite her feelings that such a board represented mainly a person's unconscious mind, she decided to give it a try.

"Who is there?" she asked.

Immediately the board gave her an answer. "Seymour," it spelled.

"Are you my Uncle Seymour?" she asked, for she could think of no relative other than her uncle who might want to communicate with her.

"No," the communicator said sternly, "Tom Seymour."

It still didn't ring any bells in her mind. "Which Tom Seymour?" she asked.

There was a pause. Then the entity operating through the board replied, "The Lord Admiral."

This gave Catharine pause for thought, and then she decided to investigate this communicator more closely.

"When were you born?"

"Fifteen o three."

"Why do you want to get in touch with me?"

"Long have I waited," the board spelled out.

"What have you waited for?" Catharine asked.

The whole thing became more and more ludicrous to her. Her suspicious mind was ready to blame her subconscious self for all this nonsense, or so she thought. She knew enough about extrasensory perception to realize that there were also pitfalls which a sensible individual had to avoid at all costs. She wasn't about to fall into such a trap.

"For you, Kate." Now, no one has ever called Catharine Warren-Browne Kate except her father, so she was rather dubious about the genuineness of the conversation.

Immediately, she thought of what she had read that could have some bearing on all this. Years before, she had read *The Wives of Henry VIII,* but that had been in her school days. More to amuse herself than because she accepted the communication as genuine, she continued working the Ouija board.

The unknown communicator insisted that he was Tom Seymour, and that she, Catharine Warren-Browne, was Katharine Parr reincarnated. The notion struck Mrs. Warren-Browne as preposterous. She knew, of course, that Katharine Parr was the last wife of Henry VIII, the only one who managed him well and who survived him, but she had never heard of Tom Seymour. It is well to state here that all her research in this came after most of the information had come to her either through the Ouija board or in dream/visions.

Today, of course, she has a fairly good knowledge of the period, having even decided to write a romantic novel about it, but at the time of the initial communications in 1968, she knew no more about Henry VIII and his queens than any well-educated Englishwoman would know.

The communicator who had identified himself as Tom Seymour advised her among other things that she was buried at Sudely. Now, Mrs. Warren-Browne had always assumed that Queen Katharine Parr was buried in the royal burial vault at Windsor, but upon checking this out, she found to her amazement that Katharine Parr had indeed been laid to rest at Sudely, an old castle at the border of Worcestershire and Herefordshire.

Later she was able to find references to Tom Seymour in historical records. It would appear that Tom Seymour and the widowed Queen Katharine had married after the death of King Henry VIII. Their marriage had lasted about eighteen months. Afterward, she had died in child-birth. Tom had survived her by about a year, when he was executed as a result of political intrigue.

At the time of the first communications through the Ouija board, Mrs. Warren-Browne did not know this, nor did she indeed know the name of the child, the only child, "she" and Tom Seymour had had. Tom referred to the child as Mary. Mrs. Warren-Browne very much doubted this, assuming that the child would have been called Jane, since Jane Seymour was Tom's sister and a close friend of Katharine Parr; however, research proved the communicator right. The child's name was Mary.

All during October of 1968 she felt herself drawn to the Ouija board and compelled to write down as quickly as she could whatever was given her by that means. She didn't want to believe the authenticity of that material, and yet she felt that in view of her earlier psychic experiences she should at least have someone look into this and authenticate the whole matter if possible or reject it, if that were to be the case.

Thus in December of 1968 she contacted me. When we met the following spring, we went over all the communications she had had until that time. "What indication do you have that you are Katharine Parr reincarnated?" I began.

"Well, this is what *he* thinks," Mrs. Warren-Browne replied politely, "unless, of course, it is something from the subconscious mind."

"What are Tom Seymour's reasons to assume you are his long-lost Katharine?"

"Well, he keeps saying that he's tried to reach me for

years, that he's been waiting and waiting, and I replied, 'Katharine Parr is dead. Why are you not together now?' "

"And how does he explain that?" I asked.

"They are on different planes, on different levels," she explained.

"But you were reborn because you were in a more advanced state."

The communications between Mrs. Warren-Browne and Tom Seymour went on for about a month. There was still some doubt in Mrs. Warren-Browne's mind as to the authenticity of the whole thing. On one occasion, the communicator referred to the date on which their child had been born. Tom had insisted that it was August 17. Mrs. Warren- Browne went to the library and looked it up and found that the child had been born on August 28, and died eight days later. The next evening she reminded her communicator that he had made a mistake in his calculation. "No," Tom Seymour replied through the board. "We have the Julian calendar, you have the Gregorian calendar." Quickly she checked this and found that he was right. The difference of eleven days was accounted for by the difference of the calendars.

"Before this communication came, did you ever have any slips in time, when you felt you were someone else?" I asked Mrs. Warren-Browne.

"Not that I have felt I'm someone else, but that I have known places that I have been to."

"For instance?"

"Pembroke Castle. When my uncle took me there, I said to him, 'Now we are going to such and such a room, which was where Henry VII was born, who was Henry VIII's father.' "

"And how did your uncle react to this information?"

"Well, he was of course surprised, but you see, if I had indeed been Katharine Parr, I would have known this, because Henry VII was her father-in-law."

"Is there anything else that reminds you of the fifteenth or sixteenth century?" I asked.

"Yes, many times I will catch myself saying something that sounds unfamiliar in today's use, and yet that fits perfectly with the earlier period in English history."

"Any strange dreams?"

"Yes, but of course I would consider them just wishful thinking. Sometimes I would see myself wearing long, gorgeous dresses, and it seemed that I was someone else."

I suggested we try a regression experiment, but since Mrs. Warren-Browne's husband was present and both were somewhat pressed for time, I felt that this was not the best moment to try it. We said good-by for the moment, and I promised myself to take the first possible opportunity to regress Mrs. Warren-Browne back into the period in which she thought she might have lived. There wasn't sufficient time the following day to call her back and to try my hand at regressing her then. Also, they lived quite a distance away, and it would seem impossible to ask them to drive all the way to Hollywood again. But my time schedule was suddenly and unexpectedly rearranged. An appointment I had made for the following morning was canceled, and so I felt almost compelled to pick up the telephone and call Mrs. Warren-Browne. I explained that I had some free time after all, and would it be possible for her to come back again so that we could attempt our first regression session. She agreed readily, and within a matter of hours she arrived in Hollywood. I then proceeded in the usual way to put her into deep hypnosis. It did not take overly long, for Mrs. Warren-Browne, being mediumistic, was already attuned to this process.

I first took her back into her own childhood, making sure that the transition to another lifetime was gradual. She had come alone this time, perhaps because the presence of her husband might, in her own mind, impede her ability to relax completely, something very necessary for a successful regression.

When I had taken her back to childhood, she spoke in great detail of her house in England and the staff they had. I then proceeded to send her back even further, and we were on our way to finding Katharine Parr.

"You're going backward into the past before your birth; way back, until you can find you're someone else. What do you see?"

"I see a home with stone . . . it's Sudely."

"Whom does it belong to?"

"Belongs to Admiral Seymour . . ."

"Do you see yourself?"

"Yes, I see myself."

"Who are you?"

"*He* calls me Kate. I'm terribly cold. I called the doctor, told him how cold it is. Dr. Tahilcus, he was so good."

"Are you ill?"

"Yes."

"What do you have?"

"A fever."

"Is anyone else with you?"

"Dr. Herk. He is the King's physician."

"Who else?"

"My sister, Anne, and Herbert, and Lucy Tibbett, my stepdaughter. Lucy was a poor girl. She didn't like me when I married her father at first. Then she grew very fond of me. Lucy was most faithful. Lucy and Anne kept our marriage secret. I'm so cold, cold, cold."

"How old are you now?"

"Thirty-six."

"I want you to look back now, see what happens to you. You recover from this illness?"

"No, no."

"What happens to you?"

"I go away. I die. I die. I knew it would happen."

"Where do you die?"

"At Sudely."

"What happens to you immediately after you die?"

"Tom is upset, he goes, I'm buried."

"Where are you buried?"

"At Sudely."

"In what part?"

"In the chapel beneath the altar."

"What is on the stone?"

"HERE LIES . . . HERE LIES KATHARINE—THE QUEEN DOWAGER—BARONESS SEYMOUR SUDELY—Kate Parr—Katharine . . . Katharine the Queen. I never wanted that irony."

"Who is buried next to you?"

"No one, no one. He was gone. He was gone and I loved him and I was angry with him. The Protector told me he was seducing young Bess. I believed it for a time."

"Who was young Bess?"

"The King's daughter."

"Who seduced her?"

"The Protector said that Tom did."

"What is his name?"

"Edward Seymour, Tom's brother. Edward Seymour hated Tom. He hated Tom's popularity. He hated the King's love for him. He was scheming. They even denied me my dowager rights. I had several manors and I had dowries from my two husbands before—Lord Latimer, John Neville—good men."

"I want you to look at the chapel now. What is next to your tombstone?"

"Next to my stone . . . It's beneath the altar, a wall, and it fell. It fell on Cromwell's men. Cromwell's men desecrated my tomb."

"Is it still there?"

"It was rebuilt in later centuries."

"Can you see the windows of the chapel?"

"It was an oriel window, but it's changed. I left because Tom is not there. They took his body."

"Where did they put it?"

"They took his body back to Wiltshire. His family took it. Tom came from Wilkes Hall, in Wiltshire."

"Is he still there?"

"I don't know. I haven't found him since."

"Do you see him now?"

"I remember him. He had black hair, dark blue eyes; he was always tanned. He was at sea a lot. His brother was a cold fish."

"When you died, what did you do immediately afterwards?"

"I remember looking at him. He was sad, and I was sorry that I had not trusted him."

"Do you see your body?"

"Oh, yes, just *as a shell.*"

"Where were you?"

"In my bedroom in Sudely. My spirit got up. My body was taken."

"What did your spirit look like?"

"How does a spirit look?"

"Did you wear clothes?"

"I suppose so. I suppose so, but they couldn't see me."

"Where did you go then?"

"I went to Hampton."

"Why?"

"That's where we had been so happy. I went to Hampton because Tom had liked to. He couldn't bear Sudely."

"Where is Hampton?"

"Hampton Court, and his house in Chelsea."

"Did anyone see you?"

"I don't know."

"What did you do there?"

"I looked around from room to room, but he'd gone. He went north to my home."

"What did you do then?"

"I went to Kendal."

"Where's that?"

"In Westmorland."

"What did you do there?"

"I looked around where I was born. And Tom *went* there. He went up there."

"Did you find him *there?*"

"I saw him, but *he* couldn't see *me.*"

"Did you make any attempt to let him know you were there?"

"Oh, yes."

"What did you do?"

"Yes, I put my arms around him, and he shivered. He was sad, and he went to my cousin's. He went to Strickland."

"Where are they located?"

"On the borders near Westmorland."

"And you followed him there?"

"I followed. Then he went away. He had to go into hiding."

"Why?"

"His brother accused him of treason."

"What had he done?"

"Nothing. He had the affection of his nephew, the little king. He had never done anything. His brother accused him of trying to wed with Bess, which wasn't true. Bess was only fifteen. He just used to romp with her. He had no children, just one baby that I left."

"And his brother, Seymour, whose side was he on?"

"He was the Lord Protector, but the little king didn't like him. They kept him short of money, and Tom used to take a little money and give it. That's why the Lord Protector took the great seal to stamp the documents. He took it away from the king."

"Who did the Lord Protector favor for the crown?"

"Jane Seymour and his son. Not James Seymour. James Seymour was his brother . . . the King's brother. Jane, Jane, she was Jane."

"And what happened?"

"Jane Grey, Lady Jane, she was only a child. She was married to Guildford. He wanted to control the children."

"But how was the Lord Protector related to Jane Grey?"

"I think he was her uncle."

"Then Jane Grey had the right of succession?"

"Rather distantly, but she thought she was a niece of the late King Henry."

"And he favored her cause?"

"Yes, because he knew that little Edward would not live. He had the lung tisk."

"And he then helped Lady Jane to become Queen?"

"Yes, but it only lasted a few days. The poor child. They beheaded just a child."

"What happened to the Protector?"

"He was beheaded too, when Mary came. Mary had her good points. Mary had grown sour, but she was a good woman."

"Did she marry?"

"Yes, she was a sad woman. If she'd married younger and been in love younger, she would have been a happier woman, but the Protector tried to kill Mary, and somebody counseled her to hide. Sawston, she hid at Sawston."

"What happened at Sawston?"

"They burned it."

"Yes, and what did she say after it was burned?"

"She said she would reward them and build them better. She was fond of them."

"Do you remember the name of the people that owned Sawston?"

"Huddleston."

"Were they Protestant or Catholic?"

"They were Catholic. The Huddlestons always were . . .
I knew a Huddleston in another life."

"You knew a Huddleston?"

"He was a Benedictine priest."

"What was his first name?"

"Gilbert, and in religion it was Roger."

"Tell me this—after you left, after you couldn't find
Tom, where did you go?"

"I wandered."

"Did you know you were dead?"

"Yes."

"Did it bother you?"

"I was sad to leave, sometimes content. I was happy
in a sense, but sad to leave, because somehow we couldn't
find each other."

"Were you aware of the passage of time?"

"Not particularly. It seems I was aware of people coming, people changing. People came where I was."

"Where were you most of the time?"

"I don't know how to describe it. It was light. I think
it was happiness, but it was not complete happiness."

"Was it a place?"

"It was not just one place. It was . . . it was space, but
I could go on the earth."

"How did you do that?"

"I could just will myself. Just will, that's all."

"Now, this place you were in up above the earth, could
you look down from it?"

"Yes."

"What did you see?"

"Just a great amount of people, people, places."

"And the place you were in off the earth, did you see
people?"

"Oh, yes."

"Did you recognize any of them?"

"My grandmother, my grandmothers."

"Did you speak to them?"

"Yes, you don't speak."

"How did you hear them?"

"We think."

"And the thoughts were immediately understood?"

"Yes, and we could will things for people. We could help sometimes, but not always. Sometimes you would want to prevent something terrible from happening."

"And?"

"So we would try, but not always, you couldn't always. People don't understand."

"Is there some sort of law you had to obey?"

"I don't know. I don't know."

"Was it anyone who took charge? Any authority up there?"

"Yes, in a sense. You felt bound by something, by someone."

"Was it a person?"

"It was a rule."

"Who made the rule?"

"It came from someone higher."

"Did you meet that person?"

"Not really. We saw a great light."

"Above you?"

"Beyond."

"What was the light like?"

"It was clear, bright, bright light."

"Did you speak to the light?"

"Yes."

"How did it answer you?"

"It said to be patient, go on, try to help. I wanted . . . I wanted. I wasn't really unhappy, but I wasn't fully content."

"Did anyone tell you how long you had to stay in this place?"

"No, they said that I could go on farther, or try to help."

"What did you choose?"

"I said I'd try to help, because time doesn't seem very long. Later, when I looked down, I knew the time *was* long."

"Who asked you whether you would want to go on farther? Who?"

"The voice from the light."

"You couldn't see a person?"

"No."

"How did the voice sound?"

"Wonderful."

"Male or female?"

"Male, male."

"Did you question who the voice was?"

"No."

"Did you know who it was?"

"I felt as though it was from God, although not Him in person. I asked, had it asked something."

"What did it tell you?"

"I asked if I had done anything wrong, not to be there where the light was. What was wrong? And he said no, that it was not wrong, that I could choose, that I could choose if I stopped grieving, that I could go ahead, or that I could go back and help."

"If you went ahead, where would you go?"

"To where the light was."

"Did He tell you where that was?"

"Not in words. I just knew that it was ultimate, ultimate peace. I came back and mothered all those children, Henry's children."

"You mothered them?"

"Henry's three children."

"Did any of them ever see you?"

"When?"

"When you were dead."

"Oh, no, but I think that's why I came back."

"When did you come back?"

"I think I had come back so much later. I took care of a lot of children. The war . . . we took care of a lot of children."

"Now, how many years after you had died did you come back?"

"In world years, a long time."

"But you say you took care of children. You mean on earth?"

"Yes, I took care of a lot of Polish children in this last war."

"You didn't come back between the time you were up there and the time you're in now?"

"I don't remember. I searched for a long time. I searched for him."

"For Tom? Did you find him?"

"I saw him, but I could never get close."

"He was not up there?"

"Yes, but he wasn't with me, but he seemed to be looking."

"But after his death, did he not join you?"

"Not closely."

"Didn't you ask for him to join you?"

"Yes, I did, I did."

"Why didn't it work?"

"I don't know. He'd look at me; he'd look at me very sadly."

"What did he say?"

"He didn't . . . I don't know."

"Did you ask the light to let you find him?"

"No, I just waited."

"Now, when you came back in your present incarnation, do you remember how you were born? Just before you were born?"

"I remember my mother. She was a beautiful woman."

"When it was time to go down again, did someone tell you when the time had come?"

"I felt it was the time. I seemed to be shown."

"What steps did you take?"

"I didn't take any real steps."

"Was it immediately?"

"No . . . I saw them, but I knew my mother before."

"How did you enter the child's body?"

"I don't think I did by myself. *I was suddenly there.*"

"And what was the first thing you remember?"

"The first thing I remember, they put me to one side because they thought I wouldn't live. They thought I was premature."

"At that moment, did you still remember your previous life?"

"No, it was so dark. There was noise, like I was going through a tunnel, terrible."

"Did you see anything?"

"It was dark and noisy."

"Did you see anything?"

"No, not until after."

"And then what did you see?"

"Then I was in a room. They wrapped me up, but they

said I wouldn't live, and I thought, Oh, I have to go back!"

"You remember that?"

"I remember that, and I thought, I must live. I must live. I had died before, and I was going to be happy. I was going to. I'd waited so long, eighteen, twenty years, and then it was so short."

"When you came back, you could actually understand what they were saying?"

"Yes."

"You understood every word?"

"I understood the words. I was premature, and it was rather difficult."

"And did this knowledge stay with you during the first few months, or did it disappear again?"

"It went after time. It went until the time when I was two. When I reached two until I was six, a great friend from the *other place* used to come and sit by me. Every night he'd come and sit by me."

"You mean, dead people?"

"Oh, it was wonderful. He came from where the light was."

"And why did he come?"

"He used to talk to me. He was someone very, very great."

"Did you remember his name?"

"We didn't call him by name because he was divine."

"Was he your master?"

"He was, yes, you would say master. He sat by my bed, and then I lost him."

"What do you mean by 'master'?"

"He was what we understood as Christ."

"Is there such a person?"

"Oh, yes."

"Is he the same as the historical Jesus?"

"I think people embellish things, but he is *Christ*. He is the son of a great spirit."

"Is God a person or is God a principle?"

"Perhaps I'd call it a spirit. I never saw God, but I knew that one day I would. I would see behind the light."

"Now, after you came back, had you forgotten these things?"

"I forgot, but sometimes you dream and remember. He left when I got older. I realize I was the cause of His leaving. I was disobedient. It was a childish disobedience, but He told me that I would find Him again, but I would have to go a long way."

"Did you ever find Him again?"

"No, but I will."

"Did you ever find Tom again?"

"I know that I will, because Tom is trying to find me. Before, he didn't *try* to find me."

"What about Tom? Where is he now?"

"He's waiting to be with me. The time will come."

"Do you think he will pass over again?"

"I think so, this time."

"Why did he have to wait so long?"

"He had things to do."

"What sort of things?"

"He had to wait. He had to *obey* someone."

"What about you?"

"I was widowed at eighteen. I was wed at sixteen to Lord Borough."

"How old were you when you married Henry?"

"I was thirty-two when I married Lord Latimer. I was married in St. Paul, Yorkshire. Latimer was a good man, but headstrong."

"Tell me about Henry. What was he like?"

"He was really not as fierce a man as they say."

"How many years were you married to him?"

"He sought my company several times when I was in mourning. He knew me from when Jane was his queen. Jane and I were friends. Jane asked me to take care of her little Edward. Jane died in childbirth fever."

"How did Henry ask you to marry him?"

"He just asked me. He said that he would wed with me. I knew inside that he was going to ask me, and I was hoping that he would ask me to be his mistress, not his wife. I didn't want either, really. I wanted Tom. We felt safer not being married to Henry. A mistress he could pension off. But he didn't have many mistresses, really. He was rather prim."

"How old was he then?"

"He was about fifty-two; he was very, very obese. He was very handsome, virile."

"Now, when you were married, did you celebrate your wedding?"

"Oh, yes."

"What were some of the songs that were sung at your wedding?"

" 'Green Sleeves' is one, and a lute song."

"Do you remember the words?"

"I remember some of 'Green Sleeves,' not much. Henry wrote music. He wrote one they do not credit him for."

"What was it?"

" 'Western Wind.' "

"How does it go?"

" 'Western wind, when wilt thou blow? With the small rains . . . I caressed my lover in my arms and lie in my bed again.' Henry wrote that, but they missed it. They missed it, I know. Henry played the lute. He was very musical. He was a very clever man. He had a very hot, angry temper, but he was quickly over it. But Gardiner and Wriothesly took advantage of this when they wanted to get rid of someone; they would pick a moment when it was easy to get him angry. That was how he got rid of poor Kate Howard. She was foolish. She was not fit to be queen, but he loved her. It was just an old man's love for a girl, and she was vain and silly, but she wasn't evil. But they took her away, and they wouldn't let her speak to him. She wanted to speak to him. She knew he would forgive her, put her aside. Henry told me that."

"What had she done?"

"She had committed adultery. She had loved someone else all her life, but she was flattered to marry the king, and you couldn't very well refuse the king's hand. But she should have told him. He begged her to tell him."

"And she didn't do it?"

"No, she was afraid. She was a foolish child."

"And was Henry upset by her death?"

"Yes, he prayed for her. He was angry. He went away. Gardiner and Wriothesly had hastened the execution. Cranmer and Austin. He didn't like the Howards, you see. The Howards were very powerful. He didn't like them, and Henry felt betrayed by them. He had two Howard queens."

"Which was the other one?"

"Anne Boleyn."

"Tell me, why did you pick *this* incarnation, *this* body, *this* person to speak through? Was there any reason, anything you wanted her to do for you?"

"I was vain. I believe I was considered a good woman, and I loved my husband and I loved Tom. But I had vanity, and I came back into a world which had frightening things. She has tried so many things."

"You mean the woman who has it hard?"

"She's a woman who loves beauty around. She loves beautiful surroundings. It happened at a time when she was young. When she was stupid. She craved for it. This would upset her vanity."

"This is your punishment?"

"Perhaps it is a punishment, but also I wanted to help those children."

I noticed that Mrs. Warren-Browne showed signs of tiring, and as time had passed rather quickly, I decided to bring her back into the present and her incarnation as Mrs. Warren-Browne. This done, she awoke without any recollection of what had transpired in the preceding hour. She felt well, and soon was on her way home to rejoin her husband.

All the historical data given by her in the hypnotic state were correct. Some of these are perhaps available in history books, and other data, while available to the specialist in that particular period, are not readily accessible to an average person. Katharine Parr had been twice widowed before she had married Henry VIII. The names of Lord Borough and Lord Latimer are historical, and her death in childbirth is also factual. After the death of Henry VIII, there was political intrigue in which Tom Seymour fell victim to the machinations of his own brother, the Lord Protector. The fact that Katharine Parr's being buried at Sudely, and the account given of the flight of Mary Tudor to escape her political enemies, are entirely correct. Mary did hide at Sawston Hall, near Cambridge, which was burned down by her enemies and later rebuilt in great splendor by the Queen. Huddleston is indeed the name of the family owning Sawston, and the Huddlestons to this day are a prominent Catholic family. The reference to the entity knowing another Huddleston in this incarnation makes sense if one realizes that Mrs. Warren-Browne was friendly with Father Roger Huddleston in her earlier years in England. Father Huddleston was a Benedictine priest.

But more than the factuality of historical data given, the descriptive passages of life between births and on the other side of life are fascinating, and matches similar accounts from other sources. It may be difficult for a non-religious person to accept the visit of the Christ to the young Catharine Warren-Browne, and yet there are other accounts of such visitations. Surely the possibility that the Master looks after His own is not entirely illogical or impossible, for even a non-religious person will generally grant the historical Jesus His great status as a teacher and healer.

One June 4, 1969, the day after our last meeting, Mrs. Warren-Browne had a meaningful dream, which she proceeded to report to me immediately. The following night she had another dream, also tying in with the regression experiment. Here, then, are her reports.

Dream #1.

I sleep badly, and was awake until after 3:00 A.M., so this took place between 3:00 and 5:00 A.M. It was in color, and voices appeared to be normal or real. We were riding through woodland or heath country, am sure it was Richmond, the Surrey side of London. I was still Latimer's wife. Lucy Tyrwhitt, my stepdaughter by Lord Borough, rode with me. We were with the King's party; he was hawking. There were bearers and hawk boys, hounds, etc. Tom was there, home from France; he and Henry wore the Tudor colors of green and white. I felt very happy; in fact, happiness permeated the dream. It was a wonderful morning, early and misty, sun breaking through, the smell of crushed grass beneath hooves and gorse. I rode a gray; Tom rode beside me whenever he could, although Henry would keep bellowing for him. They were on terms of great friendship.

Henry rode an enormous horse, dark bay. He was very heavy but rode magnificently. We cantered up a grassy slope to a clearing, and Henry released his hawk. He removed her hood, undid the leash from jesses, and threw her. She darted up in circles, and we all watched. In a very few minutes, she had sighted her quarry, then pounced in to kill. Henry was delighted. He laughed and joked. They had laid wagers. Then, in turn, the others, Tom included, released their hawks. Henry called the hawk boy to him. The boy knelt on the grass, and Henry roared, "Don't kneel, damn you. We are all men out here." He chose a small merlin and gave her to me, showing me how to carry her on my wrist. He asked after Latimer's health. Very assiduously, I told him that he seemed better, though very tired, and that he was at home translating a Greek work. Then His Grace asked me to ride beside him, and he chatted and thanked me for riding out to Hatfield House to see the children, Prince Edward and young Bess. He was in high good spirits. He waved his cap, plumes waving, and called out, "We shall meet again, my lady, at Greenwich." He led his party off at a mad gallop, leaving Tom to ride with me and Lucy and a page.

I felt very free from care. Tom took the small hawk from my wrist and gave it to the page, and he, Lucy, and I raced one another up the slope. I felt aware in the dream of a breeze, and joked with Lucy at not having to wear the awful boned corset that women wore then. Tom said that a horse felt good after days at sea, and he was going to Syon house. I felt guilty for being so happy when my husband was at home, ill.

Dream # 2.

I was back in the past, at Hampton Court, in what had been Jane's apartments. Katharine Howard had been beheaded months before. In fact, I knew that the King had been alone since her death. I was aware of the year in my dream—1543—and I was a widow; Latimer had died. I felt alone. Tom was in France about the King's affairs, and I wished that he were here. The King had sent for me, and I was afraid that I knew why he had sent for me. There was a noise outside, and the doors were flung open. The King and two gentlemen in waiting came in. I curtsied to him, and His Grace took my arm and raised me, saying to his men, "Leave me, gentlemen, I pray you. I would speak privily with Lady Latimer."

They left, and Henry led me to a window seat. He kissed my hand and held me by the arm, then kissed my cheek and said, "How fair thou art, sweet lady, and kind as thou art comely. Today I was at Hatfield, and my motherless boy told me of your visits." He was in excellent spirits. His rages after Katharine Howard's death were all gone. I felt almost choking with fear, as I knew what was to come, and yet I pitied him. He was a crumbling lion and ruled a turbulent country as only a strong man could. He said, "You could give me much comfort and peace, Madam Kate, and, who knows, perhaps more heirs for England." In the dream I felt at a loss for words. He went on, saying, "My offer does not please you? I thought to do you honor and ask you to wed with me, for truly I have grown to love you very dearly." I told him bluntly, being a North Country woman, that I had not expected this, and, while honored, also felt a little afraid to accept, seeing the fate of two of his queens.

He was not angry, but told me to ". . . have no fear." I had "twice been wed and widowed" and was "known to be virtuous," and that "no scandal could ever attach" to me; that I had "both intellect and gaiety." He asked me to let him know very quickly, as time passed and he was aging, but felt for me as any stripling. "Be kind to me. Be kind to England." Now, what woman could resist a proposal like that? Even in a dream or centuries ago? Incidentally, he removed my widow's veil and tossed it on the floor. That was Henry. We walked down the long gallery, and in my dream I knew it was where Katharine Howard had run screaming to try and reach the King. Henry seemed to sense this and told me, "Forget what has gone before." We went into another room he called his closet, and he seemed very gay, almost boyish, and told me that I could refurnish the queen's apartments as I wished; the Exchequer was low, but so be it. I told him (North Country thrift) that I had loved Jane's apartments and hangings, and that I had brocades and hangings in storerooms at Snape if he would like me to use them. He told me I was the first woman who had not sought to ruin him. And that was the end of the dream, all very domestic and practical. I remember, his eyes were small and sunk in heavy jowls, but he still had remnants of his former handsomeness, though he limped. I was aware in the dream of being sad that Tom had not returned in time and that the only way I could refuse the royal offer without offense was to enter a convent, and that did not appeal to me. I also knew it would endanger Tom to refuse Henry and hope to marry Tom later; heads fell for far less.

Mrs. Warren-Browne has, of course, read a few books on the period by now, especially Agnes Strickland's *The Queens of England,* and *Hackett's History of Henry VIII,* but she has not become a scholar on the subject. Perhaps she needn't to, having primary access to information scholars have to dig for year after year.

Is Mrs. Catharine Warren-Browne the reincarnated Queen of England, Katharine Parr, last and happiest of wives of Henry VIII? She does not claim to be, but I think that the evidence points in that direction. The manner in which the first bits of personal data were received indicates that they came from a source that knew well what the lives of Tom Seymour and Katharine Parr were like. I am satisfied that coincidence, unconscious knowledge, and other ordinary factors do not play a dominant role in this case.

There is, of course, still the question of Mrs. Warren-Browne. After all, Tom Seymour may not wish to wait forever, and then again, what happens if, many years hence, Mrs. Warren-Browne goes over to the other side of life and Tom Seymour has finally reached a state where he in turn may return to earth in another incarnation? Will they miss each other, then, again? But that much is pure speculation. My job as investigator pertains to sifting the facts, and separating them from fancy and wishful thinking.

VIII
The Many Lives of a Midwestern School Teacher

By his own request, his name and address are to be kept confidential for the time being. Much of the unusual material he has put at my disposal pertains to predictions and visions concerning the future of the world, but some of it deals with previous lives and remembrances of them.

Robert E. first wrote to me in May of 1960, after he had read my book *Predictions—Fact or Fallacy?* He, too, had had some interesting predictions and wanted someone in a position of research authority to record them toward the day when they could be proved either true or false.

But along with the ESP material, there were hints at reincarnation, and asked him to give me a full statement concerning his memories of earlier lifetimes.

On first reading, the young man sounded odd. I began to wonder if he was not indulging in a series of fantasies, since so many famous names were involved in his predictions. To be honest, I still wonder—not about his honesty, but about the nature of his strange "gift." Only the future will tell if that part of Robert E. that sees into tomorrow is for real. But I was sufficiently impressed with the tone of seriousness in his correspondence with me to seek a meeting at which I could evaluate him more fully in person.

Robert is twenty-seven years old, a native of Illinois, and holds a B.S. degree in secondary education as well as a B.A. in history and English. His father is the deputy sheriff in a small town in Illinois, and he lives with his family in a typical middle-class home. His mother is a grade-school teacher, and an only sister is still in high school. After teaching school for several years in his home town, Robert grew restless and decided to seek greener pastures in California. This turned into an economic disaster for him. He spent a year floating around California and getting oriented, or rather, disoriented. Having found California life not to his liking, after all, he returned home to Illinois to resume teaching. Unfortunately, in the small school system he had been part of, there were no extra jobs open. Try as he might, he could not get back into teaching again.

In desperation and to earn a living, Robert turned to other work. Through a friend, he was able to get a job as an ordinary workman in a local caster company. What little skill was required, he managed to acquire quickly, and he is still employed in that capacity today. While he keeps an eye open for a teaching position to open up for him, he has his much higher salary to console him.

Although he has had some ESP experiences as far back as childhood, the majority of his visions came only after he started his job in the caster company. Between the hours of 9:00 and 11:00 A.M., when he says he is most relaxed, they come to him, unsought, out of the blue, and in rapid succession. He tries to remember them, or tell them to his co-workers in order to have some witnesses, but no one takes him too seriously, including his own father, the deputy sheriff.

Between May and October, he faithfully wrote down all his impressions, both those pertaining to future events and those having to do with previous lives. Then, on October 18, 1969, we met in Chicago and I questioned him for several hours.

My first impression of the very tall, thin young man was positive. When I had secretly feared to find a neurotic, attention-starved small-town youngster, I found instead a serious, soft-spoken young man puzzled by the influx of odd information streaming through his consciousness. At no time did he want publicity or fame, and he was quick to cast doubt about the reliability of his visions himself.

I looked through the record of his training. Since he had been a teacher of history, it seemed natural for him to have a degree of historical knowledge. But after extensive questioning of Robert E., I realized that this young teacher had only a very superficial knowledge of world history. His background is English and German, and there is no connection with anything Latin either in background, upbringing, or social circles frequented by him. He has not read a great deal either, but presented a keen, grasping mind, limited educational background or not. Certainly he might have picked up information on previous cultures and periods of history in passing, or perhaps unconsciously. But he does not seem to have done so either deliberately or consciously.

I then proceeded to hypnotize the young man, which presented no problems. He went under quickly and normally. But strange as it seemed to me at the time, his hypno-regression was anything but eventful. He was able to speak of an earlier lifetime in Burgundy, apparently in addition to the waking flashes he had reported to me earlier.

He also described a life as a South American Indian, which I am not including here as it is impossible to authenticate it on the basis of the generalities given under hypnosis. This does not necessarily indicate fraud or manufacture. But no fragments of language, names, and other specifics came out to enable me to check them. What I got was a graphic description of himself as an Indian, and the migration of his tribe across an ocean.

Upon awakening, Robert E. also spoke of still another "feeling" he had not mentioned before. He had come upon the name Heydrich accidentally in a book and immediately felt a relationship with that name. He saw himself in a Nazi uniform and trembled at the thought that he himself might have been the infamous Hangman through whom the Czechs had suffered so much during World War II. But I had the feeling that this latest impression was far from complete. Perhaps at some future date more material on this period might come to him so that I could check it out.

What fascinated me was his admission that nearly all his waking impressions came to him on his job at the factory, in the morning. Apparently he was and is able to do his work at the same time as living through these visions rather rapidly.

Obviously, Mr. E. does not enjoy his work, for a teacher doing manual labor of a particularly repetitive kind is not in his proper element. Thus, his mind wanders and the condition so often found conducive to psychic experience is present; disassociation follows, and the material is able to rise from the unconscious level.

When put under hypnotic regression, however, Mr. E. does not come across nearly as well. I suspect that this is because in experimenting with me he was far more enthused than in doing his chores at the caster company. Thus the natural loosening of bonds between conscious and unconscious states did not occur as it did when he was bored with his work. To be sure, he did speak of the earlier existences during the Italian Renaissance and in Spain, but the material was not as precise as when he had first received it in waking flashes. This is a curious situation as far as regression techniques are concerned, and indicative of the tricky nature of this case.

I also tested the young man for the Italian language, which he does not speak at all in the conscious state. He spoke Italian in hypnotic regression, but it was in his own, midwestern accent!

In the following paragraphs I will let Robert E. describe his excursions into various yesterdays in his own words, adding my comments and conclusions afterward.

From about 1956 onward, Mr. E. has had some recurrent dreams in which certain scenes and events kept appearing before his mind.

It is always in a coach drawn by horses. The coach's windows are high and wide, and purple drapes are hanging at the sides—the coach is dark brown wood—and while the scene takes place, I can see a wide stretch of beach that extends quite a distance, and almost azure or turquoise-blue water far out. There are no rocks on the beach, but I saw large rocks in the distance to the right that the coach had just passed. The sand was yellowish white, and the time seemed to be in the midmorning.

There is another passenger in the coach sitting facing me next to one door, and I am sitting on the seat immediately behind the driver toward the middle of the seat, but facing and speaking to the other passenger. The carriage or coach is enclosed like a stagecoach, but the windows are taller and wider, with purple drapes.

During the dream, both I and the other passenger are very seriously discussing something—in Italian! I can pick out some Italian words when they are spoken, mostly due to Latin courses I took in high school, but in this dream both of us rattle on so rapidly I can't pick up much of anything as to the content of the discussion.

The other passenger is dressed in military clothing. He wears a blue-black uniform—the hat, coat, and pants are all black and have a bluish hue to them.

The hat is a cockade-type hat as a British admiral might wear—like a costume from *H.M.S. Pinafore*—there is silver or gold around the border of the hat. He has wide white lapels on his jacket and a red sash that crosses his chest, and a long silver sword hangs at the end of it.

He has several medals on his chest, and red, white, and green ribbons attached to them—some of the medals are in the form of sunbursts. The sword has a pearl handle but it is either very shiny steel or silver.

He wears black shoes. He looks like he's in his sixties and has graying hair on his head, and sideburns lambchop style, and a well-groomed but thick gray mustache. His skin is olive color.

In the dream I wear brown shoes and a gray tweed suit with a vest with several buttons. There is a dark brown Homburg hat lying on the seat next to me. While we are talking, I touch my upper lip and I have a rather thick, wiry mustache and my hair is very thick and wiry, much like an Italian's. Ordinarily, my hair is long and brown and straight and I do not wear a mustache.

I've looked at travel literature and in the *National Geographic Magazine*, and the nearest location I've ever seen that resembles the scene in my dream are some beaches near Amalfi, in Italy.

The second recurrent dream has been going on ever since I was in grade school. I was at baseball practice sitting along the sidelines from home plate to the first-base position, and the weirdest building formation came into my mind then, and this scene has been recurring at least once every two weeks ever since.

The surrounding area is very high and mountainous—there are sharp-peaked mountains in the distance, and there is no vegetation anywhere. During the dream I have trouble breathing, just like the air is very thin. I have the feeling the location of this place is on top of a mountain, because there is no vegetation around, and the gravel around is flintlike and very sharp; it could cut your feet if you walked barefoot.

My skin is reddish brown in color, and there is a gold band around my right biceps. I am carrying a staff that I think is a spear but is more like a knife that curves into a ball-like object. The inside of the curve is as sharp as a razor. I have on a headdress, but I don't know what kind. I'm wearing sandals that are much tougher than rope, but look like sisal. I'm wearing a faded blue saronglike skirt.

The building is shaped like a baseball diamond—if you were to see the floor plan. The walls are about ten or twelve feet high, and the stones are so well fitted together that they don't need mortar between them. There is a hallway that runs from home plate to each one of the bases inside—around the bases in the manner of a runner who has just hit a home run—but the inside "diamond" is a mystery. The top of the building is open and has no roof, but once or twice in the dream I saw a ray like a flashlight pointing upward into the heavens from the middle section. I have the feeling it is located in Bolivia or Peru: the "Andes" seem to be the most prominent name that stands out. I felt like I was a guard or sentry.

Although no actual names or place names are given in this description, the amount of detail stands out. Mr. E. is evidently very familiar with the scenes he describes. If these were mere fantasies, made up to please me or to get attention perhaps, and related as he went along, I would doubt very much that he could be so detailed and specific about them. I tested him on this and asked him to repeat the description of these two scenes when we met in person, and substantially the same story came out.

The Italian uniform Mr. E. describes does belong to the Garibaldi era of nineteenth-century Italy, and the Amalfi coast was then part of the Kingdom of Naples. The uniform sounds to me like a royal Neapolitan officer's uniform, but what was going on in that coach is, of course, as much a mystery to me as it still is to Robert E.

The Indian guard in the Andes, on the other hand, does seem to tie in with his description, while under hypnosis, of life as a South American Indian. The interesting description of the diamond-shaped temple or guard tower perhaps also has authentic overtones in the manner in which these buildings were constructed. I do not believe Mr. E. is a student of Inca architecture, but I am.

During the first week of July 1969, he had a series of waking flashes while at work. Here is Mr. E.'s own immediate report, written while the memory of his visions was still fresh in his mind.

The following took place at work on a Saturday morning, during the usual 9:00–11:00 A.M. interval, in a period of from thirty to forty-five minutes.

The first of these things, which I have a witness to, a Mr. Howard Hoffert, whom I work with, occurred over a period of two or three weeks. For the longest time, and ever since I can remember, the name "Genoa" automatically evoked anger in me. This is quite odd itself, since there are only five things I have any knowledge of concerning "Genoa." These things are: (1) Genoa is the birthplace of Christopher Columbus, (2) Genoa is an Italian coastal city, (3) it is on the western coast of Italy, (4) it is near Turin, and (5) it once owned the isle of Corsica, when it was a city-state. Other than these five enumerated facts, I know nothing about "Genoa," but whenever I heard the name or even thought about it, I was overcome with almost uncontrollable anger and repulsion.

The progression of events is as follows: For the longest time, I felt angered or repulsed by the mere mention or thought of the name "Genoa." As I concentrated on the name "Genoa," the anger and the repulsive reactions faded away, and instead, I started to get "goose bumps" whenever I thought of "Genoa." Mr. Howard Hoffert saw these several times when I talked to him about it, and he will attest to the fact that these actually occurred on my arms, because he saw them, too.

I decided to pursue this mental probing somewhat further, because as I progressed in investigating "Genoa," the "goose bumps" became prominent more often, and later on during this two weeks, I began to get chills up my spine, and my arm muscles began to tense up whenever I thought of it—it was the same sensations I get when I am frightened or scared of something—a quivering sensation in my shoulders, too. The reactions of my body were identical to the reactions I would experience if I were frightened, but consciously I was not frightened, but whenever I thought of "Genoa" these things would occur.

On that particular Saturday, scenes, names, and countenances began to shoot into my mind from nowhere. My own voice seemed to be narrating something to me in Italian: the sound of the words seemed to indicate an Italian accent with slight traces of a Castilian lisp.

I seemed to be someone named Basuleeoh (Basilio?) Marazante or Maraganti—this, unfortunately, is the closest I could come to the name. As I rattled on to myself, the "ganti" or "gantay" endings seemed intermixed—maybe there is a different ending to the name depending on how the Italians use the name in a sentence! But I'm still not sure whether the fifth letter in the last name is a "g" or a "z."

I found myself in a dungeon with green walls, and sewage and rotten rancid water on the floor—it stunk of urine and other human waste. Rats were running around through the rotting and partially decomposed hay that littered it (the dungeon). Somehow, I felt like a rebel priest or seminarian. Then the scene shifted me to another room; this was cleaner, but it was a torture room. There were two strong-armed men there, and they stretched me out on a table so I was looking upward at the ceiling. They strapped me down on the table and pulled my trousers off me. One of them stood over me with a red-hot knife. Then an older priest in purplish garments that reached to the floor demanded that I repent for something—I don't know what—but I refused.

The priest had a billy goat's beard and looked like the picture of a noble from about the Renaissance era. He had the pointed white beard and mustache and pageboy haircut, but where the hair ended around his ears it was curled.

He then told the guards to teach me a lesson and I felt a horrible pain in my groin, but only momentarily; I saw myself screaming and trying to double over—then the priest told them, "Put the dog out of his misery and save the world from more misery."

They unstrapped me, flipped me over on my stomach while I was screaming and thrashing about and swearing at the priest and spreadeagled me again. I heard the priest mutter something in Latin and say "Pater et Filio et Spiritu Sancto"; then I felt a stabbing pain like a steel shaft was run through the area of the kidneys above the right buttock and right through the table under me.

I saw myself yelling and screaming more. The priest bent over me and said something to the effect that I am experiencing a good taste of hell even before I got there—I could hear him laughing—then he got very quiet, then I felt a sharp pain like a steel shaft was rammed point first behind the left ear and at the base of my skull. Then everything went black.

In the next scene I saw a rather grubby old jailer telling some people a story about a priest named Basilio who was killed many years ago in this same prison and whose ghost stalked the halls of the prison for almost twenty years after his death. Many prisoners and guards had seen it. But the ghost disappeared forever after a certain priest named Randolphi or Gandolphi died. According to the story, that priest, Randolphi or Gandolphi, died in a state of fits after he had seen the ghost of Basilio. The guard said the priest's order had called it a "seizure" or "convulsion," but the guard added that his own guilty conscience had been the reason for his death.

Ever since this experience was unfolded to me, by means of these scenes, I have had no more feelings of hostility or anger, or chills, etc., concerning the word "Genoa." I realize this is probably pretty far out, but it happened, and my co-worker, Howard Hoffert, can attest to the "goose bumps" I got even when I discussed it with him.

Almost immediately after this thing about Basilio Marazante (Maragante) took place, a flurry of other scenes came to me—mostly from Renaissance Italy and Spain.

The first one I remember found me in a wild and undisciplined *mood—like a spoiled brat—again I was speaking in Italian, but I knew what I was saying in English, if that makes any sense. The dialect seemed to be Italian with a heavy dose* of French words and expressions mixed in. For instance, I found myself saying "ēēdăh nāy āy ōh tōh ఠonōh ఠo nōh millay nya ohinko santo—" but I knew what I was saying because the date *August 1st, 1555* stood out. My name came out as *Luigi Carragione,* but I even said I prefer to be called Luis or Louie (French accent) rather than Luigi.

Somehow I had an uncle named Balthasar Carragione, who was quite a horseman and quite a ladies' man. My mother was a second cousin to the Medicis, and I had another cousin or great-uncle, named Anselmo de Medici, who was a miser with his money, a good businessman, and who hated my father's brother Balthasar. In the chatter I even hinted at the possibility that old uncle Anselmo might have had more than a passing interest when my uncle Balthasar was shot through the chest and killed by a bolt from a crossbow while riding—the assassin was not caught.

The chatter continued on about some pranks that this Luigi and a close friend, Paolo, pulled off—like staging swordplay right in church and chopping the tops off the candles in front of statues of saints with their lunges and slashes.

He talked (I talked) about an uncle or relative of his who was the pastor of the church, who reprimanded both of them for their actions. Then the chatter shifted to women. I rambled on about some prostitute in a tavern—she must have been quite a woman and quite experienced from the way I (he) described the antics in the bedroom—her name was Maria something.

Then (I) he went on to talk about a commoner girl named Francesca; he was obviously in love with this girl, but since he (I) couldn't marry her, he wanted her to be his mistress. She was a small person with long dark hair. He said their eyes were the same color—blue, but his hair was curly and very blond.

He goes on about some pranks he pulled on an old shepherd who tended flocks near his home—the man was white-haired and had long hair and a beard like Santa Claus, and

wore clothes made of skins. He describes the shepherd as
being a mean old cuss who had once been a mercenary in
the French Army. The old man's name was Niccolo, but
the voice called him Niccolo-Piccolo said that once this
Niccolo had killed one of his hunting dogs, so he hit the
old man in the head with a riding crop when he rode by
him one day.

He keeps saying that he is a "Lombar*ding*" or "Lombardino" and that he hopes he will tame down enough to be a
good nobleman. Despite his admitted hell-raising, he seems
to be very much a papist and hotly against what he calls
the *"All-bi-gĕnti."* The name *San Mĕĕ-kāle* is a church or
seminary nearby. It may even be a political district.

Soon after Luigi faded, another voice, whose body I did
not see, began a narrative about a white villa I saw out in
the country. Again, names and places seemed to come from
almost nowhere. This narrative covers not only the villa, but
other people and places, too. The voices seemed to be that
of a priest, or someone in holy orders—the voice was not in
Italian, but in English with the r's rolled and the lilting accent
that an Italian would speak with.

The first scene was this white villa made of adobe and
covering quite an area. I don't know where it was, but it
couldn't have been too far from a place called "Poldesta"—I
had the distinct feeling that this was taking place during the
Italian Renaissance even before I saw the costumes.

Again, the white villa of adobe had bricky brown tile on
the roof and with the same-colored bordering around the
doors and windows. The voice talked about some young
woman named "Angela" who made moon sacrifices to Diana
in a meadow just east of the villa. He said, *"we burned her
for the witch she was."*

He talked about a fire that had burned down a stable or a
barn that was part of the villa complex. He said something
about two lovers—Marco and Lucia—who had made the
barn their rendezvous. Marco was killed during the fire and
was buried at the foot of an oak tree just in front of the
villa to the right; the barn that burned was just behind the
big oak. Lucia died in the fire, too.

Then the scene shifted to another place owned by "that
pig, Giulietto di Poldesta." There was a portrait hanging
inside with this name under it. The man was big and had a

long, curly beard that fell halfway down his chest; the same
curly light-brown hair formed a mustache, but he was bald
completely across the top of his head. I saw bread crumbs
in his unruly beard, and he wore an open, finely tailored
jacket which was dark green with gold buttons and gilded
lace around the buttonholes. On a table was a golden helmet
with *a cat's face* impression on it.

He had a sister named "Rosamunda," who was pretty
frail and skinny; she had long, blond flaxen hair and watery
blue eyes, and she wore a light-blue floor-length dress, and
you could see white shoes underneath. The voice said that
"Rosamunda" was "tainted," and Giulietto had had her (his
sister) put away in a convent as a mental case, but he was
as much to blame for her mental condition as anyone else.

The voice seemed to talk about the white pigs that this
Giulietto raised on his villa—it said that the "pigs were cleaner
than their owner and took better care of what they owned."

There was a skinny farmer who seemed to be the steward
or overseer of the villa; his name was Giacomo; he was tall
and had a long, hooked Roman nose; Giacomo's daughter,
Rosana, was the mother of Giulietto's child, but the pig
refused to marry her, but treated her parents well. He mentioned something about a miller named Gēē-yĕll-mō, who
had a crusty green statue in his mill that many people thought
came from China—the name he used was "Far Cathay"—the
statue had a fat belly and fangs for teeth. Then the scenes
ended.

Now the scene shifted to a church in Spain. I had the
feeling that the place was Spain because the voice spoke
with a Castilian lisp and he mentioned Margareta Teraysa
and the "Eth-kor-ēē-ăhl" (Escorial).

All I saw was a monk in the far distance of a church hallway—brownish habit with sandals and a white rope around
the waist hanging down. He was looking toward some statue
that I seemed to be standing under and next to. It was a tall
statue of a female saint, and there were many candles lit
around it, but that part of the church was dark except for
the glaring candles. In front of the statue and looking up at
the statue just in front of me was a young noblewoman
dressed entirely in black—black shoes and long, black folds
in her widening dress that spread out about her from the
waist on down. From the waist on up, the form of the dress

was skintight with ruffles of black around the bust area and
black lace leading up to the neck. She wore a black net
shawl over her head and shoulders, but her face was bare;
she had very red lips, her teeth were straight, and she had
large brown eyes. Her hair seemed to be a mixture of black
and auburn. She was very beautiful. There was a silver ring
on her finger inlaid with diamonds, and she was crying as
she stood there looking up and praying to "chaira Santa
Lucia."

The voice seemed to come from the priest in the distance,
whose name sounded like Domingo Rēē bara. He said his
name was his patron saint's name and that this woman would
have been his if he hadn't been forced to take holy orders.
Santa Lucia seemed to be her patron saint, and her last name
looked like Munoz, with a curlicue over the "n." Then the
picture was gone.

Now all this material has the ring of truth to it, partly
because of the vivid detail, the names, the historical
"feel," which is genuine as far as I can tell, coming, after
all, from a trained historian.

On the other hand, Robert E. is not nearly as con-
versant with the history of the Italian Renaissance as I
am, even though he taught history in a public school. The
names given—Anselmo, Basilio, Giacomo, Rosana, Gu-
glielmo—only a person with a good knowledge of Italian
language and history would know.

I am unable to prove, thus far, that a rebel priest
named Basilio Marazante existed in Genoa, but the name
Marazante is certainly of that area, and the name Carragione also belongs to western Italy, so the French
accent is not at all out of line. The date Robert E. remembers so vividly, August 1, 1555, is also correct for
the horrible scene of torture and murder described by
him. The Inquisition, having been quiet for some time,
was revived again in 1542, and was at its height in 1555,
when the man who had revived it reigned as Pope Paul
IV.

The family name di Poldesta may be a misspelling of
podestà, a word meaning magistrate or mayor, and also
found as a family name. The description of a girl having
worshiped Diana in "moon" sacrifices and then having

been burned as a witch is also, in my estimation, far beyond Mr. E.'s storehouse of knowledge. Connecting witchcraft with the Dianic cult requires intimate knowledge of it. "Far Cathay" is indeed a Renaissance term for China. "Lombardino" is a contemptuous description for a country bumpkin, used in the period under discussion.

The term "Albigensi" applied to heretics—those in rebellion against the Pope. The war of extermination waged by the Pope and his mundane allies against the French reform movement called Albigensi took place between 1209 and 1229, but the term itself may have been used even afterward as a word meaning heretic or rebel.

A few days before our meeting in Chicago, Robert E. had another historical flashback.

I was referring to myself as "Kedrick" and was speaking with a guttural roll to my r's. The area was something like "Leeah tū vōs" or "-vosh" where I was—the people spoke a different language than I did and they had buttery complexions and most of them had blue eyes. They were farmers, and the richest ones were very proud of their white geese. I kept calling them something like "Schloffen" or "Schlobben" or something close like that. The area was plains, and the sea didn't seem too far away—word "shay-den" came up a few times. The people were caucasoids, but they had buttery faces—I called them "Shparden" a few times. The first three digits of date were clear, but the fourth was not—I caught 123 something—it could have been a 4, a 2, or a 1— they seemed mixed, but it wasn't above 5 in value, whatever it was.

I talked of the "order" with pride and had three black crosses on the chest of my tunic, which was white—the crosses formed a diagonal from my left shoulder to my lower right ribs. My hair was long and blond and I had a droopy blond mustache—I looked like a Swede—my hair was straight and hung down to my shoulders. I wore chain mail under the tunic, and it pinched and felt heavy, tight, and confining as I walked. I didn't like it that the "order" had sent me down here for seven years as an overseer. I couldn't wait for the last three years to end so I could return to "Loybeck" or "Rockenstock."

A man named "Agst," but sounded like "August," was my sponsor—he carried a large curved sword he had found in Turkey. He had blond hair and hazel eyes, but was much older than I. He was a "Danch" (sounded more like "dŏnch") and had gone twice to the Holy Land.

I spoke of a "Shaldon Teeth"—some kind of a tax or charity contribution everyone was supposed to pay. I wanted to go on the next expedition, but I knew it was impossible. I was stuck here.

My helmet was burnished and looked like copper—it was a dome-shaped helmet with small holes for clasps called "bolden" at the base; the nose guard was in the form of a cross, and the crossbar center covered my nose; the lateral shafts were under my eyes and there were clusters of three lobes at the four points of the cross; the hinge at the top of the cross allowed the whole nose guard to be lifted up like a window; the clusters at the four points of the cross made it look like a Maltese cross.

I mentioned "Zont Jawnen" several times—he seemed to be a leader of the order or someone connected with it in the past—I thought he was a great man.

This latest flashback I found particularly intriguing, since it dealt with a period in history even a specialist might have trouble with. By chance, or perhaps by design of fate, I am quite familiar with the period of the Crusades. It so happens that my wife is descended from a family active in the orders that emerged from the crusades, and as a consequence of this personal interest, I became a student of the period and of the entire structure of those orders.

Robert E. speaks of a farming people in a plain area not far from the sea, and he mentions the name "Leatuvos." The area is indeed all that and its people even today are called Lithuanians, or, in their language, Lietuvos.

The name Kedrick and the date 1231–1234 are given. Kedrick probably is Frederick, a personal name much used by the Teutonic Knights and the Livonian Brotherhood of the Sword. Also, Emperor Frederick II's crusade to the Holy Land took place in 1228–1229. The person

Robert E. describes wears a white tunic with three black crosses as insignia. So did the Knights of the Livonian Order, also known as Brotherhood of the Sword. These were returning crusaders who were sent by the Pope to christianize the European East, especially parts of Poland, East Prussia, and the Baltic states, which include Livonia, Lithuania, Estonia, and Latvia. He describes himself as a blond man with a large mustache.

The knights crusaders were German or of Germanic stock, as different from the farmers, who were native Slavonic people. The man Robert E. feels he once was complains of being stuck on his job and not being able to return to the pleasures of "Loybeck" and "Rockenstock."

"Loybeck" is today's Luebeck, and "Rockenstock" is now Rostock, both for centuries involved with the fate of the Baltic orders, though nominally independent city-states. The superior Robert remembers as "Agst" or "August" may well have been "Danch"—Danish—because fighters of many nationalities were gathered at that time for the common crusade. The helmet described is correct for the period and style used amongst the participants of the Crusades.

The name "Zont Jawnen," as Robert spells it phonetically, must refer to the illustrious Knights of St. John, who had already played a prominent role in the earlier crusades and were now in possession of Jerusalem.

So it all adds up, and I doubt that Robert E. has the kind of detailed knowledge of the period to have manufactured this bit.

The case of the midwestern school teacher will continue to interest me, of course, but the evidence thus far gathered does indicate that the young man has strange powers of the mind, to say the least. Incidentally, he has a clean record healthwise, and the only incident involving psychological counseling happened when he was a high-school student and needed advice about a problem at home. He has derived no profits from his involvement with the past, and in view of his requested anonymity, he is not likely to become a public hero. But it must be frustrating working in a caster plant in Illinois when you've once been a knight crusader.

IX
Techniques
of Regression

If someone comes up to you at a party and asks, "Can you find out who I was in a previous lifetime?" the best thing is to smile and say, "Perhaps." To make reincarnation into a party game is not only ludicrous, but perhaps even dangerous. Surely, if all of us were to know what we did in previous incarnations, the purpose of karma would be defeated, but there are enough cases where conscious information makes a person wonder about previous lifetimes, and in *such* cases the technique of regression seems to be in order.

To begin with, no one should undertake regression experiments unless he or she is fully qualified to do so. By qualification, I mean not simply a knowledge of hypnosis —that, of course, is necessary—but I also mean a deeper understanding of the problems involved in bringing a person back, through childhood and the threshold of birth, into an earlier lifetime. Only a trained psychic researcher and hypnotist should undertake this.

When *The Search for Bridey Murphy* was a best seller, a great deal of attention was focused on this technique. Morey Bernstein had come to the field as a novice, and hypnosis to him was nothing more than a hobby at first. That his book was honest and authentic is the more to his credit. Despite those who tried to discredit it, it was later fully exonerated, but the danger is always present when those unfamiliar with the technique are involving themselves with it. There is always the possibility that a person may have unresolved psychiatric problems in this lifetime that can become acute or aggravated by simple hypnosis. If such is the case, the operator, that is to say, the hypnotist, must be qualified to deal with them so that no damage may result to the psyche of the subject.

Assuming, then, that those who wish to regress another person are fully qualified to undertake this task, I will proceed to explain the techniques I find most useful and successful in obtaining the desired information.

To begin with, the majority of individuals who feel they might be good subjects generally are not. Just because someone claims that hypnosis would yield good results with him or her doesn't mean that this will in fact take place. Many people harbor resentments and other forms of resistance, usually on an unconscious level. They are the kind that cannot be hypnotized even though consciously they are willing to go under the hypnotist's spell.

I find that no more than one fourth of those who are willing subjects can actually be brought under hypnotic control, and only one in ten people make excellent hypnotic subjects. There is no hard and fast rule as to the kind of person that can be easily hypnotized. Generally, women are easier to hypnotize than men. This is true, but even among women there are exceptions, for hysterical conditions may very well prevent them from letting go control over their bodies and personalities, something absolutely essential if genuine hypnosis is to take place. Emotional people are probably more prone to be good subjects than logical and reserved individuals.

A positive attitude toward the experiment is valuable, but not essential. On the other hand, a negative attitude, which includes unwillingness to let go of one's self-control, may frequently thwart the efforts of the operator. I usually suggest that the subject make himself or herself comfortable on a couch or in an easy chair, remove shoes if they are too confining, and relax for a few moments before beginning the actual verbalization. I then suggest that the person close his or her eyes and listen to my voice. I will usually count from one to ten and suggest that at the count of ten the person be fully relaxed. This is followed by instructions to the various limbs of the person's body, saying that the limbs are becoming heavier and heavier, and that the whole body finally feels as if it were sinking down into the couch.

I then proceed to suggest that the individual is quite alone and can only hear my voice coming to him or her from a distance, but that no extraneous noises will be heard by him or her. Again I count to ten, suggesting that at the end of the second ten the individual will float out into the distance, far away from his or her usual surroundings, but that my voice will always be heard.

Depending on the success of the first stage, I will then suggest that the individual will be able to hear everything I say and will not awaken until I awaken him or her, that, however, he or she will answer all my questions without awakening.

All this time I observe very closely and carefully whether hypnosis is in fact taking place, or whether the person is still fully awake. I do not test my subjects with needles or in any other physical manner. This is strictly for stage hypnotists, and I view their work with both alarm and disdain, for hypnosis is too serious a subject to be used for entertainment purposes only.

To reach the third or deepest stage of hypnosis, I will suggest another ten steps down an imaginary staircase, toward the sea or toward some pleasant open area such as a meadow. I suggest conditions symbolizing freedom from all problems, total aloneness and a happy climate, such as a blue sky, clouds overhead, a sunny day, or some other form of atmospheric condition symbolic of well-being. At this point, most subjects are indeed under hypnotic control. I test this by asking the individual for his or her name and age, and if he or she is not hypnotized at this point I will be told, "But, I am not under yet, Mr. Holzer." In that event I would have to start all over again, and if I do not succeed the second time, I will generally dismiss the subject and ask him or her to return some other time, for it can very well happen that a subject feels tense on first meeting me, and may be relaxed a second time. If after the second visit no hypnosis results, I regretfully dismiss the subject and turn to another person for further research.

No one can be hypnotized against his will, or without his express wish to go under, at least, not in the total sense in which I use hypnosis. People have fallen under spells through repetition, through advertising, and through slogans that they may hear or see on such mass communication media as television or on stage. But specific personal hypnosis, especially the kind needed for regression, is possible only with the co-operation of the subject.

Assuming that my subject has now gone down to the third, or deepest, stage of hypnosis, I will suggest age regression. This means that I will say, You are now so many years old and so many years old, and gradually will suggest the person at a younger and earlier period in his or her life. Having suggested a specific date in the person's lifetime, I will then request information about the circumstances he or she lives under at that time. I will ask for the name of a school teacher, or an address where he or she and her or his parents lived at the time, the sort of information that only a person would know if he or she were indeed at that age and the kind of information that one is prone to forget at a later stage in life. This, of course, proves that under hypnosis one remembers a great deal more than one is aware of in the conscious, or ordinary, state.

Gradually, I will then regress the person back to childhood and to the moment of birth. After this I suggest that he or she cross the threshold of birth into another lifetime. Sometimes I will give a figure, such as fifty years before your birth, a hundred years before your birth; or at other times I will simply direct that the person go back until he or she meets an earlier incarnation, until he or she comes up to another person in another lifetime. When this happens, I ask for specific details and a description of the person, the period, and the circumstances under which the scenes now described take place.

Having obtained information of this kind, I will then bring the individual back into the present by easy stages, making sure that he or she is not taken out of the hypnotic stage too quickly. Just before bringing him or her back to ordinary consciousness, I will suggest that nothing be remembered from the discussion or conversation held between the subject and myself under hynosis. To the contrary, I will then add a feeling of well-being to be experienced immediately upon awakening. If the individual has requested that I help him or her fight against abuses or bad habits, such as excessive smoking or drinking, I will at that moment insert a message to the unconscious to the effect that the person will not be able to smoke or drink as much as before, or not at all, depending upon the desire of the individual. After that, I will count to ten once again, instructing the individual that, at the second count of ten, he or she will be fully awake and in good spirits.

This happens quickly, and the individual generally does not remember much or anything of the conversation that has taken place between him or her and myself while under hypnotic regression. If some parts are remembered, this indicates that hypnosis was not as deep as desirable and that on future occasions I must correct this condition. However, even a full remembrance of everything said under hypnosis does not prove that the state of hypnotic regression was not in fact successful. Some individuals have total recall even when instructed not to do so.

A few minutes later, the subject will be allowed to get up and go home. Generally I need between one and five sessions to establish a full character in the case of previous lifetimes. On occasion, a single session has done what four or five sessions might do in other cases. This all depends on the depth at which the earlier lifetime material is buried in the unconscious of the subject.

I never do any corroboration or research while still working actively with a subject, but begin my conscious research only after I am satisfied that I have obtained all the possible material that I can from this particular subject.

There is, of course, the problem of fantasy, which one must always reckon with. Some researchers feel that reincarnation material in general consists only of fantasy manufactured by a willing unconscious to please the researcher. I do not for a moment accept this version, but there are cases where fantasy may play a part. However, in my many years of reincarnation research, I have never encountered a seemingly genuine case where fantasy played a significant role, but I have encountered cases of hypnosis in which subjects related fantasy stories in order to work out some depressed material or some unattainable goal in real life. These, however, pertain solely to the present incarnation and not to earlier lifetimes.

When dealing with genuine or seemingly genuine material, it is always imperative to try to corroborate as much of it as possible. Only when at least a portion of the information can be traced and is not due to other factors, can we assume reincarnation to be the explanation. Then, too, we must realize that reincarnation does not work, apparently, in the same way for everybody, and that it is a highly individual and sophisticated process in which each case must be taken on its own merits. There are rules, but they do not apply to everyone in exactly the same way. How the law works is still partially a mystery, but that it *exists,* I do not doubt in the least.